The Social Impact of Sport

This book critically examines the ways in which sports contribute to, or inhibit, social well-being, the directions these impacts take and the conditions necessary for sport to have beneficial outcomes. The themes addressed in the book demonstrate the diversity and versatility of the social impacts sport can potentially achieve as well as the variable benefits of sport in different social contexts. The contributions are focused around four major themes:

- Sport development and social change: intended and unanticipated consequences
- Empowerment and personal change through sport
- Sport participation, social inclusion and social change
- The impact of sport in society: historical and comparative perspectives

The volume constitutes the first scholarly attempt to locate, compare and conceptualize the social impact of sport in different local, national and international contexts. Through international comparison and empirically grounded case studies the book provides an important new departure in the study of the social meanings of sport in society, linking themes and areas that have previously been studied separately from one another.

This book was previously published as a special issue of *Sport in Society*.

Ramón Spaaij is a Research Fellow at the La Trobe Refugee Research Centre and School of Social Sciences, La Trobe University. He is also a Research Fellow at the Amsterdam School for Social Science Research, University of Amsterdam.

The Social Impact of Sport

Cross-Cultural Perspectives

Edited by Ramón Spaaij

Routledge
Taylor & Francis Group
LONDON AND NEW YORK

First published 2011 by Routledge
2 Park Square, Milton Park, Abingdon, Oxon, OX14 4RN

Simultaneously published in the USA and Canada
by Routledge
270 Madison Avenue, New York, NY 10016

Routledge is an imprint of the Taylor & Francis Group, an informa business

This book is a reproduction of *Sport in Society*, vol.12, issue 9. The Publisher requests to those authors who may be citing this book to state, also, the bibliographical details of the special issue on which the book was based

Typeset in Times New Roman by Value Chain, India
Printed and bound in Great Britain by MPG Books Group, UK

British Library Cataloguing in Publication Data
A catalogue record for this book is available from the British Library

ISBN13: 978-0-415-58394-7

Contents

Part 4: The impact of sport in society: historical and comparative perspectives

Sport in the Global Society – Contemporary Perspectives

Series Editor: Boria Majumdar

The Social Impact of Sport
Cross-Cultural Perspectives

Sport in the Global Society – Contemporary Perspectives

Series Editor: Boria Majumdar

The social, cultural (including media) and political study of sport is an expanding area of scholarship and related research. While this area has been well served by the Sport in the Global Society Series, the surge in quality scholarship over the last few years has necessitated the creation of *Sport in the Global Society: Contemporary Perspectives*. The series will publish the work of leading scholars in fields as diverse as sociology, cultural studies, media studies, gender studies, cultural geography and history, political science and political economy. If the social and cultural study of sport is to receive the scholarly attention and readership it warrants, a cross-disciplinary series dedicated to taking sport beyond the narrow confines of physical education and sport science academic domains is necessary. Sport in the Global Society: Contemporary Perspectives will answer this need.

Other Titles in the Series

Australian Sport
Antipodean Waves of Change
Edited by Kristine Toohey and Tracy Taylor

Australia's Asian Sporting Context
1920s and 1930s
Edited by Sean Brawley and Nick Guoth

'Critical Support' for Sport
Bruce Kidd

Disability in the Global Sport Arena
A Sporting Chance
Edited by Jill M. Clair

Diversity and Division – Race, Ethnicity and Sport in Australia
Christopher J. Hallinan

Documenting the Beijing Olympics
Edited by D. P. Martinez

Football in Brazil
Edited by Martin Curi

Football's Relationship with Art: The Beautiful Game?
John E. Hughson

Forty Years of Sport and Social Change, 1968-2008
"To Remember is to Resist"
Edited by Russell Field and Bruce Kidd

Global Perspectives on Football in Africa
Visualising the Game
Edited by Susann Baller, Giorgio Miescher and *Raffaele Poli*

Global Sport Business
Community Impacts of Commercial Sport
Edited by Hans Westerbeek

Governance, Citizenship and the New European Football Championships
The European Spectacle
Edited by Wolfram Manzenreiter and Georg Spitaler

Indigenous People, Race Relations and Australian Sport
Edited by Christopher J. Hallinan and *Barry Judd*

Reviewing UK Football Cultures
Continuing with Gender Analyses
Edited by Jayne Caudwell

South Africa and the Global Game
Football, Apartheid and Beyond
Edited by Peter Alegi and *Chris Bolsmann*

Sport – Race, Ethnicity and Identity
Building Global Understanding
Edited by Daryl Adair

Sport and the Community
Edited by Allan Edwards and David Hassan

ABSTRACTS

The transnational view of sport and social development: the case of Dominican baseball

Alan Klein

This essay examines social benefits of Major League Baseball's half century of dealings with the Dominican Republic. While the relationship was built along neo-colonial lines that heavily favoured the North American partner, structural events have unfolded in the past decade that have resulted in a levelling of the political-economic playing field. This is the outcome, not so much of MLB's sense of corporate responsibility, as it is the unforeseen consequences of its actions and the ability of Dominicans to take advantage of opportunities.

The glue that holds the community together? Sport and sustainability in rural Australia

Ramón Spaaij

Drawing on the author's research in northwest Victoria, Australia, this essay examines the forms of capital that are created in and through rural sport as well as the processes of social inclusion and exclusion that structure access to social networks and to the resources these networks contain. In the face of economic and social changes that affect the region, rural sport participants view local sport clubs as vital community hubs fostering social cohesion, local and regional identities and a shared focus and outlet. Sporting competitions in northwest Victoria also contribute to cultural and economic capital for some participants, and to relatively limited stocks of linking social capital. While the creation and transference of these capitals are to a large degree regulated by wider social divisions, structural changes in the area present increased opportunities for other people, including young women, to take on leadership roles and to develop new skills and knowledge through sport participation.

Sport as a post-disaster psychosocial intervention in Bam, Iran

Valeria Kunz

In the field of humanitarian assistance, sport and play have recently gained attention as innovative instruments to support a psychosocial rehabilitation process in post-disaster and post-conflict situations. The project 'Sport and play for traumatized children and youth', implemented by the Swiss Academy for Development after the earthquake in Bam, Iran, was a pilot project conducted in this field. This essay discusses the experiences gained and lessons learnt from the project, indicating the advantages and limitations of using sport and play as tools to support psychosocial rehabilitation in a post-disaster situation. Positive effects of the project were identified on both group and individual levels, but they cannot be attributed to the use of sport alone. The findings rather suggest that the coaches and their efforts to create a supportive environment have played a crucial role for the success of the project.

Esther Phiri and the Moutawakel effect in Zambia: an analysis of the use of female role models in sport-for-development

Marianne Meier and Martha Saavedra

In the burgeoning field of sport and development, 'role models' have been invoked as an important element to increase the participation of girls and women in sport. Grounded in the African sport-in-development experience and in a case study of Zambian women's sports and the boxer, Esther Phiri, this essay examines the discourse around the use of 'role models' and begins to elaborate a theory around the use of this hitherto elusive notion specifically in the experience of sport-in-development projects and programmes which have gender-specific outcomes. We consider how role models may function to encourage and sustain female involvement, as well as to contribute to achieving goals set for sport and development projects, including (positively) altering gender roles and expectations. We conclude with a look towards promising areas of future research as well as a critical reflection on the limits of role models as a tool, especially given real-world intrusions.

Developing through sport: evidencing sport impacts on young people

Tess Kay

The use of sport in pursuit of international development goals is broadening, with widespread policy support for sports-based programmes that promote social, educational and health goals. Academic assessment has however been more critical, posing searching questions about the paucity of evidence that justifies the use of sport in these roles. Recent growth in evaluation studies has increased the evidence-base but carries some risks of privileging positivist forms of knowledge and fails to engage with issues surrounding decolonization of research. This essay suggests that reflexive qualitative studies that capture authentic local knowledge can help address both of these issues, illustrating this through an exploratory study conducted with young women and adult sport workers involved in a 'successful' community-based sports programme in Delhi, India (n ¼ 38). It is argued that the form of data obtained can enhance academic understanding and assist in the process of decolonization of sport-in-development research.

Engaging sport-for-development for social impact in the South African context

Cora Burnett

The politics of development ideology and global leadership set the scene for sport (for) development in South Africa. Academic inquiry followed in an ad hoc way, mostly in the wake of contracted and/or externally and diverse disciplinary infused research paradigms. Diverse research agenda and donor requirements set the scene for Participatory Action Research as an enabling tool for researchers, funders and research participants whereby indigenous knowledge systems can be accessed and enriched in a collaborative venture of knowledge production. Four case studies of sport-fordevelopment projects in the South African context explain the evolving architecture in this field. A discussion of three distinct and interrelated models, based on the rationale of Mintzberg (2006), affords insights within a social capital framework of a top-down, bottom-up and outside-in approach in various integrated formats. It is apparent that social impact and networking evolved around strategic alliance formation and development agendas of major stakeholders.

Participation in sport: bonding and bridging as identity work

Jeroen Vermeulen and Paul Verweel

Nowadays sport is assigned a crucial role in solving social problems, especially those relating to social cohesion. Participation in sport is assumed to build relevant bonding and bridging social capital that generates reciprocal contacts and trust in others. In this essay we will present findings of two, mainly qualitative studies on participation in sport in the Netherlands. We argue that while sport indeed makes contributions to the development of social capital, bonding and bridging are much more complex and differentiated processes than is usually assumed in both social policies and social capital theory. An argument is made to view bonding and bridging as identity work

Race relations, Indigenous Australia and the social impact of professional Australian football

Chris Hallinan and Barry Judd

We consider how Indigenous athletes have become symbols of what is perceived by white Australia to be progressive race relations. In particular, the men's professional sports of Australian football and Rugby League draw the most heavily mediated attention as well as significant numbers of Indigenous players. We draw upon the narratives of key advocates of Indigenous participation and performance in professional Australian football: journalists and recruiting managers. The emergent theme of white privilege is used to examine how their advocacy of Indigenous performance masks shortcomings in access and opportunity beyond playing roles. We conclude with the idea that race relations progress fulfils the needs of white Australia but fails to sufficiently deliver genuine opportunity for Indigenous Australian participants.

Social functions of high school athletics in the United States: a historical and comparative analysis

Ruud Stokvis

In the United States competitive sport is part of the extra-curricular program of high schools. In the Netherlands, on the other hand, competitive sport is practiced in private clubs which are completely independent of the high schools. The consolidation and continuity of this difference can be explained by the importance of the integrative function athletics acquired in the US high schools. These schools have a much more heterogenic body of pupils in terms of talents and social class than most Dutch schools. The prevalence of ceremonies, rituals and symbols surrounding high school games in the US enhances this integrative function. In Europe these ceremonies are nearly absent in games and matches between private clubs for boys and girls of high school age. The integrative function of athletics in American high schools contributes to the motivation of students to participate in the school system and to the prevention of students dropping out.

The social construction and impact of champions

Joseph Maguire

This essay addresses the belief that the performances of champions are attributable to either the genetic make-up, or to some notion of genius of athletes. Individualistic and/or behavioural explanations tend to dominate. Yet, such explanations provide a very limited grasp of the genesis of performances and reveal nothing about the stage on which the 'act' is performed, the theatre in which the 'play' takes place or the impact that sport has on society. In emphasizing the cultural making of sport, this is not to dismiss the notion of genius, or overlook the creativity, expressiveness and existential experiences that are part of sport. In fact, champions of sport perform powerful functions for the societies they represent. This essay, then, seeks to capture both the construction of genius and what it tells us about the societies which such champions represent.

The social impact of sport: diversities, complexities and contexts

Ramón Spaaij

School of Management, La Trobe University, Australia; Amsterdam School for Social Science Research, University of Amsterdam, The Netherlands

There is a widespread belief that sport (broadly defined) has the power to make 'society' more equal, socially cohesive and peaceful. The potential of sport as a tool for development and peace is being harnessed by an ever-expanding range of organizations at local, national and international levels, engaging in ever-evolving public-private partnerships. Whether a transnational corporation committed to corporate social responsibility, an international aid organization pursuing the Millennium Development Goals or a grassroots non-governmental organization (NGO) seeking to meet the everyday needs of disadvantaged communities in the Global South, it is increasingly common to herald sport as 'a new engine of development'[1] and social development through sport as a 'new social movement'.[2] A typical statement representing the aspirations of this movement stresses how:

> Through sport and physical education, individuals can experience equality, freedom and a dignifying means for empowerment, particularly for girls and women, for people with a disability, for those living in conflict areas and for people recovering from trauma.[3]

This heralding of sport as an agent of personal and social change has, of course, not gone unchallenged. It is by now commonplace to point to the absence of 'hard' evidence needed to 'test' whether and how sport programmes actually work, to criticize the shortcomings of 'anecdotal evidence', and to stress the need for better monitoring and evaluation of 'sport-for-development' programmes.[4] Aside from methodological considerations, there is a danger that social development through sport is imposed on disadvantaged communities in a top-down manner, lacking community engagement and shared ownership.[5] Instead, sport-for-development programmes should be participatory, promote self-reliance and empowerment, use indigenous understandings and knowledge, take an interest in both the means and ends of development, and be concerned with ethical and moral issues as well as practicalities.

One of the cornerstones of alternative development in the Global South, in which local NGOs play a critical role, is the belief that the state is often part of the problem and that alternative development should occur outside, and perhaps even against, the state.[6] This alternative perspective is directly at odds with mainstream approaches to development through sport which promote 'linked-up' partnerships between states, international NGOs, transnational corporations and international organizations such as the United Nations, UNICEF or FIFA. For example, the Sport for Development and Peace International Working Group posits that the future of sport as an instrument for development and peace ultimately depends on national governments; hence the need to convince governments in both the Global North and the Global South of the potential of sport as a development tool. In practice, partnerships of this kind can be problematic, masking existing power relations between international donors, states and NGOs and creating challenges for NGOs in a context where organizations are competing for similar sources of funding.[7]

More fundamentally, this example underlines the lack of consensus surrounding what development actually means. While development can generally be taken to mean 'the processes by which there is an attempt to improve life chances throughout the world but particularly in countries considered to be low income',[8] development is always contextually defined. A striking example of the use and abuse of development discourse, the Developmentalism doctrine of Soeharto's New Order government in Indonesia, driven by a desire for economic growth and political stability, generated a growing gap between the rich and the poor as well as the suppression and destruction of certain disadvantaged communities, and became known for its corruption, collusion and nepotism.[9] History shows that several governments put 'development' ahead of 'democracy' to the point of strengthening military regimes in order to provide the stability that is supposed to promote (economic) development.[10] It is unsurprising, therefore, that experienced grassroots activists in countries such as Indonesia are very wary of attempts by government officials to co-opt their community initiatives for political purposes. In theoretical or abstract terms, the state can be as much part of the problem as the solution. In any event, the performance of the state in alleviating social inequalities is susceptible to empirical evaluation.[11]

The above discussion raises all sorts of interesting and relevant questions regarding the rationales, design, implementation and outcomes of sport-for-development programmes. Arguably, the main limitation on producing evidence for policy-making and practice is 'the absence of an understanding of processes and mechanisms which either produce, or are assumed to produce, particular impacts and outcomes': what 'works', what processes produce these effects, for which participants, in what circumstances, and what are their limitations?[12] Several of the chapters in this book address these questions, drawing on detailed empirical investigation of sport-for-development programmes that target a range of social change objectives, including empowerment, peer leadership, gender equity, post-disaster psychosocial intervention and community development.

Yet although the sport-for-development debate holds a prominent position in these chapters, this book is not limited to it. In fact, my concern about the almost exclusive focus on *specifically targeted* sport programmes within policy and academic discourses on sport as an instrument for personal and social change acted as a catalyst for this particular volume. The idea that sport has certain wider social 'functions' beyond the game itself is of course not new; social development through sport has a long history. As Kidd notes, its aspirations can be traced back to the 'rational recreation' interventions in the late nineteenth century, the 'playground' movement of the early twentieth century, and the confessional and workers' sports movements of the interwar period, among other antecedents.[13] Its current manifestation is different in, among other developments, the rapid explosion of the agencies and organizations that are involved and the extent to which it has been championed by the United Nations and other significant international governing bodies.[14] As part of this process, we have increasingly come to understand sport as a programme that needs to be consciously and carefully designed for social benefits to accrue. In turn, global coordination and an agreed institutional framework are deemed necessary to enable coherent policy and the implementation of professional, well-designed programmes.[15]

A major limitation of this perspective on the social impact of sport is that it tends to gloss over the fact that social benefits which may accrue from sport participation cannot simply be imposed artificially by political decree or through social engineering.[16] Local, autonomously run sport teams and competitions, which are primarily concerned with playing (competitive) sport and maintaining sports facilities rather than with broader social development objectives, may also generate certain social benefits, but this is not an initial incentive to compete. Most people do not engage in sport to achieve certain societal ends, but rather for enjoyment, health or to spend time with friends and family.[17] As several contributions to this special edition demonstrate, such voluntary sport activities often serve as sites for the creation and maintenance of different types of capital (as well as particular forms of social inclusion and exclusion).[18] This underlines Seippel's observation that social capital 'is not necessarily the result of intentional investments aimed at future benefits' but, to a large extent, 'probably the unintentional consequences of instrumental, normative and/or expressive actions.'[19]

But also in its more general forms sport should of course not be regarded as inherently wholesome or socially cohesive, or as exclusively or automatically generating beneficial outcomes. Change represents a process that may have positive or negative consequences, as perceived by those affected by it. Hence, sport has the potential of (simultaneously) producing both positively and negatively perceived outcomes, and it often reflects or even reinforces social inequalities. One of the major challenges scholars face, Vermeulen and Verweel argue in their chapter, is to consider the social impact of sport from the perspective of socio-cultural diversity and from the perspective of localized processes of social inclusion and exclusion. From a different angle, Maguire conveys the apt metaphor of sport as a symbolic dialogue involving a dramatic representation of who we are and who we would like to be.

Levermore and Beacom identify two layers of potential exclusion within international development through sport.[20] The first layer relates to sports, communities and regions that currently lie outside of the parameters of the sport-for-development focus. The second layer of exclusion relates more specifically to the unequal power relations in sport. While sport can be viewed as a form of resistance that might occasionally challenge dominant systems and processes, far more prevalent is the largely one-way communication process whereby Northern governments, development agencies, foreign NGOs and sport associations provide support, information and advice and set up sport programmes in the Global South. For Levermore and Beacom, this is 'inevitably a problem that is concerning from dependency and post-colonial perspectives, especially when programs and policies are initiated with excessive influence from powerful institutions and actors'. Related to this is exclusion in terms of stereotyping and representation of the disadvantaged that takes place through the representation of sport.[21] This form of social exclusion features prominently in Hallinan and Judd's chapter on Indigenous representation in Australian football. They demonstrate how Indigenous players and their supporters are complicit in a sport system that generates a form of organizational practice that contains and stereotypes Indigenous ambition and performance to on-field involvement, representing a form of 'enlightened racism'.

This special edition of *Sport in Society* aims to highlight the diversities, complexities and contexts of the social impacts of sport. Its overall objective is to critically examine some of the ways in which sport contributes to, or inhibits, personal and social change, the directions these changes take, and the circumstances and wider social conditions in which they occur. This volume not only explores these themes in an interdisciplinary manner, but also seeks to move beyond policy-related and practical issues concerning sport activities in general and sport-for-development programmes in particular. It also recognizes and addresses the different levels of sport – elite, sub-elite, grassroots, school sport – and their inter-relationships. We have invited authors from a variety of academic and professional backgrounds to reflect upon particular themes relating to the role and influence of sport as an agent of personal and social change. Their geographical scope ranges from small scale, localized sport practices to transnational analyses and comparisons, including countries from South Asia, the Middle East, Africa, the Caribbean, Oceania, North America and Europe. The contributions highlight the multitude of theoretical approaches, methodologies and loci that can be employed to study sport's contributions to personal and social wellbeing as well as the potentially detrimental effects of sport in that regard.

The purpose of this special edition, then, is to raise new theoretical, methodological and policy-related questions that serve to enrich and stimulate contemporary academic and policy debates on the social impact of sport. The major significance of this special edition arguably lies not so much in the answers it generates, but rather in the new questions it raises. These questions require a profound rethinking of modes of research into the social and cultural outcomes that sport produces at an individual, interpersonal, national and international level.

Overview of this book

This book has been grouped into four broad sections in such a manner that different dimensions of the social impact of sport are addressed. Though I have organized the chapters in a particular manner for the purpose of thematic structure, I acknowledge from the outset the various ways in which they cut across categorization. The chapters serve as a starting point for examining the ways in which sport contributes to, or inhibits, particular social outcomes. The epilogue addresses and compares, in a concise and exploratory way, some of the main cross-cutting themes that emerge from the individual contributions as a basis for further discussion and research.

Part 1: Sport development and social change: intended and unanticipated consequences

Emphasizing the counter-intuitive and unintended effects of the growing entrenchment of Major League Baseball (MLB) in the Dominican Republic, Alan Klein argues that although it is tempting to regard MLB's increased embeddedness as a setback to Dominican baseball's structural autonomy, increased interactions of this nature can actually result in local empowerment. Interpreting this process in a uniformly negative way misses a very significant counter-result: MLB is having a positive impact on communities throughout the country and Dominicans are actually becoming more politically and economically powerful. Klein analyses the major direct and indirect economic and social consequences of MLB involvement in the Dominican Republic, including community development, social capital and economic aid. Klein's analysis confirms the point made earlier: social benefits of sport do not necessarily accrue intentionally as a result of well-designed sport-for-development programmes, but can actually emerge as unanticipated outcomes of the drive towards sustainable competitive advantage in a globalizing context. These outcomes cannot be ascribed to MLB's sense of corporate social responsibility, but should be understood as the unforeseen consequences of its actions and the ability of Dominicans to take advantage of opportunities.

Some of the issues addressed by Klein are examined further, from a different perspective, in my chapter on the social impact of sport in northwest Victoria, a predominantly rural region of Australia. The perceived significance of sport in the social life of small towns in northwest Victoria should not merely be understood as a historically evolved cultural pattern, but also within the context of relatively recent structural changes in local economies and demographics. The region has experienced profound social and economic changes in recent decades that impact not only on the general social and cultural life of small towns, but also specifically on the ways in which local residents perceive and experience sport. It is demonstrated that some of the beneficial outcomes in relation to bridging social capital and economic capital are actually unintentional consequences of the adaptive strategies of sport clubs and local residents to cope with structural changes. Population decline and technological changes, for instance, have intensified the social connections between residents of different towns, generating new relationships, forms of knowledge and economic opportunities. Voluntary community sport organizations are vital nodes in the creation and maintenance of these resourceful social networks.

Part 2: Empowerment and personal change through sport

The second part of this special edition shifts the attention more explicitly to the level of individuals. Valeria Kunz notes how sport and play are increasingly being used in psychosocial interventions targeted at children and youth. Her contribution is focused on a project in Bam, Iran, which was established after a devastating earthquake struck the city of Bam on 26 December 2003. Kunz concludes that sport and play have had a positive impact on the wellbeing and development of the participating children. But she also points out that these positively perceived effects cannot be isolated to the use of sport alone. Coaches play a crucial role in the post-disaster psychosocial rehabilitation of children and youth through sport and play. They are actively involved in relationship building, seeking to encourage young people and to open up potential personal development pathways.[22]

Working on a similar terrain, Marianne Meier and Martha Saavedra explore the notion of role models as a tool within sport and development practice in Africa (particularly Zambia). They discuss how female role models might operate to increase girls' participation in sport and contribute to achieving goals set for sport and development projects, including positively altering gender roles and expectations. A major concern for Meier and Saavedra is how historical, spatial and cultural contexts affect the nature and efficacy of female role models. They explore these issues through life histories of the Zambian boxing champion Esther Phiri and the Moroccan former Olympic champion Nawal El Moutawakel.

The final chapter in Part 2 draws on research undertaken in Delhi, India. Tess Kay reflects on young women's experiential accounts of sport as an agent of personal and social change. She argues that qualitative investigations may help capture the complex and multi-faceted process through which individuals experience beneficial social outcomes from sport. More fundamentally, she states that qualitative methodologies are required to help address a neglected issue within sport-for-development research: the need to subvert enduring 'colonial' power relationships. Whilst she acknowledges that qualitative methodologies do not magically transform and democratize underlying power relationships between researchers and the objects of their study, she does believe that reflexive forms of research provide a mechanism for the expression of local understandings and knowledge that are crucial to the assessment of the social impact of sport in development contexts. This argument raises vital epistemological and methodological questions that remain seriously undervalued in the contemporary social development through sport movement.

Part 3: Sport participation, social inclusion and social change

Part 3 of this special edition focuses on the relationship between sport participation, social inclusion and social change within a range of socio-cultural settings. Reporting on sport development in South Africa, Cora Burnett argues that the multilevel manifestations of development dynamics and interrelatedness of different components of sport activities necessitate a multidisciplinary and/or integrated theoretical approach. She sets out to explore conceptual frameworks rooted in social capital theories and to reflect on three distinct development approaches: top-down, inside-up and outside-in. These frameworks and approaches are discussed in relation to four sport-for-development programmes in South Africa, which illustrate the development dynamics of such models in a context of poverty where individuals, collectives and communities have been targeted for sports-related development.

Jeroen Vermeulen and Paul Verweel present findings from studies on sport and social participation in the context of ethnic diversity in the Netherlands. They argue that sport participation can help individuals to develop competence in the sometimes subtle and situational processes of social inclusion and exclusion. Sport provides ways to be included, to attain recognition and self-esteem. They assert that while sport may make important contributions to the development of social capital in terms of useful and reciprocal relations and trust in others, bonding and bridging practices are far more complex and differentiated processes than usually assumed. The authors propose to understand bonding and bridging processes in terms of identity: participation in sport is to be regarded as identity work.

The chapter by Chris Hallinan and Barry Judd moves the issue of sporting inclusion into the arena of race relations. The authors are particularly critical of White Australia's celebration of race relations progress in sport. Their chapter discusses how the containment of Indigenous participation in professional Australian football is framed along common assumptions centred on biological determinism and stereotyped ideas about ambition, many of which have enjoyed currency in Australian society since the early nineteenth century. Drawing on both the evolving political-cultural context of Indigenous Australia and the contributions of Indigenous Australians to professional Australian football, Hallinan and Judd conclude that the race relations in the Australian Football League reconfirm colonialism rather than forge a situation of reconciliation, which remains far from complete.

Part 4: The impact of sport in society: historical and comparative perspectives

Part 4 takes a wider historical and comparative approach to the social impact of sport. In his comparison of the social functions of athletics in high schools in the United States and the Netherlands, Ruud Stokvis draws on the work of James Coleman (1961) and others to explore how the integrative function of athletics in US high schools contributes to the motivation of students to participate in the school system and to the prevention of students dropping out. For Stokvis, the integrative function of athletics in US high schools works in three ways. First, students with athletic ambitions are being drawn into the school system not only to become popular at school, but also because of potential rewards. The 'no grade, no play' rule – which establishes that students are not allowed to play unless they attain a certain minimum standard necessary to complete their school year – forces them to concentrate their efforts as much on their schoolwork as on sport. Second, students with fewer athletic ambitions are drawn into the school system via activities that are associated with the athletic events. Finally, students are drawn into the school system because they identify with their school teams as fans. Through their participation as fans, students and staff acquire positive 'emotional energy' and a collective school identity.[23]

Also analysing the social impact of sport from a historical-comparative perspective, Joseph Maguire argues that sport champions, as socially constructed phenomena, perform powerful functions for the societies they represent. For Maguire, sport is a modern morality play that reveals fundamental truths about individuals, their societies and their relations with others. Sport champions express myths and revered social values of a society, as well as the sports ethic that underpins involvement in sport. Maguire argues that because sports are a separate world that suspends the 'everyday world' they enable the celebration and reinforcement of shared cultural meanings that are expressed through and embodied by champions. While in 'real life' social divisions along class, gender, ethnic and religious lines interfere with, and rig, social life and its outcomes, with its champions being 'profane deceptive illusions', on the field of play sport outcomes are sacred and authentic. Maguire portrays sport champions not only as talented individuals but as modern heroes whose lives tell stories about ourselves to ourselves and to others.

Acknowledgements

I would like to acknowledge the assistance of Sean Brown, who was committed to the realization of this project from its early beginnings. I also thank the participants to the panel on 'Sport for Development and Peace' celebrated as part of the 50th Annual Convention of the International Studies Association in New York City (15–18 February 2009) for their helpful suggestions and comments.

Notes

[1] Levermore, 'Sport: A New Engine of Development'.
[2] Kidd, 'A New Social Movement'.
[3] Beutler, 'Sport Serving Development and Peace', 365.
[4] It is common to distinguish between 'sport development' and 'sport for development'. The former implies the development and diffusion of sport itself, whereas the latter implies using sport as a tool in development assistance and poverty reduction, for example in relation to the Millennium Development Goals. E.g. Bartlett and Straume, *Sports-for-Development Monitoring*, 10. The concept of sport within the context of sport for development tends to be broadly defined to include all types of organized physical activity that may serve as a tool for development and peace. Levermore and Beacom adopt the term 'sport-in-development' as representative of the perception that the use of sport *may* assist the international development process. They privilege this term above 'sport for development' because the latter term implies that the use of sport in the development process is an overwhelmingly positive one and tends to preclude the argument that sport might be detrimental to societies in the Global South. Whilst fully acknowledging the potentially detrimental aspects of sport, in this introduction I use the term 'sport-for-development' because it captures more fully the diversities and complexities of the social impact of sport, taking it out of the limited context of development studies and applying it to the more general notion of sport as an agent of personal and social change. Sport-for-development programmes have a wide variety of aims, objectives and methodologies, as Burnett's contribution to this volume demonstrates. Levermore and Beacom, 'Sport and Development', 9; Coalter, *Sport-in-Development*, 1; Green, 'Sport as an Agent'.

[5] See also Skinner, Zakus and Cowell, 'Development through Sport', 270.

[6] Rigg, *Southeast Asia*, Chap. 2.

[7] E.g. Banda *et al.*, *Partnerships involving Sports-for-Development NGOs*.

[8] Levermore and Beacom, 'Sport and Development', 7.

[9] For an excellent analysis of Developmentalism in Indonesia and the ways in which social scientists served this ideology, see Hadiz and Dhakidae, *Social Science and Power in Indonesia*.

[10] Kahl, *Three Latin American Sociologists*, 181.

[11] Dean, Cimadamore and Siqueira, 'Introduction', 17.

[12] Coalter, *A Wider Social Role for Sport*, 2–3.

[13] Kidd, 'A New Social Movement', 371; see also Dunning and Waddington, 'Sport as a Drug', 355

[14] Kidd, 'A New Social Movement', 371.

[15] E.g. Beutler, 'Sport Serving Development and Peace', 366–7.

[16] Cf. Hughson, Inglis and Free, *The Uses of Sport*, 68.

[17] Spaaij and Westerbeek, 'A Healthy Active Australia?'

[18] Several contributors address the concept of social capital. Each contributor tends to define and measure social capital in slightly different ways, underlining the broader lack of consensus in academia and policy-making concerning the conceptualization and measurement of social capital. E.g. Bailey, 'Evaluating the Relationship', 74.

[19] Seippel, 'Sport and Social Capital', 171.

[20] Levermore and Beacom, 'Opportunities, Limitations, Questions', 253.

[21] Ibid., 254.

[22] Cf. Crabbe, 'Avoiding the Numbers Game', 29–30.

[23] On the concept of emotional energy see Collins, *Interaction Ritual Chains*.

References

Bailey, R. 'Evaluating the Relationship between Physical Education, Sport and Social Inclusion'. *Educational Review* 57, no. 1 (2005): 71–90.

Banda, D., I. Lindsey, R. Jeanes, and T. Kay. *Partnerships Involving Sports-for-Development NGOs and the Fight against HIV/AIDS*. York: York St John University, 2008.

Bartlett, S., and S. Straume. *Sports-for-Development Monitoring and Evaluation Consultancy: Final Report*. Washington, DC: Inter-American Development Bank, 2008.

Beutler, I. 'Sport Serving Development and Peace: Achieving the Goals of the United Nations through Sport'. *Sport in Society* 11, no. 4 (2008): 359–69.

Coalter, F. *A Wider Social Role for Sport: Who's Keeping the Score?* London: Routledge, 2007.

Coalter, F. *Sport-in-Development: A Monitoring and Evaluation Manual*. London: UK Sport, 2006.

Coleman, J. 'Athletics in High Schools'. *Annals of the American Academy of Political and Social Sciences* 338 (1961): 33–43.

Collins, R. *Interaction Ritual Chains*. Princeton, NJ: Princeton University Press, 2004.

Crabbe, T. 'Avoiding the Numbers Game: Social Theory, Policy and Sport's Role in the Art of Relationship Building'. In *Sport and Social Capital*, edited by M. Nicholson and R. Hoye, 21–37. Oxford: Elsevier Butterworth-Heinemann, 2008.

Dean, H., A. Cimadamore, and J. Siqueira. 'Introduction'. In *The Poverty of the State: Reconsidering the Role of the State in the Struggle against Global Poverty*, edited by A. Cimadamore, H. Dean and J. Siqueira, 1–37. Buenos Aires: CLACSO, 2005.

Dunning, E., and I. Waddington. 'Sport as a Drug and Drugs in Sport: Some Exploratory Comments'. *International Review for the Sociology of Sport* 38, no. 3 (2003): 351–68.

Green, C. 'Sport as an Agent of Social and Personal Change'. In *Management of Sports Development*, edited by V. Girginov, 129–45. Oxford: Elsevier, 2008.

Hadiz, V.R., and D. Dhakidae. *Social Science and Power in Indonesia*. Jakarta: Equinox, 2005.

Hughson, J., D. Inglis, and M. Free. *The Uses of Sport: A Critical Study*. London: Routledge, 2005.

Kahl, J. *Three Latin American Sociologists: Gino Germani, Pablo González Casanova, Fernando Henrique Cardoso*. New Brunswick: Transaction Books, 1988.

Kidd, B. 'A New Social Movement: Sport for Development and Peace'. *Sport in Society* 11, no. 4 (2008): 370–80.

Levermore, R. 'Sport: A New Engine of Development'. *Progress in Development Studies* 8, no. 2 (2008): 183–90.

Levermore, R., and A. Beacom. 'Sport and Development: Mapping the Field'. In *Sport and International Development*, edited by R. Levermore and A. Beacom, 1–25. Houndmills: Palgrave Macmillan, 2009.

Levermore, R., and A. Beacom. 'Opportunities, Limitations, Questions'. In *Sport and International Development*, edited by R. Levermore and A. Beacom, 246–68. Houndmills: Palgrave Macmillan, 2009.

Rigg, J. *Southeast Asia: The Human Landscape of Modernization and Development*. London: Routledge, 2003.

Seippel, Ø., 'Sport and Social Capital'. *Acta Sociologica* 49, no. 2 (2006): 169–83.

Skinner, J., D. Zakus, and J. Cowell. 'Development through Sport: Building Social Capital in Disadvantaged Communities'. *Sport Management Review* 11, no. 3 (2008): 253–75.

Spaaij, R., and H. Westerbeek. 'A Healthy Active Australia? Sport and Health Policy in Australia'. In *Using Sport to Advance Community Health: An International Perspective*, edited by H. Westerbeek, 59–89. Nieuwegein: Arko Sports Media, 2009.

The transnational view of sport and social development: the case of Dominican baseball

Alan Klein

Department of Sociology and Anthropology, Northeastern University, Boston, USA

This essay examines social benefits of Major League Baseball's half century of dealings with the Dominican Republic. While the relationship was built along neo-colonial lines that heavily favoured the North American partner, structural events have unfolded in the past decade that have resulted in a levelling of the political-economic playing field. This is the outcome, not so much of MLB's sense of corporate responsibility, as it is the unforeseen consequences of its actions and the ability of Dominicans to take advantage of opportunities.

Introduction

Views – academic and other – of the impact of global sport in developing nations typically project a gloomy picture. The expansion of sporting giants emanating from the developed world is perceived as threatening to the well-being of local institutions by leeching their most valued resource – labour – and/or wreaking havoc on their autonomy.[1] There is, in this perspective, a strong element of World Systems and Dependency thinking that correctly identifies the political and economic power differentials that negatively impact local sport.[2] It would seem, then, that any discussion of social benefits accruing from such a skewed international relationship would be suspect. However, I will show that there are 'unintended consequences' in these neoliberal models that can, at times and unwittingly, promote positive outcomes.

It would be hard to find a better illustration of the social benefits of sport than the case of baseball in the Dominican Republic.[3] Two factors make this so: poverty and baseball excellence. Over the course of a century, these factors have worked to build Dominican baseball into a sport juggernaut.

Factor one: poverty

Despite economic gains made during the past 20 years, the Dominican Republic remains a country with excessive poverty and a vulnerable economy:

> This [World Bank] report finds that poverty and the incomes of the poor saw virtually no improvements during the growth bonanza of 1997–2002, and that the 2003–2004 economic crisis brought dramatic deterioration of real incomes and poverty levels. About 16% of the Dominican population ... became poor in those two years. In 2004, 42 out of each 100 Dominicans were poor, and 16 of them living in extreme poverty.[4]

There is a saying in the Dominican Republic that, 'When the United States sneezes, the Dominican Republic gets pneumonia', a reference both to the heavy reliance upon the US and to the fragile nature of their economy. So, it should come as no surprise that the current recession in the US is wreaking havoc upon the Dominican Republic. In one month (December 2008) at only one Free Trade Zone, 4,000 workers lost their jobs. Between 2007 and 2008, over 103,000 Dominicans lost jobs in 40 of the country's Free Trade Zones.[5]

Currently, poverty blends into the overall lack of economic opportunity; and this in turn fosters intensified searching on the part of the economically challenged for options offering an escape. The opportunities associated with baseball represents one of those rare bright spots.

Factor two: baseball excellence

In a country with little to boast of, the highly visible success of Dominicans in baseball represents a valued window to the world. The Dominican Republic has become synonymous with baseball excellence, producing more Major League Baseball (MLB) players per capita than anywhere else on earth. Players from this tiny island country of 9 million, last year represented 12% of players on Major League rosters (98 of 849 total players). Dominicans have won every major award in the sport and are beginning to gain entrance to the upper echelon of the administration of the sport (the ranks of coaches, managers and general managers). Additionally, almost 25% of all Minor League players working their way up the ranks of professional baseball are Dominican.[6]

The intense national pride that baseball provides Dominicans has been building for the past several decades. It has evolved into a substantial industry, with social and economic impact for Dominicans, particularly the hard-pressed. How it came to be, what it portends for the disadvantaged and the benefits accruing to communities are the subjects addressed in this study.

The study

To accurately assess the social benefits accruing to Dominican communities from baseball we have to use a transnational model, specifically one which begins using the frame of reference of Dependency Theory and progresses to a globalization model. It rests on 'core' (developed processes) and 'periphery' (developing processes) that projects into a sport globalized context.[7] Whereas in a developed nation sports franchises have the ability to draw players to them from anywhere in the world, in the Third World sport leagues often have been compromised by being unable to hold on to their local talent who leave for Europe and North America. This 'brawn drain' is facilitated by the development of 'academies', that enable them to find and train talent before shipping it abroad. Depending upon how regulated the industry is – either by its own organization or through the host nation – the relation can vary wildly from exploitive to beneficial.

A Dependency model only succeeds in establishing some structural parameters however. To more accurately assess this relationship between sport and social development in a transnational context one must use an expanded view. The relationship between a sport behemoth and a developing nation can create a myriad of features, some of which can result in displacing the normal hegemonic mechanisms of control. These opportunities occur as a result of unintended results of programmes and policies which tend to mutate from the way they were spawned. Additionally, because sports clubs vary widely in the way they operate in the periphery, we should seek to examine the role of the industry as it functions, not in any particular area, but throughout the nation. This holds as much for the Dutch football club Feyenoord working in Ghana as it does for the Boston Red Sox in the Dominican Republic.

The following study examines this process at the level of specific teams, entire industries and, finally, the players and other agents that impact both the communities and the production of players. To gain a structured understanding of how this system works across international boundaries and among so many different types of people and communities, I am looking at two paradigms: global value chains and social capital as mechanisms for getting resources to embattled communities.

Global Value Chains

The Global Value Chains (GVC) model for looking at transnational economic flow stems from Wallerstein's World Systems Theory.[8] Proceeding from the view that capitalism has been a global system since the sixteenth century, production, trade and consumption cross national boundaries as a matter of course. By linking Global Commodity Chains (as it was originally termed) with development sociology and globalization, Gereffi and Korzeniewicz brought this discussion to a sociology audience.[9] Global Value Chain research allows us to see the specific links between developed and developing economic enterprises in dynamic ways. By focusing upon the way a commodity is produced, enters the global chain that moves it through layers of marketing and institutional regulation, until it gets into the hands of the consumers around the world, the GVC model allows one to specifically see how various institutions and agents can impact the way this process is produced and reproduced. Three basic variables are central to the model: governance, institutional relations and political geography.

Importantly, with GVC research we have the capacity to introduce a wide range of variables into the production and consumption of commodities, thereby gaining insight into relations between nations and economies. We can, for instance, gauge the role and import of consumers in advanced sector countries, just as we can the role of informal middlemen and production relations in developing nations. And, most importantly, we can join these seemingly disparate elements into a unified system.

Social capital

In an important review essay on social capital, sociologist Alejandro Portes points out that the concept of 'social capital' is not at all new, having been well developed in both Marxist discussions of class and Durkheimian views of group life as an antidote to anomie.[10] Social capital has, in recent years, become a popular term in policy circles and fashionable in sociology again, bringing back the notion of 'sociability' as an overlooked mechanism for gaining access to resources and power. Bourdieu was most instrumental in reintroducing the concept to sociology, but virtually anyone writing of it points to the soft properties of social capital: sociability – trust and support – as integral to the attainment of economic goals.[11] In this sense sport is a form of social capital that can 'bridge' social relations effectively, fostering community development, upward mobility and attainment of individual or social goals. The following study of Dominican baseball draws upon the notion of social capital as developed by Putnam,[12] Bourdieu[13] and Portes,[14] but attempts to move it into the interstices of globalized relations between nations.

Setting up the Dominican study

My work in the Dominican Republic began in 1987 and has gone on intermittently since. The latest round of research began in 2002 and consists of two to three field trips per year, each lasting from one to two weeks. I am looking at several things. First, the baseball academies run by Major League teams now define the sport within the country. Their domination and key outcomes of this hegemonic relationship is central to the study. Second, the Dominican Office of the Commissioner of Major League Baseball is also a focus of study. Finally, studying the operatives themselves, the players and other agents (e.g. unregulated Dominican agents who find and train pre-signing aged players (younger than 16), hoping to get them signed at the earliest opportunity and collect their commissions), is also investigated. I have ongoing relations with organizations and people in all three areas and rely on interviews and observations to generate my data.

While the notion of social capital has been looked at, primarily, in micro terms, i.e. as networks impacting families and communities, my work is exploring the concept in the service of global interactions. Hence, when I speak of community development, I am looking at the way certain transnational relationships work toward that end. When I am considering notions of sociability, I am thinking of this with regard to the way Dominicans bound up in the global value chain of MLB, fashion and maintain such relations at the local level.

By considering the production of Major League players within the Dominican system of player development, we can construct a global value chain that places all entities and relationships within a temporal and global arrangement.[15] How social capital is developed, by whom, and for what ends, within such a system are the questions to be answered.

The baseball academy

The most dramatic structural development to have taken place in the past half century in Dominican baseball is the rise to dominance of Major League baseball academies.[16] Academies were designed to allow Major League teams a local space within which to fashion Dominicans that had been signed into players that they could comfortably send on to their teams in the US. From only two in the 1980s (Toronto and Los Angeles), these baseball academies now include all 30 Major League teams. Most importantly, they have deepened their roots in the country.

The contemporary academy bears little resemblance to the majority of academies that existed even as late as 2000. Few Major League clubs spent much time, money or personnel on finding and training Dominicans as professional players until 2000. Formerly, Major League teams approached player development in the Dominican Republic haphazardly, thinking only that quickly plugging a player into the team's minor league system was sufficient. In the early academy – beginning in 1986 – Dominicans would often be trained in a setting that Americans would consider unacceptable for players back home in the States, but adequate for Dominicans. *Pensiónes* (apartments, most often substandard) would house players in nearby towns. Food, while in relatively abundant supply, was not considered in terms of nutritional content. Playing conditions were makeshift and often rough, and coaching was often not that well thought out. Although most foreigners observing these early 'academies' commented on their poor condition, locals considered them to be an improvement upon their overall situations.[17]

It was the Los Angeles Dodgers International Director (later Vice President), Ralph Avila, who pioneered the first modern academy.[18] He conceived of and built the first academy in Latin America in the mid-1970s, and soon began envisioning a more comprehensive and evolved form. Campo Las Palmas was opened in 1987, located about an hour outside of the capitol city of Santo Domingo. It was the most complete facility ever devised: sitting on 250 acres, containing a modern dormitory, kitchen, clubhouse administrative offices and exercise facility. Most importantly, it had two complete baseball fields that at the time of its opening rivalled those to be found at professional parks in the country. It even contained its own farm which grew a large amount of the food that was consumed.

Avila single-handedly pioneered the idea of full-time scouting presence by Major League representatives when he moved to Santo Domingo in 1972. Soon after, he conceived of the concept of creating a system by which Dominican players he signed could be trained as the club would like them to be. He saw the value of using the time in training as a way to educate them: developing language skills and cultural remediation. By isolating players, one could limit distractions, control nutrition and conditioning, and promote training and playing according to the team's philosophy.

It took more than a dozen years before his idea and the model of Campo Las Palmas took hold with other Major League teams. Only when the numbers of Dominican players who succeeded in North America rose to a critical mass was the lesson of Campo Las Palmas learned and replicated. Currently, all Major League teams have moved into new academies that they either had built for them or which they lease.

The political economy of player production in the Dominican Republic

The base of this global value chain involves four links rooted in the Dominican Republic. Discovering and cultivating young talent is a complex set of relations that involve social agents, families and parts of communities in an effort to get players into the ranks of professionals. It takes years and involves ever-changing configurations of people that are, for the most part, invisible to outsiders and representatives of professional North American baseball. The point at which a young player auditions (tries out) for a Major League team, through his signing and time spent at the Dominican academy is the second phase of this Dominican-based odyssey. It, too, can take years; and in the end – if successful – will see him promoted to the US minor league system. What most do not understand is that by the time this young player arrives on the shores of the US as what most North Americans think of in terms of a fresh-faced rookie, he is in reality a weathered veteran.

Finding talented youth

Early identification of talent used to occur within the context of the amateur baseball system in the Dominican Republic. Word would spread of the best young players as they rose through the amateur ranks, culminating in their being placed on the national teams. Scouts would hear of the best of them and hold tryouts to see if they would be signed by Major League clubs. Others could find a future in playing in the professional Dominican Winter League.

The rise of the Academy System weakened this path to signing players, creating a structural void for early spotting and developing of the most talented players.[19] The *buscón* ('searcher', who is part scout, trainer, boarding house and agent) filled this void. He would quickly become the primary agent in developing young talent for Major League teams.[20] One Dominican *buscón*, Carlos Christopher, summed up his role: 'We're the eyes and ears. It's our job to know what's going on, where a player might have the best opportunity.'[21]

The first *buscónes* were scouts or 'bird dogs' who, working part time for Major League teams, would have spotted a talented 14-year-old playing in various amateur leagues and still a few years away from signing. Whereas, previously the *buscón* would have passed this prospect along to a Major League scout, in the Academy era he found the players and began training them himself. With many fewer leagues around, the *buscón* sought to develop the skills of the player until he could arrange a try out with a Major League team. Upon signing, the young player paid a substantial percentage of the signing bonus to his *buscón*. Anticipating the outrage associated with the 25% to 50% commission of the players signing bonus, one *buscón* defended himself: 'We don't work free. Nobody works free. We work them out (train them) and try to get them into professional baseball. We train the kids and they probably would never play in baseball if we weren't there.'[22]

This new way of developing players quickly established itself and the numbers of *buscónes* swelled as more and more Dominicans were signed and moved through the minor league, increasingly getting on Major League rosters. Throughout the 1990s Major League teams began to acknowledge the calibre of player coming out of the Dominican Republic by upgrading their presence on the island. This, in turn, further fuelled the numbers of *buscónes*. No one is sure of just how many of them there are in the country at present, but Ishmael Cruz, International Scouting Director for the New York Mets, confirms the view of the ubiquitous *buscón*, 'Everybody in this country is a *buscón*. Priests, teachers, doctors, politicians, even maids say, "Hey, I got a player for you".'[23] While an obvious exaggeration, Cruz wanted to communicate the rapid proliferation of *buscónes*. Baseball insiders estimate between 800 and 2,000.

Structurally, they are indispensible. In developing young players, *buscónes* are the spigot of the Dominican talent flow. Former Major Leaguer and now Red Sox academy Director, J. Alou summed up the view of many Dominicans: 'I think they're benefiting baseball … They are getting kids interested in playing … They might not know how to teach kids the proper way to play baseball, but they've got them in camp. They've got them interested in baseball, and that keeps them away from bad things.'[24] Because they have emerged from every corner of the country, *buscónes* have information and access that no one else has, furthering their importance to the process. Luis Silverio, former Director of the Kansas City Royals' academy, shook his head admitting, 'This may sound nuts, but they go where some of our scouts don't go. There are some dangerous places here, places where you cannot [have a] try out … Those *buscónes* cover those areas.'[25]

Training young prospects for turning professional

The youth who impresses a *buscón* is either directly approached, or his parents are, with an offer to develop him and get him signed to a professional contract with a Major League team. Successful *buscónes* are usually known to the young prospects and their parents, and they generally do not have to do much to bring the player under their tutelage. There are promises made to train the young player and, depending on the *buscón*, house and feed him; and these days a contract between the boy's family and the *buscón* is signed in which a large commission is to be paid upon signing with a professional team.

The conditions provided by these *buscónes* run the gamut from programmes that are clearly substandard to those that are on par with anything in the US. The former train their players under the worst of conditions: dilapidated fields and with inferior equipment. If they house players, these fiscally strapped programmes have boys sharing cramped quarters in poor sections of towns. The food is usually modest – rice and beans with some meat – but in adequate quantities. North Americans would condemn these conditions, but it should be noted that they most often represent an improvement over what these young players experienced before signing. At the other end of the spectrum are 'programmes' that faithfully mimic the academies themselves. Ramon Martínez, a former Major League star with the Los Angeles Dodgers, opened up his academy soon after he retired in 2002.

He had a dormitory built that could house about 50 players, along with a cafeteria. Martínez's academy fielded two squads, nicely attired in uniforms and playing with new equipment on well cared-for baseball diamonds.[26]

This relationship between *buscón* and player may last for several years, in which they train every day and occasionally play games. It will end when either the player tries out and is signed by a Major League team or when the boy is deemed no longer a genuine prospect.[27]

Age is an important factor in all this. Picked up early (let's say at around 14 years old), the player is judged to have a longer gestation period and may be held on to for several years. If picked up at an older age (perhaps 16 years old) he will be pushed to succeed more quickly because what drives both Major League teams and *buscónes* is the 'July 2nd' signing. According to this, a boy who is 16 years old, but will turn 17 before the onset of the next Dominican Summer League (see below) season is highly prized and can sign for seven figure bonuses. The older the prospect, the less interested are Major League clubs. The rationale behind this arrangement is that Dominicans are not subject to the amateur player draft that Americans are. They also have no organized league structures (post adolescent leagues, high school or collegiate) which foster the keeping of statistics on players. Therefore, the Dominican prospect has no empirical history of performance, only hearsay and physical attributes. Allard Baird, when General Manager of the Kansas City Royals, relied heavily upon what he called 'projectable bodies': 'Our approach is to go younger – higher risk, higher reward ... When you project, its more dangerous because you're anticipating based on physical attributes. "Well, he doesn't have a good arm right now, but he does have a good body. He's got good arm action".'[28] This approach reaches its highest expression in the Dominican Republic.

Try-outs and signings

The better young players are brought to try out with Major League teams. Since there is no baseball resumé that accompany these young players, the try-out is the only criteria used in decided whether or not to sign a Dominican player. Try-outs will consist of presentation of basic skill sets: fielding, throwing, hitting and running. They may last an hour or more depending on how many candidates are present.[29]

If the personnel at the academy like what they see in the try-out they will begin the negotiation with the *buscón*. The parties, of course, have differing agendas: Major League teams want to sign him for as little as possible, while *buscónes* want to get the largest signings possible. This is affected by such things as whether the team is a large market or small market team with budgets to match.[30] The size of signing bonuses has dramatically escalated in recent years and it is not at all uncommon to find six-figure bonuses being given to 16-year-olds. Through the first nine months of 2008, Major League teams spent $15.8 million on just 16 Dominican 16-year-olds.[31] Many club scouts and directors will go so far as to interview the player's family and friends, wanting to try to limit social and psychological flaws in the candidate that will prevent them from developing into successful players. This is what Major League scouts and others term 'makeup'.

Should the young player impress people at the academy's try-outs and pass their questioning, the conversation turns more seriously to validation of identities. Considering the impoverished backgrounds of so many of the players and with so much money at stake, there is a temptation to pass oneself off as younger than they are to take advantage of the July 2nd bonus money. Since the Major League Commissioner's Office began to work at cutting down identity fraud in 2000, teams have been made more responsible for screening their prospects. The Commissioner's Office and the US State Department follow up these initial efforts. The consequences for being caught are severe: the contract is nullified and the prospect is banned from coming to the US. Nevertheless, attempts to pass a boy off as younger continue.[32]

The actual signing usually takes place in the Santo Domingo MLB Office (if the bonus is over $25,000). At that point the young player will pay a commission to the *buscón*. This is anywhere from 25% to 50%, a figure which has resulted in the demonization of *buscónes* as thieves and exploiters.[33] For the successful prospect, a formal signing of a contract with a Major League team represents his passing through the portal into the world of professional baseball.

The academy

Officially a rookie in professional baseball, the Dominican player will attempt to learn the game as configured by his team and, ultimately, get promoted to play in the US minor league system. To accomplish this, a player has to perform well in a number of areas. First and foremost, he must play impressively in the Dominican Summer League (DSL). The DSL was formed in 1986, when the number of academies in the country had reached a critical threshold. It was then decided to have the rookies regularly play against each other and thereby develop statistics that gauged their progress and skills. In a 72-game season, the rookies compete against other teams as well as within their own club. These figures are monitored and become the primary currency, along with the intangibles of playing (e.g. one's psychological make-up) that eventually come to represent the player's profile.

In the academy players are also given language instruction and cultural remediation training in the hopes that this will shorten the cultural learning curve they will have to face upon arriving in the US. While this is considered less essential than his baseball accomplishments, everyone recognizes that a player who can master these aspects will tend to advance more quickly.

Players have up to three years to convince their organizations that they are worthy of getting promoted. At any point along the way they may be promoted to the organization's Florida Rookie League or be released. From the moment that they are sent to the US, they enter the minor league system where they try to move through the ranks, hoping eventually to play for the parent team.

This is the point of the Global Value Chain where the Dominican Republic ends and the US begins. We will stop at this point, turning our attention to the relationship between MLB and Dominican community development.

Dominican baseball as socially beneficial

Because it examines interactions at all levels, Global Value Chain research can reveal the local benefits coming from foreign influences. Here we can look more directly at how baseball-related activities and organizations function as social capital, which Alejandro Portes defines in the following manner: 'Social capital stands for the ability of actors to secure benefits by virtue of membership in social networks of other social structures.'[34]. Social benefits of sport can be measured in a variety of ways. In this study benefits are measured in more economic ways:

1. Direct benefits to communities from nearby academies and Major League teams;
2. Indirect benefits to communities from academies and MLB teams, e.g. educating players at the academies or after their careers;
3. Baseball as social capital in a variety of forms: *buscónes*, academies and players all function as social capital-creating agents;
4. Remittances as economic aid.

Direct community benefits

Academy in community development

Even though academies are intentionally located at a distance from surrounding communities, they still develop relationships with them. The Los Angeles Dodgers were the first to provide aid to their neighbours. The hamlet of Guerra is less than two miles from the academy. The Dodgers became involved with it shortly after opening their academy in 1987, when the organization's Dominican Director, Ralph Avila, arranged for the team to support a school in the town.[35] This relationship has continued after Avila's retirement and the sale of the club out of the O'Malley family's hands. No systematic pattern of community help by Major League teams' has emerged. The Oakland As, for example, fund a school near their facility and, in 2007, went on to buy and distribute 2,000 wheelchairs to the handicapped.[36] Yet, other teams do nothing.

Some Major League teams have linked with non-profit organizations that are not identified with any specific town or community but work to benefit communities at large. The Boston Red Sox and New York Mets have each entered a working relationship with very different NGOs. The Red Sox were approached by one of their wealthier fans, philanthropist Charlene Engelhard, with a project that became named, *Lindos Sueños* (pretty dreams). It calls for a dozen Dominican youth and an equal number of Americans to be brought together in the community of El Mamón where they jointly work on a community project during the day and play baseball at night. Their first project was building a day-care centre. The NGO went on to fund families in need, purchased an ambulance for the nearby town, and in 2008, initiated a project assisting an orphanage in the city of San Pedro de Macoris.

Taking a different tack, the New York Mets have joined with Esperanza International, an NGO that is heavily involved in micro financing as a vehicle for community development. It is typically clusters of 4–5 women that apply for very small loans (around $150) for a wide variety of tiny start ups. They can, upon paying the initial loan back, reapply for additional loans thereby growing their businesses. The Mets General Manager, Dominican Omar Minaya, has personally shepherded this project which has the most development potential. Both cases represent mergers between NGOs in the US, teams and Dominican communities.

Players benefiting communities

Many players have given back to their communities and the nation as a whole; and they do so through dense social networks that they remain a part of. It might take the form of building sport (usually baseball) facilities for youth and supporting the playing of the game with equipment. Or, it might involve creating badly needed edifices for communities. Pedro Martínez built his hometown a new church, while funding many small projects and directly aiding many in his community. His efforts prompted one local to claim, 'Pedro

Martínez is the best form of government we have had'.[37] Another Dominican superstar, David Ortiz, has helped build a hospital in his community.

Indirect community benefits

The buscón *as social capital*

In his role as the link to a professional baseball career for young players (through his incessant building of relations with young players and their families), the *buscón* represents a vital link between the resource goal (a professional contract) and the local community. The *buscón*'s programmes are nothing less than tiny social networks of people brought together to gain access to resources. Insofar as he can reject people at the player's end, while directing his charges to those in MLB he most favours, the *buscón* is the highly influential gatekeeper in that he takes on only the most advanced and talented young players, either rejecting or deferring until later others.

Education as community development

Since 2005 or so, a few Major League organizations have gone in the direction of creating a compulsory educational component in their academies. In this programme, all players are required to partake in formal schooling, usually consisting of classes three times a week, following games or practices. This I touted as enabling players to become productive members of their communities when their playing days are behind them. The vast majority do not have long to wait as they never proceed far up the baseball ladder. Being able to speak English and have a grasp of what is required in the baseball world makes them attractive as future employees in a rapidly growing sector of the Dominican economy.

Academy as social capital

The academy is also a social hub, a centre that collects a diverse set of individuals and forms them into a working community. Any particular class of academy players has to form itself into a community, and in doing so will influence the behaviour and outlook of anyone in it.[38] A key way in which a cohort reflects social capital is in the mutual dependence that is formed during their stay there. The bonds can aid them while there, but also for years after. Players may wind up in far-flung corners of the baseball universe (as in those who climb the rungs of the minor league system more quickly than others; or those who get to the big leagues versus those who do not), but through their earlier ties they can foster continued mutual aid. Former teammates may wind up in joint ventures especially when new academies are developed, when positions open up, or, as often happens, former players are hired by the very academies that they attended in their youth.

For the people of nearby towns, the academy is also an employer. It is estimated that almost 1,000 people are directly employed by the academies to help run the operations (e.g. guards, cooks, groundskeepers). Here, being in proximity to the academy works to facilitate employment potential, but having the contacts among those who have already been hired is an even bigger aid. This works both ways. For the academy, hiring locals also cuts down the theft by locals. The Mets were happy to have left their former location in an urban area where their efforts were never widespread enough to promote mutual goodwill – the result was regular theft from the academy.[39] In contrast, the Red Sox Director commented that now that they hire locals, theft has decreased significantly.

Playing baseball as social capital

A small – but influential and growing in number – set of players have become brokers in the world of Dominican baseball. For those fortunate enough to have played in the Major Leagues, their celebrity (and in many cases acquired wealth) has put them in touch with others, at times forming investment networks that build academies. The most famous, though not the only, example is Junior Noboa. Noboa gave me a tour of his most recent development project in 2007, a sports/education complex that was being funded by Yankee pitcher Mariano Rivera (a Panamanian). He began his post-baseball-playing career by brokering the building of a twin-complex (an academy for two teams) capitalized by Dominican investors. It was then leased to two Major League teams. This was followed by the building of 'Baseball City' a mammoth undertaking that housed six Major League teams. Other former players followed suit (e.g. Jose Rijo, Melido Peréz). What is clear is that their playing celebrity has helped foster a network or, put in other terms, a fraternity of players and those with wealth to find projects of mutual interest.

Pedro Astasio, a former Los Angeles Dodger pitcher, invested some of his money in the purchase of land next to his former academy. Years later, when the Tampa Devil Rays (a Major League team) sought to build its academy, they wound up buying the land from Astasio. This same scenario was at work while the New York Mets team leased its facility (before building their own). Former Dominican pitcher Melido Peréz had become a successful economic presence in his community and built the facility on his land, with his cement company providing the materials for construction. Here we see that Dominican capital is the new feature and that it functions to put people to work in a variety of ways.

Remittances as economic aid

In 2006, Dominicans working abroad (almost all in the US) sent back more than $2 billion dollars.[40] This constitutes an important lifeline for Dominican families remaining at home. 2007 estimates by MLB studies have baseball players repatriating $52.5 million by fewer than 100 Dominicans playing in the Major Leagues. Additionally, there are almost 3,000 Dominicans playing Minor League Baseball and earning salaries. No study exists of their remittances, but it might be as high as $20 million.

Baseball as an industrial complex: the Boca Chica area

Beginning around 2003, the academies that had been found in three disparate areas of the country (east of Santo Domingo, west of Santo Domingo and in the Cibao) began relocating to the Boca Chica area, east of the capitol. One of the reasons most given for this was the proximity to the international airport outside of Santo Domingo. In this location the teams' senior administration and ownership could easily visit the academy, making it one of their regular stops. By 2008, 29 of 30 teams had moved into this general area, creating a critical mass. Not only are there more than 1,000 players in this general area, but also the support people, such as coaches, trainers and outside administrators, are all found within a compact area. With so many clubs in the area, the level of Dominican Summer League (DSL) play was made easier – games involved little more than 20 minutes of travel time – but there is also evidence to suggest that the amount of economic opportunity for non-players mushroomed. A sector of people arose who provided services to academies. Samuel Herrera, for instance, was a *buscón* who shifted gears to become a vendor for the academies. He built a small business that provides clean sheets and laundry to several academies. Typical of developing nations, his business also sought to sell other things, such as cleaning services.[41] With so many clubs concentrated in an area, people along the route might wind up trying to sell any number of things to the increased (and anticipated) traffic of players, teams and assorted personnel. I know of several employees of teams who make it their business to stop at certain places to pick up specialty items (e.g. fish) that they cannot get in the capitol.

Conclusion

I have tried to show that the intensification of Dominican-MLB baseball relations has resulted in an array of social and economic benefits to communities in particular and to the nation as a whole. The irony is that these benefits have come in the wake of MLB's increased structural presence in the country (i.e. the Academy System and the MLB Commissioner's Dominican Office). While it is tempting to regard MLB's increased embeddedness as a setback to Dominican baseball autonomy (as would a Dependency Model), in a globalized context, increased interactions of this nature can result in a local empowerment. There is a trade off in which, while the amateur system became weakened and increasingly subordinated to the MLB production of labour, a course of events unintentionally unfolded: Dominicans playing Major League baseball achieved a level that had far-reaching and positive consequences back home. Dominicans have actually grown in political-economic power within the baseball relations it has with MLB.

The impact of Major League Baseball in the Dominican Republic might be objected to on the basis that in selecting only the most talented players it's social benefits do not reach down far enough into communities.[42] That is an assessment that can only be significant within the confines of the industry itself. Playing professional sport is, by definition, exclusive; that is, it selects only the best and rejects all others. But, within that structure there is the potential for significant shifts in the parameters of inclusion and exclusion. That is, over time the sport can mature in a country or region sufficiently to bring in increasing numbers of players and to allow them more direct and indirect opportunities.

The Dominican Republic was, until the past decade, disregarded by MLB clubs and operatives. It is now recognized as important enough to invest in and, by extension, to empower in the ways discussed above. One final illustration: in late 2008, it was announced that Major League Baseball in conjunction with US Aid for International Development and the Peace Corps were each putting $1 million into a fund that would be run through Dominican non-profit organizations to help poor Dominicans get a leg up.[43] What is significant about this is that MLB had come to the point where it considered projects that better the Dominican Republic as a whole as important enough to partner with international agencies. A decade ago, such a move would have been beyond the realm of comprehension. It is important to keep in mind that it is not that MLB has arrived at some enlightened position regarding this prized source of baseball labour. Rather, it is that it has come to realize that investing in the Dominican Republic makes good business sense.

The continued entrenchment of MLB in the Dominican Republic has without doubt weakened the structural sovereignty of the sport, but interpreting that in a uniformly negative way, misses a very significant counter-result. The initial colonialist relationship that MLB had with Dominican baseball actually metamorphosed into something unplanned: a mounting body of evidence that shows that MLB is having a positive impact on communities throughout the country and, moreover, that Dominicans are becoming more politically and economically powerful.

Notes

[1] Klein, *Sugarball*.
[2] Wallerstein, *The Modern World System*; Frank, *Capitalism and Underdevelopment in Latin America*.
[3] Klein, *Sugarball*; Klein, *Growing the Game*.
[4] World Bank, *Dominican Republic Poverty Assessment*, 3.
[5] *DominicanToday.com*, December 21, 2008.
[6] Klein, 'The Dominican Republic'; Klein, 'Latinizing the "National Pastime"'.
[7] I use this model in a heuristic fashion and include semi-periphery nations as peripheral. In global sport, Europe and North America represent the core from which sport emanates.
[8] Hopkins and Wallerstein, 'Commodity Chains in the World Economy'.
[9] Gerrefi and Korzeniewicz, *Commodity Chains*.
[10] Portes, 'Social Capital', 2.
[11] Bourdieu, 'The Social Space and Genesis of Groups'.
[12] Putnam, *Bowling Alone*.
[13] Bourdieu, 'The Social Space and Genesis of Groups'.
[14] Portes, 'Social Capital'.
[15] Klein, 'Global Value Chains and Dominican Baseball'.
[16] Klein, *New Pride, Old Prejudice*.
[17] Klein, *Sugarball*; Klein, 'The Dominican Republic'.
[18] Klein, *Sugarball*, 58–79.
[19] Ibid., 63.
[20] Ibid.; Klein, 'Progressive Ethnocentrics'.
[21] J. Strauss, 'Caribbean Baseball Agents Ruling the Roost'. *SportsBusinessNews.com*, December 25, 2005.
[22] T. Jacobson, 'Buscones M.O.: Find, Train, Reap: Dominican Agents Develop Talent, Then Take a Cut'. *Fredericksburg.com/News*, December 18, 2006.
[23] Author's interview with Cruz, May 22, 2007.
[24] Interview with J. Alou, cited in Klein, *Sugarball*, 110.
[25] Author's interview with Silverio, June 12, 2002.
[26] Klein, *Growing the Game*, Chap. 6.
[27] There is a Japanese academy in the country as well.
[28] Klein, *Growing the Game,* 40.
[29] Ibid., 48–50.
[30] Ibid., Chap. 2 and 3.
[31] Badler, 'International Roundup', 11.
[32] Klein, *Growing the Game*, 56.
[33] Klein, 'Progressive Ethnocentrics'.
[34] Portes, 'Social Capital', 6.
[35] Klein, *Sugarball*, 103.
[36] Current information in this area has come from fieldtrips taken in 2007–08.
[37] Klein, *Growing the Game*, 90.
[38] Klein, *Sugarball*.
[39] Author interview with Perez, May 13, 2007.
[40] J. Díaz, 'Dominicans Cast Ballots'. *Boston Globe*, May 17, 2006.
[41] Klein, *Growing the Game*, 106–7.
[42] Portes, 'Social Capital'; Putnam, *Bowling Alone*.
[43] See http://www.MLB.com.

References

Badler, B. 'International Roundup'. *Baseball America*, November 3–16 (2008): 11.
Bourdieu, P. 'The Social Space and Genesis of Groups'. *Social Science Information* 24, no. 2 (1985): 194–220.
Frank, A.G. *Capitalism and Underdevelopment in Latin America*. London: Penguin Books, 1974 [1967].
Gerrefi, G., and M. Korzeniewicz, eds. *Commodity Chains and Global Capitalism*. Westport, CT: Praeger, 1994.

Hopkins, T., and I. Wallerstein. 'Commodity Chains in the World Economy Prior to 1800'. *Review* 10, no. 1 (1986): 157–70.

Klein, A. *Sugarball: The American Game, the Dominican Dream*. New Haven, CT: Yale University Press, 1991.

Klein, A. *Growing the Game: Globalization and Major League Baseball*. New Haven, CT: Yale University Press, 2006.

Klein, A. 'The Dominican Republic: Forging an International Industry'. In *Baseball Without Borders: The International Pastime*, edited by G. Gmelch, 117–35. Lincoln, NE: Bison Books, 2006.

Klein, A. 'Latinizing the "National Pastime"'. *The International Journal of the History of Sport* 24, no. 2 (2007): 296–310.

Klein, A. 'Progressive Ethnocentrics: Ideology and Understanding in Dominican Baseball'. *Journal of Sport and Social Issues* 32, no. 2 (2008): 121–38.

Klein, A. 'Global Value Chains and Dominican Baseball.' Submitted to *Sociology of Sport Journal*.

Klein, A. *New Pride, Old Prejudice: The Second Coming of Dominican Baseball*. Manuscript.

Portes, A., 'Social Capital: Its Origins and Applications in Modern Sociology'. *Annual Review of Sociology* 24, no. 1 (1998): 1–24.

Putnam, R. *Bowling Alone: The Collapse and Revival of American Community*. New York: Simon & Schuster, 2000.

Wallerstein, I. *The Modern World System*. 3 Vols. New York: Academic Press, 1986.

World Bank. *Dominican Republic Poverty Assessment. Report 32422-DR*. Washington, DC: World Bank, 2006.

The glue that holds the community together? Sport and sustainability in rural Australia

Ramón Spaaij[1]

School of Management, La Trobe University, Australia; Amsterdam School for Social Science Research, University of Amsterdam, The Netherlands

Drawing on the author's research in northwest Victoria, Australia, this essay examines the forms of capital that are created in and through rural sport as well as the processes of social inclusion and exclusion that structure access to social networks and to the resources these networks contain. In the face of economic and social changes that affect the region, rural sport participants view local sport clubs as vital community hubs fostering social cohesion, local and regional identities and a shared focus and outlet. Sporting competitions in northwest Victoria also contribute to cultural and economic capital for some participants, and to relatively limited stocks of linking social capital. While the creation and transference of these capitals are to a large degree regulated by wider social divisions, structural changes in the area present increased opportunities for other people, including young women, to take on leadership roles and to develop new skills and knowledge through sport participation.

Introduction

The extrinsic significance of sport has emerged as a major theme in contemporary sports research. Several studies address sport's contributions to regeneration and community development in urban areas. Coalter and his colleagues have noted that there has been little systematic analysis of the precise role that sport can play in the regeneration of local urban economies.[2] While urban aspects of 'development through sport' have recently gained increased academic attention,[3] this is not the case for rural areas, some of which experience multiple forms of social disadvantage.[4] There is an odd paradox with regards to rural sport: while many people living in rural areas herald what they consider as the profound contributions of sport to the social fabric of rural communities, these perceived effects remain seriously under-valued in the thriving sport-for-development debate. Illustrative of this point is that the few recent influential studies that specifically address rural sport tend to focus on social exclusion and deprivation in the rural context, rather than to critically and empirically scrutinize the ways in which sport (organizations) may contribute to social wellbeing in rural areas.[5]

The objective of this essay is to rectify this omission. It aims not only to empirically assess the social benefits associated with rural sport, but also to formulate a conceptual-analytical framework, albeit sketchy, which enables such analysis. This twofold task will offer the reader insight into how the people under study experience and make sense of their sporting experiences, while grounding the subjective perceptions and lived experiences of rural sport participants in the wider academic and policy debate on the social impacts of (rural) sport. In doing so, this esssay addresses the following question: which types of benefits accrue to people living in rural communities as a result of sport participation, either in playing or non-playing roles, and sporting competitions more generally? This question will be investigated by means of a case study of sporting competitions in the northwest of the state of Victoria, Australia.

The major significance of this question is that it enables us to deconstruct and contextualize the argument put forward by academics and policy-makers alike that beneficial outcomes of sport are most likely to be achieved through well-designed sport-based development programmes that are 'consciously and systematically organized to maximize the possibility of achieving such outcomes'.[6] The realities of sport in rural Australia contradict this assumption in that voluntary, autonomously run sporting competitions have been generating certain social benefits (and related forms of social inclusion and exclusion) for decades against the backdrop of profound structural changes. A recent study concluded that the contributions of sport to rural life should not be underestimated: 'Its role in fostering social interaction, a sense of place and community, and the range of physical and mental health benefits contribute significantly to the well-being of rural citizens.'[7] Such outcomes, as we will see, do not usually result from socially engineered and carefully crafted policies, but rather from the intersection of subtle and complex socio-cultural processes and the adaptive strategies and identity work of individuals and local sport organizations.

This essay is divided into three main parts. The first part discusses the conceptual-analytical framework of the study, focusing on the interplay between economic, social and cultural capital and its applications to rural sport. I argue that the social benefits of sport in northwest Victoria can be usefully analysed in terms of the creation, maintenance, transference and diminution of these different forms of capital. The second part describes the research methods and the wider social context in which northwest Victorian sport is embedded. The final part of this essay presents the study's findings regarding the social benefits that accrue from rural sport and the processes of social inclusion and exclusion that structure access to these benefits. The findings highlight the central arguments made in this essay: firstly, while influential studies on rural sport emphasize exclusion, this study also finds potent processes of social inclusion; and secondly, voluntary community sport organizations in small rural towns tend to be effective vehicles for the creation and transference of social, cultural and economic capital resources.

Social and cultural dimensions of sport in rural Australia

Studies of rural communities tend to highlight the important role that sport plays in the social and cultural fabric of these communities. Robert and Helen Lynd's well-known study of life in a small regional American town compared leisure activity of the late nineteenth century with the 1920s, noting the impact of considerable changes in technology and communications.[8] Mass production and the availability of the automobile led to greater mobility, in turn affecting communal activities such as church attendance. The Lynds argued that previous types of association and communally organized leisure had weakened or disappeared as new cultural forms took hold, with leisure involvement becoming more passive. At the same time, they indicated that high school basketball provided a renewed means of associational engagement fostering a sense of belonging, group cohesion and community spirit.[9] The Lynds viewed basketball as a unique form of social cement, drawing residents together across suburban, class and religious divisions.

Hughson, Inglis and Free make the important point that the rhetoric on which arguments for the integrative function of sport are pegged should not be taken for granted.[10] Sport is not an inherently wholesome or socially cohesive force. Rather, sport has the potential of producing both positively and negatively perceived outcomes, and it often reinforces social inequalities.[11] In their study of ice hockey culture in Canada, Gruneau and Whitsun warn that sport can work against, as much as it creates, a sense of belonging in small town life.[12] They note that 'visible minorities' are sometimes ostracized from social life in small towns because they do not become involved in sporting activities. In such cases sport provides a social norm of inclusion for those who play the game, and one of exclusion for those who do not.

These themes have been addressed to some degree in publications on sport in rural Australia. Sport organizations are commonly regarded as an important forum of civic engagement in Australian rural communities. Local sport clubs are a major focus of rural community life, and participation in (or exclusion from) sport clubs affects residents' social status, social networks and access to resources.[13] It has been argued that at a time when other social institutions were diminishing, organized sport remained, providing a sense of social cohesion and belonging. In 2004, a Parliamentary Inquiry into Australian football in Victoria concluded that 'football/netball clubs are, to a significant degree, the "glue" holding many small rural communities together'.[14] The report acknowledged a range of positive outcomes associated with organized sport, including individual benefits (e.g. skill acquisition and greater social connectedness), economic benefits (e.g. increased revenue and tourism) and broader social outcomes (e.g. a sense of local community and improved public health). Below I will conceptualize these outcomes in relation to forms of capital.

Capital formation in and through rural sport

Contemporary research into rural sport draws heavily on the concept of social capital, as we will see. Social capital is generally viewed to stand for 'the ability of actors to secure benefits by virtue of membership in social networks or other social structures'.[15] Three types of social capital can be distinguished: bonding, bridging and linking social capital.[16] Bonding social capital refers to ties between like people in similar situations, such as immediate family, close friends and neighbours. Putnam notes that bonding social capital 'is good for undergirding specific reciprocity and mobilizing solidarity'.[17] At the same time, bonding social capital, by creating strong in-group loyalty, may also create strong out-group antagonism and social exclusiveness. Dense social connections that reinforce homogeneity are more likely to build high social walls and be less tolerant of diversity. Bridging social capital, on the other hand, refers to more distant ties with like persons, such as loose friendships and work colleagues. Bridging social capital can generate broader identities, mutually accepted norms of trust and reciprocity. Bridging networks are viewed to be 'better for linkage to external assets and for information diffusion'.[18] Bridging is nevertheless essentially a horizontal metaphor, implying connections between people who share broadly similar demographic characteristics. A potentially troublesome aspect of this type of social capital is that the social connections tend to be weaker and are generally more fragile.

Putnam emphasizes that bonding and bridging social capital 'are not "either-or" categories ... but "more or less" dimensions along which we can compare different forms of social capital'.[19] He asserts that the 'right mix' is required for benefits to accrue. One question this interpretation of social capital raises is whether bridging social capital can be imposed artificially by political decree or through social engineering. Hughson, Inglis and Free point out that bridging social capital will accrue as individuals and groups seek out contact with others for whatever social reasons or through whatever institutional means.[20] Improving community relations and networks might be an outcome of collective sporting engagement, but it is not an initial incentive to compete. As I will demonstrate, in northwest Victoria these outcomes principally accrue from voluntary contact between residents of different country towns rather than through socially engineered sport-based development programmes.

A major limitation of Putnam's interpretation of social capital is its failure to adequately address power relations, social inequalities and subtle processes of social inclusion and exclusion. In Putnam's analysis 'social capital becomes divorced from other forms of capital, stripped of power relations, and imbued with the assumption that social networks are win-win relationships and that individual gains, interests, and profits are synonymous with group gains, interests, and profits'.[21] Social capital also has a vertical dimension, which has been termed linking social capital. Linking social capital is concerned with relations between individuals and groups in different social strata. Linking social capital reaches out to unlike people in dissimilar situations, such as those who are entirely outside the community, thus enabling members to leverage a far wider range of resources than are available within the community.[22] Woolcock has extended the notion of linking social capital by including the capacity of individuals and communities to leverage resources, ideas and information from formal institutions beyond the immediate community.[23]

In his study of competitive sport in a rural region of Western Australia, Tonts suggests that sport plays a significant role in the formation of social networks that contribute to bonding social capital. According to Tonts:

> Residents saw sport as a focal point of community life that brings people together and creates an opportunity for meaningful social interaction. The role of bonding capital was particularly evident, with numerous people discussing the way in which sport creates a sense of local pride and forms the basis of a 'tight knit' community.[24]

These findings correspond to Atherley's study of sport and social capital in another rural region of Western Australia. She found 'a strong connection between sport and important assets such as community cohesion, identity and pride'.[25] Indicators of bonding social capital, such as elements of trust and cooperation, were particularly evident.

For Tonts, rural sport also contributes to bridging social capital. Local residents placed considerable emphasis on the way in which sport was able to transcend class, ethnic, religious and other barriers. Residents claimed that networks created through sport can connect different social groups that might otherwise remain disconnected from one another.[26] At the same time, Tonts acknowledges that sport is often not the egalitarian and socially inclusive institution that many residents claim. Even in those clubs thought of as egalitarian and inclusive, there appear to be social divisions along class, gender, ethnic and status lines as well as in relation to the length of residence.[27] Aboriginal participation in organized rural sport remains comparatively low and tends to be restricted to a small number of sports, notably Australian football, basketball and netball. Female residents also feel excluded to some extent. A number of women pointed out that they were not welcome at some of the functions at football clubs. The division of labour at club functions in a range of sports was also noted, with women usually responsible for activities such as preparing food, cooking and cleaning.[28] This division of labour often contributed to a spatial division of labour within clubs, with women and men often occupying different parts of a club or venue, with little interaction. Dempsey has also noted the significance of rural sport clubs as a site for male bonding and for the construction and reproduction of masculinities, with sport arguably providing the strongest marker of masculinity in country towns.[29] Notwithstanding these cultural norms and pressures, Tonts concludes that sport's positive contributions to rural life outweigh its more problematic aspects, especially in its role in fostering social interaction and a sense of place and community.[30]

Social benefits of sport in northwest Victoria: methods and context

In my analysis of the benefits that accrue from sport participation in northwest Victoria, I aim to expand the narrow focus on (bonding and bridging) social capital in the existing literature by arguing, following Bourdieu, that different species of capital are inextricably intertwined.[31] Applications of the concept of social capital to the realm of sport tend to incorrectly divorce the notion of social capital from other forms of capital, ignoring Bourdieu's point that capitals are more or less fungible. For the present purpose, I will analyse the close interrelationships between economic, cultural and social capital and the ways in which rural sport participation influences the creation, maintenance, transference or diminution of capital resources. Economic capital corresponds to material wealth, as capital that can be readily transformed into money and that can be institutionalized in terms of property rights. Cultural capital (broadly defined) refers to cultural goods, knowledge, experience, education, competencies and skills which a social actor possesses and which confer power or status in the social hierarchy.[32]

The research on which this study is based was carried out in small rural towns in northwest Victoria in 2008 and 2009. These rural localities consist of population clusters of 400 to 1,600 people primarily living on farms or in agricultural service centres. The research incorporated five sports: Australian football, netball, hockey, cricket and tennis. Within each sporting environment, semi-structured interviews and focus group discussions were held with participants, volunteers, club and league organizers, and local residents who did not participate in any of these sports. Group sessions focused principally on participants' experiences and their views on the impact of sport participation on their lives and on the wider community.

Several local residents are involved in more than one of the above sports as part of their multiplex sporting relations.[33] These sporting relations are often seasonally based, with some male residents participating in football during the winter season and in cricket during summer. As I will demonstrate, these multiplex relations allow resources embedded in one particular sport-based relationship to be appropriated for use in others and, more importantly, in interpersonal contacts outside the realm of sport. This is particularly the case for those individuals who hold positions within sport clubs or leagues that convey considerable social status, such as the roles of president, treasurer or secretary. In other words, the potential social benefits of sport are not only to be fostered through direct participation; involvement in the organization and provision of opportunities for sport can assist in the development of transferable resources and skills.[34]

The case study included individual and paired interviews with people in the following categories ($n = 59$):[35]

- Australian football players, league/club officials and volunteers ($n = 20$);
- Netball players, league/club officials and volunteers ($n = 5$)
- Hockey players, league/club officials and volunteers ($n = 5$)
- Cricket players, league/club officials and volunteers ($n = 2$)

- Tennis players, club officials and volunteers ($n = 3$)
- Non-playing residents ($n = 6$)
- Council members ($n = 3$)
- Representatives of local schools ($n = 5$)
- Health providers ($n = 3$)
- Local businesspeople ($n = 5$)
- Local journalists ($n = 2$)

Although Australian football is by far the most popular sport in terms of the number of participants and spectators in northwest Victoria, the comparatively large number of interviews with persons in this category may leave the other sports slightly under-represented. The popular over-representation of Australian football and its particular cultural norms (e.g. male bonding, drinking culture) has in fact been raised by some residents as an issue of concern, especially in relation to local government funding for sport. Most residents, and especially men, will nevertheless argue that 'football is the dominant sport' and that 'football is unique' in terms of its community appeal.[36] Other sport clubs 'do not necessarily have the same standing as football/netball clubs in terms of their ability to act as a "community hub", facilitate broad-based social interaction and engender a sense of collective, locally-based pride'.[37] However, there is often a high level of interdependence between football/netball clubs and other sport clubs.

Structural changes in northwest Victoria: implications for sport and communities

The perceived significance of sport in the social life of small towns in northwest Victoria can be viewed as a historically evolved cultural pattern. Sport formed a large part of the social life of many of these towns from the very beginning. In most cases, the first sport to begin, the most popular and the most enduring was Australian football.[38] In some towns other sports such as racing emerged even earlier than football.[39] But the particular benefits local residents assign to sport should also be understood within the context of more recent structural changes. Northwest Victoria, like several other rural regions in Australia,[40] has experienced profound social and economic changes in recent decades that impact not only on the general social and cultural life of small towns, but also specifically on the ways in which local residents perceive and experience sport. Lack of space prevents me from discussing these changes in full detail in this essay. The main social and economic changes in rural Victoria are summarized below.

The economic restructuring of agriculture, driven in part by technological changes, has resulted in a situation where farm incomes have steadily fallen and forced many families to leave the industry. The total number of farms operating in Australia fell from around 201,000 in 1960 to just over 130,000 in 2004. Australia experienced a decline of 20,000 farms between 1994 and 2004.[41] These families rarely remain in rural areas and tend to migrate to cities or coastal areas.[42] Changes of this kind have been exacerbated by policy changes whose effects have been to link the Australian economy more tightly into the global economy and to make it more responsive to market forces, including deregulation in the finance sector and labour market, privatization of government business enterprises, reduction in general levels of government assistance to industries, and wider application of the 'user pays' principle.[43] These changes are reflected in a general shift from government policies based on socio-spatial equity to those that emphasize economic efficiency, with many services relocating from rural communities into regional centres or capital cities.[44] This transformation has resulted in the loss of facilities and services that are deemed essential to the survival and identity of small rural towns (i.e. schools, banks, post offices, hospitals), and therefore an erosion of the roles and functions performed by these towns.[45]

The rapidity of economic and social changes in the past three decades has generated particular difficulties for several rural communities. Many small rural towns have experienced a contraction of local economic activity (business closures, fewer employment opportunities), further outmigration of young adults and families with children, and the breakdown of certain local social institutions and networks.[46] McManus and Pritchard note the fundamental problem of population decline, locking some communities into a vicious cycle, where the removal of services not only contributes to population decline, but often results in the more entrepreneurial and higher spending members of a community moving elsewhere in search of opportunities.[47] We should add to this the impact of long periods of drought on agriculture in northwest Victoria, which has been an integral part of the economic, social and environmental issues facing farmers in the area for more than a century.[48] Drought has also affected the maintenance of sport facilities in the region, urging clubs to implement strategies for sustainable water usage on sport grounds.

The consequences of these developments are distributed unevenly across Victoria. There is a growing division between those (mainly coastal, accessible or environmentally attractive) rural areas experiencing population growth, and those (mainly inland agricultural regions) experiencing decline. The wheat and sheep belt of northwest Victoria falls into the latter category, with many of its towns experiencing (either slow or more rapid) depopulation accompanied by the gradual withdrawal of public services.[49] In some cases the closure of public services has had a significant psychological impact on rural towns, arguably signalling the 'death' of the town.[50] Such changes may also affect the sustainability of voluntary organizations and sport clubs. All towns witness the 'flight of youth' to seek education, training and employment in regional and metropolitan cities (mainly Melbourne, Ballarat and Bendigo).[51] This has an impact on the social structure and amenity of each town. It also has an impact on sporting and social events and affects the supply of able-bodied volunteers for vital community work.[52]

Again, this development is more noticeable in some small towns than in others. Certain towns in northwest Victoria appear to have been relatively successful in retaining or attracting young people, for example through establishing cutting-edge agricultural organizations or by attracting new industries. These organizations have successfully tempted young professionals to move into the area. Many of these young professionals perceive sport as an important means for meeting new people and settling into the community, and some of them are prominent figures in the management of local sporting competitions. One male resident explained:

> I have only been in the town for five years. Being involved in hockey and football is a great way to integrate and to get to know people, especially for my wife because she was a school principal in the past so she used to have a large social network.

Atherley argues that processes of restructuring are having direct impacts on rural sport clubs. The adaptive strategies of sport clubs in Western Australia are a direct result of the clubs being exposed to these processes and include amalgamation and the spatial reorganization of sporting competition locations.[53] The extent of these impacts appears to be less pronounced in northwest Victoria, where the loss and amalgamation of sport clubs has been a less frequent, but nevertheless significant, occurrence. In recent years there have been two amalgamations of football/netball clubs in the area under study, as well as an amalgamation of tennis clubs. The loss of a local sport club has the potential to impact negatively on existing social networks and community identity, cutting deeply into the pride of the town. For example, a male resident interpreted the amalgamation of his football/netball club with a club in a neighbouring town (with the latter club functioning as the club's new home base) as follows:

> The end of the footy club was due to the loss of population, which in turn is due to changes in farming. This has signalled the death of the town, loss of a community hub. Now the club is amalgamated but only in name. It has lost most of its community appeal.

Furthermore, many football/netball clubs in northwest Victoria struggle to retain young people who have moved to Melbourne or other regional centres for work or education. They encourage them (especially talented players) to return 'home' on weekends to play football or netball by paying their petrol costs and/or offering playing fees. While this appears to have been a reasonably successful strategy, individuals rarely continue to do this for more than a few years. One former football player, who is now a league representative, explained how 'young players only travel back for two or three years normally, then you lose them because they settle down and have family or job obligations'.

Sport clubs as community hubs fostering social interaction

> 'Sport is the soul of the community.' (local male teacher)

Many participants and volunteers emphasize the contributions of local sporting competitions to social networks. Sport clubs, and especially football/netball clubs, are viewed as important hubs for social interaction, providing a shared focus and outlet. Football/netball clubs play a vital role in maintaining and improving community facilities, such as leisure centres and social club rooms. For many residents, the significance of sport as a site for social interaction has increased in recent decades as a result of mostly negatively perceived structural changes. It was observed that some of the historically dominant forms of associational engagement, such as church groups, had diminished and that few major forums for social interaction remain, with sport clubs occupying a prominent place in the towns' social and cultural landscape. Participation in sport clubs, whether as player or volunteer, is predominantly motivated by the fun, friendship and social aspects associated with club membership.

Given the relatively small population sizes of the towns, it is perhaps unsurprising that several residents indicated that they already knew most club members before they joined the club, for example through school or work. Involvement in sport clubs allows them to get to know others better and to develop closer ties. This social aspect of sport does not interest everyone to the same degree. While some spend a large amount of their leisure time at the sport club, others are more pragmatic in their sport participation. For example, a man who recently moved into the area stated: 'My two sons play junior football. They enjoy football and have made new friends through their involvement. I take them to the games, but I do not stay around all day. I usually go home straight after the game to do things around the house.'

Sport clubs in northwest Victoria not only foster the creation of bonding social capital, but also facilitate social connections between people from different walks of life. Residents tend to argue that 'at the footy social barriers don't exist' or that 'in tennis you mingle with people in different age groups ... who you wouldn't normally meet'. For some farmers, Saturday afternoon sport is quite literally a principal form of social interaction. One farmer commented:

> I live on a farm 12 kilometres from the town, quite isolated. If it wasn't for sport, I would probably stay on the farm to fix a fence or something. At footy I talk to other farmers about

sport and farming issues, for example new methods, machinery and funding options. It is also a great way to meet other types of people, like teachers and doctors.

In times of drought and economic hardship, involvement in sport is believed to have a positive impact on physical and mental health. Another farmer stated: 'For me it is a switch-off cue, to get away from the farm and a sort of outlet, fun, to release tensions and stress. To share experiences or just to crack jokes. It gets you out of your isolation.' Comments of this kind are fairly common and underline the belief of many local residents that 'sport gets people out of their homes' and that sport allows one to 'meet people you wouldn't meet in a social context otherwise'.

The significance of sporting competitions in the creation of bridging social capital in northwest Victoria is enhanced by two characteristics of the regional sport landscape. Firstly, population decline has forced some football/netball clubs to merge. Although this is interpreted by most local residents as a loss of identity and local pride, amalgamations also provide new opportunities for social connections between people of different towns, enhancing trust and cooperation in both an economic and a social context. One female resident commented:

> You mix more with ferals through football now [after the amalgamation], for example a few players and fans from a lower socio-economic background from the other town. They blend in very well at footy and have made valuable contacts. If not for sport you wouldn't engage with them.

However, this comment also reveals that bridging connections at sport matches are situational and do not necessarily challenge existing social inequalities, but rather reproduce them through subtle mechanisms of social distinction (e.g. stereotyping). Furthermore, growing contacts between people living in different towns cannot be attributed to sport only. Young people generally have more, and more intensive, contact with their peers in other towns than in the past, partly owing to increased mobility and the availability of Internet and mobile telephony. This wider trend is reflected and enhanced in sport, with young players at times staying in town the evening after an away match to catch up with opposing players and other friends or acquaintances. One netball player explained how she sometimes stayed over after a night out in another town instead of having to drive home. She described sport as a way to get away from parents and visit other towns as part of away games.

Secondly, the league under study is unique in that it incorporates three sports at both junior and senior levels: football, netball and hockey. Match days feature a large number of matches involving people in different age groups (from juniors to seniors) in male and female sport teams. This set up stimulates interaction between different generations and between men and women, diverging to some extent from the more traditional view of rural sport as heavily male dominated. This particular configuration of the league is principally a consequence of adaptive strategies of sport clubs to cope with wider social changes, such as population decline. Many teams struggle to field the required number of players, especially the lower-level teams, and teams therefore regularly borrow each other's players, generating more multiplex sporting relations. Consider the following observation by a female resident:

> One team has too many junior players, so they are on a roster system and each week some players have to play for the opposing team, but not just the worse players. They see this as a fair play system, and it brings kids into contact with each other and as a consequence their parents as well.

The shortage of players appears to reduce to some degree the talent barrier of sport participation and to enhance the inclusiveness of sport clubs. A female resident gave the following example of sporting inclusion in northwest Victoria, drawing a comparison with sport in urban areas:

> Our league is very inclusive. You don't have to be talented to be able to play. New residents told me that their kids wanted to play football when they were living in the city, but they were not selected because apparently they were not good enough. Now they have moved here they can play. We are very happy to have them.

Another implication of the shortage of players and volunteers has been that, in addition to hockey and tennis clubs, women increasingly occupy leadership positions within football/netball clubs, enabling them to acquire greater social status, broaden their social networks and develop new skills in management, finance and diplomacy. This issue is discussed below.

Developing skills and knowledge through sport

Several interviewees argued that they can acquire new skills and new forms of knowledge and experience through sport participation. Although the development of cultural capital through sport is commonly presented as open to all participants, in reality it is mainly confined to those who occupy leadership positions within sport clubs and leagues. The former president of a football club described how he, a farmer in his late 50s, learned about administration and management through his roles in the club. The professional skills he claimed to have developed include public speaking, engaging with government and sport organizations, conflict resolution and people management. Additionally, in his previous role as club treasurer he was responsible for the financial business of the club with an annual turnover of $200,000. Stressing that he never completed secondary education, he argued that he uses these skills in his profession and that this has opened up new opportunities and networks. Another male farmer similarly stated that his role as club president enabled him to learn to speak in public, manage people, lobby at a political level and work in a team, leading him to gain access to new business networks. Both men emphasized the importance of these experiences for young people with little or no previous (work) experience. Older, more experienced people, they felt, should guide and mentor them and act as role models. This belief was shared by a local businessman who stressed that he learned many skills at a relatively young age through his involvement with football. He became the secretary of his local club at the age of 21, which he sees, in hindsight, as a major life experience that has helped him to set up his own business.

While these opportunities for skill development are presented as egalitarian and open to everyone, access to status positions within clubs and leagues is in many cases regulated by wider social divisions. People in certain occupations, such as managers, teachers or doctors, are relatively often in managerial positions in sport clubs. Recruitment is regularly based on pre-existing skills in particular areas and/or social status as a (former) player rather than on expected future outcomes in relation to skill development and cultural capital. There thus exists a pattern of social reproduction in which people with relatively large stocks of cultural and symbolic capital are most likely to obtain prestigious and culturally beneficial positions in sport clubs and leagues. However, given the shortage of qualified volunteers in most small towns, there are also regular opportunities for younger or less educated people (including young women) to take up leadership roles in sport clubs and to use these roles to expand their social networks and acquire new skills and knowledge.

Another important aspect of the creation of social and cultural capital in and through sport is the way in which these practices are gendered. Sporting fields have long been identified as 'sites of masculine power and privilege' as indicated, for example, by the almost total absence of women from rural media reports of sport.[54] Gender relations permeate northwest Victorian sport clubs in several ways. Some residents commented on the pressures associated with the cultural perceptions of different sports, with football being regarded as a 'man's game' compared to games such as hockey, while netball is traditionally viewed as the most prestigious and culturally appropriate game for women, with talented players often having substantially more social status than female hockey players. But although these cultural images persist, there have been some changes in recent years, partly as a result of depopulation. There are now more men who play hockey in all male or mixed hockey teams in the region, with hockey providing new participation opportunities for men who dislike Australian football or its culture. Some parents actually discourage their sons from playing football due to fear of injuries. A number of reserve football players also play hockey, which at times has concerned football teams for fear of decreased interest in Australian football. The latter point indicates that while there are major overlapping sporting networks in northwest Victoria, there are also variable degrees of competition between different sports, generated in part by demographic changes and evolving cultural norms.

Another way to interpret gender relations in northwest Victorian sport is in terms of the division of labour at sport clubs, leading some female club members to feel partially excluded. In most sport clubs women are usually responsible for activities such as preparing food, cooking and cleaning, limiting their interaction with players and fans of opposing teams. At most sport venues I have visited women run the catering, bar and kitchen, with very few men taking on these tasks. But also in this area gender relations are subject to a variable degree of change. While football is still a man's game in most respects, women are now more centrally involved. A few women occupy leadership positions in football/netball clubs, for example in junior football. Social roles are also no longer as traditional as they once were. At some sport clubs all members are on the roster to cook and clean, and not just the women. These practices appear to have transformed traditional gender roles to some degree. Local residents explained these changes in terms of the shortage of volunteers (resulting in increased opportunities for women to take up leadership roles) and the fact that more women in small towns work nowadays. As the secretary of a local hockey club, who is a teacher, asked: why would we have to do all the work at the club when we also work during the week?

Social capital and economic opportunities

Sport clubs in northwest Victoria have a significant economic impact. The fortunes of sport clubs and small town economies are linked to a considerable degree. This interrelationship is based on sponsorship of sport clubs by local business and reciprocal support from football/netball clubs for local businesses, especially shops and hotels. Fundraising activities can raise significant amounts of money, representing a high level of local investment in sport clubs.[55] Economic opportunities also accrue at the level of individuals as part of the social networks that are created and maintained through sport participation. For example, sport clubs sometimes organize fundraising campaigns to provide much-needed financial support for fellow residents experiencing hardship, for example after a house fire or to pay for expensive surgery.

Some residents stressed that it is 'good for business' to be involved with a football club. A tradesman argued that some of his football-related contacts have resulted in new business opportunities, such as being contracted to work at the farm of another club member. The owner of a local hotel stated that many of his customers visit his hotel because of his status as a key representative of the football league. Access to job opportunities is not restricted to individual towns based on bonding social capital, but extends to other towns in the region as a consequence of relatively loose sport-based ties between people in different towns. For example, the abovementioned tradesman claimed to have acquired several short-term plumbing and trading jobs in other towns in northwest Victoria through his multiplex sporting relations.

Conclusion

This essay has addressed the types of benefits that accrue to people in rural northwest Victoria as a result of their participation in sport, either in playing or non-playing roles. I have drawn on the work of Pierre Bourdieu to analyse in conjunction different forms of capital that are created and converted in, and through, sport. While Bourdieu's approach may be too instrumental in its focus on deliberate strategies by individuals to acquire capitals (most people do not play sport principally for these reasons), most applications of the concept of social capital to the realm of sport can be criticized for divorcing social capital from other forms of capital. A major limitation of Putnam's influential interpretation of social capital is its failure to adequately address power relations and the subtle processes of social inclusion and exclusion that structure access to social networks and to the resources these networks contain.

Highlighting these processes of social inclusion and exclusion serves to counterbalance romanticized communitarian generalizations about sport's potential to transcend class, gender, ethnic, religious and other divisions. Although there is robust evidence for this potential in the rural context, it should also be noted that social networks and status positions in sport generally tend to reproduce social divisions rather than contest or resist them. Not only is rural sport gendered (as is urban sport!), but the perceived centrality of football/netball clubs to the social and cultural fabric of rural communities in northwest Victoria can actually create social pressures to become involved in sporting activities. The data presented in this essay confirms Gruneau and Whitsun's finding that 'visible minorities' are sometimes ostracized from social life in small towns because they do not become involved in sporting activities.[56] It is for this reason that some local residents argue that although 'sport is crucial to the community', facilities (e.g. for the arts) also need to be provided for those who are not interested in sport to enable them to access similar social networks and to prevent them from being socially excluded.

Another conclusion that can be drawn from the data presented in this essay is that compared to bonding and bridging capital, opportunities for linking social capital in and through sport are relatively limited in northwest Victoria. Some representatives of local sport leagues have leveraged resources, ideas and information from institutions beyond the immediate community (e.g. regional sport organizations and health providers), and these resources can contribute to their personal stock of linking social capital and cultural capital. However, for the vast majority of sport participants, who do not occupy leadership roles within their clubs or leagues, linking opportunities are far more limited due in part to the wider economic and social changes discussed in this essay, notably the decline of public and private services in the area. In the face of these changes, sport participants nevertheless view voluntary sport organizations, especially football/netball clubs, as vital community hubs fostering social cohesion, identity and a shared focus and outlet.

Notes

[1] I thank Dr June Senyard for her helpful comments on an earlier version of this article.
[2] Coalter, Allison and Taylor, *The Role of Sport*.
[3] E.g. Coalter, *The Social Benefits of Sport*; Long and Sanderson, 'The Social Benefits of Sport'.
[4] Vinson, *Dropping off the Edge*; Alston, 'Social Exclusion'.
[5] Collins and Kay, *Sport and Social Exclusion*, 194–216.
[6] Coalter, 'Sport-in-Development', 62; cf. United Nations Inter-Agency Task Force on Sport for Development and Peace, *Sport as a Tool*.
[7] Tonts, 'Competitive Sport and Social Capital', 149.
[8] Lynd and Lynd, *Middletown*.
[9] Ibid., 485–7.
[10] Hughson, Inglis and Free, *The Uses of Sport*, 63.
[11] E.g. Eitzen, *Fair and Foul*; Coakley, *Sports in Society*.
[12] Gruneau and Whitsun, *Hockey Night in Canada*, 203.
[13] Bourke, 'Rural Communities'.
[14] Rural and Regional Services and Development Committee, *Inquiry into Country Football*, 50.
[15] Portes, 'Social Capital', 6.
[16] E.g. Putnam, *Bowling Alone*, 22–3; Woolcock, 'The Place of Social Capital'. The literature on social capital and its applications to sport and leisure have been reviewed elsewhere, e.g. Blackshaw and Long, 'What's the Big Idea?'
[17] Putnam, *Bowling Alone*, 22.
[18] Ibid.
[19] Ibid., 23.
[20] Hughson, Inglis and Free, *The Uses of Sport*, 68.
[21] DeFilippis, 'The Myth of Social Capital in Community Development', 800.
[22] Woolcock, 'Social Capital and Economic Development', 13–14.
[23] Woolcock, 'The Place of Social Capital'.
[24] Tonts, 'Competitive Sport and Social Capital', 143.
[25] Atherley, 'Sport, Localism and Social Capital', 355.
[26] Tonts, 'Competitive Sport and Social Capital', 144; see also Townsend, Moore and Mahoney, 'Playing their Part'.
[27] Cf. Dempsey, *Smalltown*, 60–2.
[28] Tonts, 'Competitive Sport and Social Capital', 147.
[29] Dempsey, *A Man's Town*, 52–8, 77–83.
[30] Tonts, 'Competitive Sport and Social Capital', 149.
[31] Bourdieu, 'The Forms of Capital'.
[32] Ibid.
[33] See Coleman's use of Max Gluckman's distinction between simplex and multiplex relations. Coleman, 'Social Capital in the Creation of Human Capital', 108–9.
[34] Coalter, Allison and Taylor, *The Role of Sport*, 60.
[35] The total *n* is higher than the total number of interviews due to the existence of multiplex sporting relations. For example, some people participate in both netball and hockey clubs, while others are involved in both football and local business. These people have been included in all relevant categories.
[36] Excerpts from field notes, July 2008.
[37] Rural and Regional Services and Development Committee, *Inquiry into Country Football*, 48. In most small towns in Australia, there exists a partnership between football and netball teams.
[38] E.g. Senyard, *Birchip*, 170.
[39] Kirk, An *Introduction to Donald*.
[40] E.g. Cocklin and Dibden, eds, *Sustainability and Change*; Black *et al.*, *Rural Communities*.
[41] *The Age*, 31 August 2005; Data collated by the Australian Bureau of Statistics.
[42] McKenzie, 'Population Decline'.
[43] Black *et al.*, *Rural Communities*, 13; Lawrence, 'Globalisation'.
[44] Tonts, 'Government Policy'; Alston, 'Gender Perspectives', 146–7.
[45] Budge, 'The Changing Dynamics', 56.
[46] Tonts, 'The Restructuring', 52; see also Stayner, 'The Changing Economies', 128.
[47] McManus and Pritchard, 'Introduction', 10.
[48] E.g. Kirk, *An Introduction to Donald*; Cf. Alston and Kent, *Social Impacts of Drought*.

[49] Budge, 'The Changing Dynamics', 56.
[50] McKenzie, 'Population Decline'.
[51] Rural and Regional Services and Development Committee, *Inquiry into Retaining Young People*. It should noted that this development is by no means new.
[52] Martin, 'The Study of Small Towns', 63.
[53] Atherley, 'Sport, Localism and Social Capital'.
[54] Alston, 'Gender Perspectives', 142–3; cf. Dempsey, *A Man's Town*.
[55] Driscoll and Wood, *Sporting Capital*, 77–8.
[56] Gruneau and Whitsun, *Hockey Night in Canada*, 203.

References

Alston, M. 'Gender Perspectives in Australian Rural Community Life'. In *Sustainability and Change in Rural Australia*, edited by C. Cocklin and J. Dibdin, 139–59. Sydney: University of New South Wales Press, 2005.

Alston, M. 'Social Exclusion in Rural Australia'. In *Sustainability and Change in Rural Australia*, edited by C. Cocklin and J. Dibdin, 157–70. Sydney: University of New South Wales Press, 2005.

Alston, M., and J. Kent. *Social Impacts of Drought*. Wagga Wagga: Charles Sturt University, 2004.

Atherley, K.M. 'Sport, Localism and Social Capital in Rural Western Australia'. *Geographical Research* 44, no. 4 (2006): 348–60.

Black, A., J. Duff, S. Saggers, and P. Baines. *Rural Communities and Rural Social Issues: Priorities for Research*. Canberra: Rural Industries Research and Development Corporation, 2000.

Blackshaw, T., and J. Long. 'What's the Big Idea? A Critical Exploration of the Concept of Social Capital and its Incorporation into Leisure Policy Discourse'. *Leisure Studies* 24, no. 3 (2005): 239–58.

Bourdieu, P. 'The Forms of Capital'. In *Handbook of Theory and Research for the Sociology of Education*, edited by J. Richardson, 241–58. New York: Greenwood, 1986.

Bourke, L. 'Rural Communities'. In *Rurality Bites: The Social and Environmental Transformation of Rural Australia*, edited by S. Lockie and L. Bourke, 118–28. Annadale: Pluto Press, 2001.

Budge, T. 'The Changing Dynamics of Small Towns'. In *Towns in Time 2001 Analysis*, ed. Victorian Government Department of Sustainability and Environment, 45–61. Melbourne: Victorian Government, 2007.

Coakley, J. *Sports in Society: Issues and Controversies*. 8th edn. Boston: McGraw Hill, 2004.

Coalter, F. *The Social Benefits of Sport*. Edinburgh: Sportscotland, 2005.

Coalter, F. 'Sport-in-Development: Development for and through Sport?' In *Sport and Social Capital*, edited by M. Nicholson and R. Hoye, 39–67. Oxford: Elsevier Butterworth-Heinemann, 2008.

Coalter, F., M. Allison, and J. Taylor. *The Role of Sport in Regenerating Deprived Areas*. Edinburgh: The Stationery Office, 2000.

Cocklin, C., and J. Dibdin, eds. *Sustainability and Change in Rural Australia*. Sydney: University of New South Wales Press, 2005.

Coleman, J. 'Social Capital in the Creation of Human Capital'. *American Journal of Sociology* 94 (1988): 95–120.

Collins, M., and T. Kay. *Sport and Social Exclusion*. London: Routledge, 2003.

De Filippis, J. 'The Myth of Social Capital in Community Development'. *Housing Policy Debate* 12, no. 4 (2001): 781–806.

Dempsey, K. *Smalltown: A Study of Social Inequality, Cohesion and Belonging*. Melbourne: Oxford University Press, 1990.

Dempsey, K. *A Man's Town*. Melbourne: Oxford University Press, 1992.

Driscoll, K., and L. Wood. *Sporting Capital: Changes and Challenges for Rural Communities in Victoria*. Melbourne: RMIT, 1999.

Eitzen, D.E. *Fair and Foul: Beyond the Myths and Paradoxes of Sport*. Lanham: Rowman & Littlefield, 2006.

Gruneau, R., and D. Whitsun. *Hockey Night in Canada: Sport, Identities and Cultural Politics*. Toronto: Grammond Press, 1993.

Hughson, J., D. Inglis, and M. Free. *The Uses of Sport: A Critical Study*. London: Routledge, 2005.

Kirk, L. *An Introduction to Donald*. Donald: Donald History Group, 2006.

Lawrence, G. 'Globalisation, Agricultural Production Systems and Rural Restructuring'. In *Sustainability and Change in Rural Australia*, edited by C. Cocklin and J. Dibbin, 104–20. Sydney: University of New South Wales Press, 2005.

Long, J., and I. Sanderson. 'The Social Benefits of Sport: Where's the Proof?' In *Sport in the City*, edited by C. Gratton and I. Henry, 187–203. London: Routledge, 2001.

Lynd, R.S., and H.M. Lynd. *Middletown: A Study in Contemporary American Culture*. London: Harcourt, Brace & World, 1956 [1929].

McKenzie, F. 'Population Decline in Non-Metropolitan Australia'. *Urban Policy and Research* 12 (1994): 253–63.

McManus, P., and B. Pritchard. 'Introduction'. In *Land of Discontent*, edited by B. Pritchard and P. McManus, 1–13. Sydney: University of New South Wales Press, 2000.

Martin, J. 'The Study of Small Towns in Victoria Revisited'. In *Towns in Time 2001 Analysis*, ed. Victorian Government Department of Sustainability and Environment, 62–70. Melbourne: Victorian Government, 2007.

Portes, A. 'Social Capital: Its Origins and Applications in Modern Sociology'. *Annual Review of Sociology* 24, no. 1 (1998): 1–24.

Putnam, R. *Bowling Alone: The Collapse and Revival of American Community*. New York: Simon & Schuster, 2000.

Rural and Regional Services and Development Committee. *Inquiry into Country Football: Final Report*. Melbourne: Parliament of Victoria, 2004.

Rural and Regional Services and Development Committee. *Inquiry into Retaining Young People in Rural Towns and Communities*. Melbourne: Parliament of Victoria, 2006.

Senyard, J. *Birchip: Essays on a Shire*. Birchip: Shire of Birchip, 1970.

Stayner, R. 'The Changing Economies of Rural Communities'. In *Sustainability and Change in Rural Australia*, edited by C. Cocklin and J. Dibbin, 121–38. Sydney: University of New South Wales Press, 2005.

Tonts, M. 'The Restructuring of Australia's Rural Communities'. In *Land of Discontent*, edited by B. Pritchard and P. McManus, 52–72. Sydney: University of New South Wales Press, 2000.

Tonts, M. 'Competitive Sport and Social Capital in Rural Australia'. *Journal of Rural Studies* 21, no. 2 (2005): 137–49.

Tonts, M. 'Government Policy and Rural Sustainability'. In *Sustainability and Change in Rural Australia*, edited by C. Cocklin and J. Dibbin, 194–211. Sydney: University of New South Wales Press, 2005.

Townsend, M., J. Moore, and M. Mahoney. 'Playing their Part: The Role of Physical Activity and Sport in Sustaining the Health and Well-being of Small Rural Communities'. *Rural and Remote Health* 2, no. 109 (2002): 1–7.

United Nations Inter-Agency Task Force on Sport for Development and Peace. *Sport as a Tool for Development and Peace*. New York: United Nations, 2003.

Vinson, T. *Dropping off the Edge: The Distribution of Disadvantage in Australia*. Melbourne: Jesuit Social Services, 2007.

Woolcock, M. 'Social Capital and Economic Development: Towards a Theoretical Synthesis and Policy Framework'. *Theory and Society* 27 (1998): 151–208.

Woolcock, M. 'The Place of Social Capital in Understanding Social and Economic Outcomes'. *Isuma: Canadian Journal of Policy Research* 2, no. 1 (2001): 1–7.

Sport as a post-disaster psychosocial intervention in Bam, Iran

Valeria Kunz[1]

Swiss Academy for Development, Biel, Switzerland

In the field of humanitarian assistance, sport and play have recently gained attention as innovative instruments to support a psychosocial rehabilitation process in post-disaster and post-conflict situations. The project 'Sport and play for traumatized children and youth', implemented by the Swiss Academy for Development after the earthquake in Bam, Iran, was a pilot project conducted in this field. This essay discusses the experiences gained and lessons learnt from the project, indicating the advantages and limitations of using sport and play as tools to support psychosocial rehabilitation in a post-disaster situation. Positive effects of the project were identified on both group and individual levels, but they cannot be attributed to the use of sport alone. The findings rather suggest that the coaches and their efforts to create a supportive environment have played a crucial role for the success of the project.

The use of sport in post-disaster psychosocial interventions

A natural disaster, such as the earthquake that struck the city of Bam, Iran in the early morning of 26 December 2003, not only destroys infrastructure and buildings, but also affects individuals on a mental level and disrupts society as a whole.[2] The destructive force of a severe natural disaster is beyond the experience and imagination of most people. It is also beyond any one person's ability of control and it threatens individuals or their loved ones with death or severe injury.[3] Stress reactions are therefore normal responses of the affected individuals to such extraordinary events.[4] We speak of psychological trauma 'when a person is exposed to a life-threatening event and in the experience of this serious threat to life, the person's response is one of intense horror, fear and/or helplessness'.[5] Experiencing such feelings in the wake of a disaster event does not necessarily mean that a person becomes permanently traumatized. In fact, most people return to a pre-event level of mental health after some months through their individual coping mechanisms and resilience. Resilience is 'a dynamic process of positive adaptation within the context of severe adversity'[6] and is a key factor for mental healing after a traumatic event. A person's resilience does not only depend on his or her individual characteristics, but also on family relationships and social networks.[7]

The concept of psychosocial intervention has emerged in recent years as part of the search for ways to support the psychological rehabilitation process in a post-disaster situation. Psychosocial interventions follow a non-medical model of rehabilitation and try to address the dynamic relationships between psychological and social effects at the same time. Instead of focusing on the vulnerability and psychopathology of the affected individuals (as it is often the case with interventions tailored according to the western mental health paradigm[8]), psychosocial interventions focus on community empowerment and on helping community members to support each other.[9] Therefore, psychosocial interventions are often better tailored to specific situations in order to meet local needs and to operate with local resources and cultures.[10]

Sport and play are increasingly being used by grassroots organizations, NGOs and international humanitarian organizations in psychosocial interventions, especially for children and youth as a target group. In a post-disaster intervention, sport and play can be valuable tools for building resilience and helping children and youth overcome trauma. The use of sport and play by psychosocial sports programmes draws on a natural predilection of children to play. Well-designed sports and play activities offer children and youth a safe, structured and friendly environment in which to verbally or non-verbally encounter, express and address their problems and fears. Since children and youth have often not yet developed the intellectual or emotional capacity to deal with such problems otherwise, sport and play offer a good opportunity to address these in a less confrontational way.[11] Sport and play activities fit well into the psychosocial approach because of their potential to build social cohesion, and to encourage community members to interact and communicate with each other.

Although a number of different actors are already using sport and play in post-disaster psychosocial interventions[12] and some research has been conducted to assess the potential of this approach in theory,[13] little empirical evidence exists to date which can provide insights into the effectiveness of the use of sport for trauma relief in the framework of humanitarian assistance.[14] By sharing the experiences from the project 'Sport and play for traumatized children and youth' implemented by the Swiss Academy for Development (SAD) in Bam with a wider public, this essay attempts to add some empirical evidence from a specific project to the theoretical discussion on development through sport. After a short introduction into the project background and its activities and some methodological explanations, the experiences and lessons learned from the Bam project will be presented.

The project in Bam

On 26 December 2003 a devastating earthquake struck the city of Bam and its surroundings. The historic citadel of Bam, an ancient Silk Road city in Iran, mostly consisting of mud brick constructions, was almost entirely destroyed in the earthquake. Around 30,000 inhabitants died, similar numbers were injured and over 75,000 became homeless. A worldwide appeal for help was issued by the United Nations and by the Iranian government and several national and international humanitarian aid organizations started their work to address the urgent needs of the affected population and to facilitate a smooth transition from the immediate rescue and relief phase to a medium and long-term reconstruction and recovery phase. The survivors of the earthquake were relocated to refugee camps, where they were accommodated in prefabricated housing units. The living situation was often precarious in these camps, the space for each family being severely restricted and equipped with the most basic infrastructure.

The most vulnerable sections of the population in such times of crisis are children and youth. Official numbers stated that 6,500 children had become orphans due to the earthquake. All children had suffered losses among their family members and friends and had lived through terrible experiences during the earthquake. Many of them had been hurt and a significant number remained permanently disabled. Displaced into the refugee camps, they were torn out of their familiar environment and were forced to live under precarious living conditions, without anything to do. For them, the project 'Sport and play for traumatized children and youth' was designed. By means of sport and other game-based activities, the project intended to offer children and youth a stable pastime structure, to provide them with the opportunity to channel emotions, to improve their mental and physical wellbeing and to promote values such as teamwork and fair play that are the basis for a peaceful environment. Funding was received from the Swiss Agency for Development and Cooperation (SDC), the Degen foundation, the federation 'Ready to Move', Holcim, Nestlé Iran and Sika.

Two protected warehouses in two refugee camps and a sports stadium in a nearby village were allocated for the sport and play activities to be run. All three locations were equipped with sports tools such as football goals, table tennis tables, rackets, mattresses for gymnastics, and so forth. Professional and experienced sports coaches were selected among the local population to perform the activities with the children and youth. A talented young Iranian woman was recruited as a local project manager. By the end of October 2004, all three centres were open and activities began. On average, around 300 girls and boys between 6 and 18 years old were participating in the activities.

Bam is a small city where most people adhere to conservative values and where rather patriarchal gender norms prevail. It was therefore important for project staff to consider the gendered aspects of the project in order to achieve equal participation of both girls and boys. Due to the social norm that women should not practice sports in public, appropriate infrastructural conditions had to be provided. These were set up in two warehouses and a stadium in Baravat, which allowed the girls to participate in the sports activities, to remove their veil and to wear more comfortable clothing while playing indoors. Additionally, curtains covered the windows, so that no one could see them from outside the centres. Having mixed classes with boys and girls playing together was also not possible in this context. Participants were therefore separated into girls' and boys' classes and the centres were reserved for either one of them at specific times. The sports activities with the girls were led exclusively by female coaches. An important factor was also to counteract safety concerns about the girls getting to, and returning from, the sport and play activities. By explaining the aims of the project to parents and by reassuring them that the coaches and the project management would keep an eye on the participants during the activities and on their way to and from the activities, the concerns of most parents could be eliminated and a participation of over 50% girls could be achieved.

Sports such as football, volleyball, basketball, gymnastics, karate and table tennis were offered by the coaches in 12 different classes. On average, around 20 children and youth were participating in every class. Over the course of 2005, daily recreational activities were expanded to include information and education on health, nutrition and drugs, as well as conflict management and violence prevention programmes. Parallel to this, workshops were offered to further educate the coaches in sport didactics and psychosocial issues.

From December 2005 onwards, the camps were gradually dissolved and most families moved back to Bam or nearby villages. In order to ensure its long-term sustainability, the project was transferred into local structures. Since 2006 a local project management team (mainly consisting of the former coaches) runs the activities with the children and youth. Thanks to the support of the authorities and generous donors, a new sports centre was opened in Bam, in which the activities are now held.

Sources of data

The data used for this research is drawn from several monitoring methods and from further information provided by the local and the Swiss project managers. The weekly reports of the coaches were the main source of information. They took the form of a structured interview, held by the local project manager with mostly open questions, plus a table to collect some quantitative data (number and age of participants, injuries, material broken/lost, etc.). The open questions covered issues such as the general atmosphere, group dynamics, individual 'troublemakers', children and youth who they perceived as suffering mentally, the relationship between the coach and the participants, changes in their behaviour, measures taken by the coach, and so on. A second source of data consisted of structured interviews with some of the participants' parents about their attitudes towards the project and its perceived benefits for their children. The interviews were conducted by the local project manager in March 2005 with a total of 15 parents. Both the statements of the coaches and the parents were translated into English by the local project manager for analysis.[15] Besides these internal monitoring methods, questionnaires were formulated for the coaches, parents and children involved in the project in Bam in the context of a research project by the Swiss Academy for Development (SAD) titled 'Gender, Sport and Development'.[16] The questionnaires from this gender survey provided further information on the project activities, especially with regard to gender-specific issues.

When looking at the effects which the sport and play activities have had on the psychosocial rehabilitation process of the participating children and youth, it must be kept in mind that such a rehabilitation process is complex and involves rehabilitation on the level of the individual, of social relations (groups, families, friendships), and of society as a whole, which are all mutually dependent and influenced by a variety of factors. To control these external influences for measuring the project activities' direct effect on the participating children and youth would have required conducting detailed questionnaires (adapted to the cultural context and emotional state of the children and youth) with the participants and a control group. Besides the ethical problems that might arise when using a control group (which receives no psychosocial support), such a method would have been difficult to implement under the encountered circumstances and it would have gone beyond the time and resources afforded to this project. Possible external influences must therefore be kept in mind when looking at the observed changes among the participants.

Experiences and lessons learnt from the project

In order to assess the effectiveness of the project in supporting the psychosocial rehabilitation process, several questions about the mental state of the participants were asked in the weekly reports. However, direct questions – such as 'Did you have any children that were mentally absent [depressed, very sad, traumatized, etc.]? How did you deal with them?' – were not answered in great detail by the coaches. A possible explanation for this could be that the question is posed in too specific a way for a post-disaster context, in which mental problems are generally widespread. When asked about the prevalence of *specific* children who were 'mentally absent', the coaches' answer was mostly 'no'. However, in their answers to other questions, observations pointing to mental problems are mentioned, but they are apparently considered too 'normal' or too widespread to be made explicit. The following statement made by a boys' football coach in a weekly report in February 2005 illustrates this point:

> I think most of these children have some serious mental problems, because they are all either nervous or depressed ... So far I think I couldn't succeed to be accepted as their coach or somebody they can trust or learn something from, but I will do my best for the next coming sessions.

Initial difficulties

All coaches described the children and youth as being very nervous in the beginning, and the atmosphere in the classes was perceived hostile with both boys and girls showing physical and verbal aggression: they hit each other and pulled each other's hair, there were verbal attacks and weaker participants were made fun of. It was very difficult for the coaches to control participants in order to be able to conduct some activities with them.

The nervous, disorganized and 'agitated' behaviours, as well as the hostile and aggressive conduct, correspond to the typical reactions of school-aged children to traumatic events[17] and can thus be related to what they had experienced. Interestingly, it was observed that the initial atmosphere was far less hostile in the village of Baravat than in the two refugee camps. The previously cited coach explained in a May 2005 weekly report:

> Even when they are talking to each other, they are using rude words. Unfortunately, I noticed that the general atmosphere of this camp is like this and all the ones who are living here are not good to each other! Maybe the environment has affected them to treat each other like this.

The precarious living conditions in the camps and the fact that families from different areas of origin were gathered there, who had been forced from their familiar social and geographical environment and who had lost everything, could be a possible explanation. In the village of Baravat on the other hand, where the children and youth knew each other and a certain degree of social cohesion already (or still) existed, the psychosocial rehabilitation process seemed positively influenced by these environmental factors that also helped the children and youth to cope with the traumatic events.

The nervous and sometimes aggressive behaviour stands in sharp contrast with the high motivation of children and youth to participate in the project activities. When asked about their motivation for participation in October 2005, all of the 50 participants in the survey fully agreed with the statement 'Sport and play activities are very important to me', and 96% of them agreed with the statement 'I am usually looking forward to go to the sports and play activities'. Interestingly, 54% of the interviewed children did not agree with the statement 'The main thing is to have fun' – a source of motivation that we would generally expect when children do sport and play together. But in their situation, it seems that being able to engage in sport and play has a more serious importance than 'just' doing it for fun. The statement of a girls' volleyball coach in one of the camps in May 2005 exemplifies this:

> As they are telling me now, this centre has become their second home and they are much dependent on coming to the class. They are saying that they are gaining peace and relaxation here. These things give me a new energy to go on with the work!

Overall improvements

The activities seemed to support the psychological rehabilitation process of the participating children and youth. All coaches observed improvements in fairness and in dealing with aggression among the children and youth over time. They learned to play together, they supported each other in learning exercises or in including newcomers or younger children, instead of playing aggressively, making fun of weaker participants and insulting each other. The girls' table tennis and basketball coaches describe this development in spring 2005:

> What was interesting here was that there was no entertainment or any other place for children, so when they came to the class they were just trying to grab the ball and play by themselves but now they are fond of playing with each other.

> We have developed a good team spirit so far and it is working well; there is a sense of team play while they are practicing and playing – it has improved a lot, maybe not a big change to last week, but much from the first months!

Even in the most difficult classes, the boys' football classes in the two camps, there was improvement over time. The boys showed more respect towards the coaches and accepted the rules he set. For instance, they would apologize when they had insulted each other upon the coaches' notice. Through learning to accept the rules of the game, it seemed that the boys gradually channelled some of their individual aggression into a sense of competition on the team level: 'This week it seems to be better, at least the struggles were among the teams and only a few of them were among team members', one of the boys' football coaches stated in February 2005.

The team spirit that developed among the children and youth during the sport and play activities also spread to their daily lives. Many participants met with each other outside the project activities; they formed groups to learn for school exams together and became friends. Such processes were especially important in the two camps, where they often did not know any other children and where families from different areas of origin often had conflicts with one another.

To enhance mutual exchange and to build trust among the participating children and coaches, several measures proved effective. In order to strengthen the cohesion among the children and youth, it was helpful to incorporate other games besides the scheduled sport into the lessons. Various group games were introduced by some of the coaches, at the beginning of every lesson for the children and youth to 'arrive' in class, to concentrate on the sports activities and to involve them in the group. External activities besides the classes, such as tournaments with other teams or a picnic in the countryside, were also very much appreciated by them and helped to establish friendly relationships between the participants. Because it was possible for newcomers to join existing classes at any time, it was sometimes difficult to strengthen the team spirit among the participating children and youth. Effective measures to integrate newcomers were to make former participants responsible for introducing the new ones into the activities and into the group or to form smaller sub-groups, in which a team spirit was easier to establish.

Positive individual examples

Improvements could be observed not only on the group level, but also on the level of individual children and youth that were particularly affected. At the beginning, mentally or physically affected children and youth were often made fun of by the others. Through the team activities and the integrative measures of the coaches, such as appointing them as their 'coaching assistant' or giving them other specific tasks, these participants could strengthen their self-confidence and were gradually respected in the group. One of the boys' football coaches stated in May 2005: 'We had nervous and depressed children, who are now much different from the first days.' Most parents interviewed in March 2005 also observed an improvement in the physical and mental wellbeing of their children. The following statements illustrate this: 'Before, she was very nervous and she was losing her temper over nothing, but now she is more calm and patient'; 'My son is very shy and before, he was hardly getting along with the others, but now he has made some friends there and he seems braver to express himself'; 'Before, she was very depressed and now she has improved a lot; she is excited and she is getting along with her sisters better now'; 'She is happier, that's what I can see in her behaviour'.

Positive individual examples are mentioned by the coaches in some of the weekly reports. There was a boy in one of the camps, for example, who had lost his brother in an accident. One week later, he came back to the football class and 'he mentioned that the only way he could forget is to come to the centre to play with his friends', his coach reported. Another very positive example is the case of a girl who had fallen from a roof during the earthquake and suffered both physically and mentally from that experience. Because she developed so well during her participation in the table tennis and volleyball classes, the coaches mentioned her improvements recurrently in the weekly reports. In January 2005, her coaches stated:

> she has fallen from the roof and it has affected her memory, so she would prefer to play alone and not with anybody, so I talked to her and tried to be a friend of her and now she is coming to the class regularly and her mom said that she has been better from the time she has attended the class.

> To me, it is a nice experience, because I am seeing the difference in the participants' behaviour comparing to the first sessions, even there is one girl who has mental problems [the girl who had fallen from a roof] and now mostly when we come, she is sitting behind the door waiting for us.

> The improvement is obvious in the behaviour of that girl with mental problems and the happiness her mother showed made me happy too.

Three months later, one of her coaches said: 'She is now one of our good players and she has lots of friends compared to the first days when she was not getting along with anybody.'

Apparently, the attempts of both coaches to integrate this girl into the classes, to improve her self-confidence and to be a trusted person for her, were vital to this success. In their statements below, the coaches describe how they let the girl take over some responsibilities in class, thereby giving her more self-confidence and greater appreciation from other participants: 'Our girl was present this week and she was helping me a lot and I can say as I have mentioned before, she has improved a lot comparing to last weeks'; 'She has got some responsibilities, too, in order to give her more self-confidence'. Her mother has also observed considerable improvement. Interviewed in March 2005, she said:

> My daughter had some mental problems as she had fallen from a roof, but from the time she is going to the classes, she has changed a lot; she is trying to be more kind to her friends and she is helping me at home; even her grades at school have become better.

The importance of the coaches

Another indicator for positive development is that after some months a trusted relationship between the coaches and the participants could be established in almost all classes. When asked about their relationship to their coaches in October 2005 in the gender-survey, 49 out of 50 participants fully agreed with the statement 'My coach is like a friend to me'. The statement, 'I usually share my private problems with my coach' was fully agreed by 74% of the participants interviewed in the survey. The coaches and the local project manager became trusted persons for the children and youth; coaches were entrusted with their personal or familial problems, their fears and sorrows. When participants had to choose what kind of characteristics they found most important for a coach, the features 'understanding and caring about people' were the most often-mentioned (compared to 'good in sports' and 'setting strict rules') by both girls and boys.

In order to establish a trusted relationship between coaches and participants, several methods were applied, which helped to improve mutual exchange. It was helpful, for instance, to invite participants to write (anonymous) letters to their coaches, if they wanted to. Thereby, even shyer children, who did not dare to address the coach directly, were offered a chance to express what was on their mind. For boys, hesitance to talk to their coaches about personal problems was further reinforced by socio-cultural ideals of masculinity, according to which boys should not talk openly about their feelings and problems, especially not to adult men. Letters did not prove effective here, since they were considered 'girlish things' by most boys. But forms of indirect mutual exchange with their coaches did nevertheless emerge in the boys' classes; they mostly did not approach the coach themselves, but other boys of the class told the coach if one of their friends had a problem, so that the coach could go and talk to that boy. Another useful method for both girls and boys were the 'friendship circles' at the end of every lesson, in which the coach discussed selected topics such as fairness, mutual trust and health issues with participants and addressed problems that many of them were facing individually in a more general group setting. The coaches also actively sought out dialogue with children whom they felt were in trouble. The example of a table tennis coach, speaking to one of the girls in her class, gives a good illustration of this method:

> On Monday, I saw one girl sitting and not playing with the others. I sat down beside her and talked to her and she said that she had some fighting with her father. She seemed very nervous about it and she said that she didn't have anybody to advise her what to do. So, I talked to her and tried to explain to her that this is normal for her age and that she had to control herself little by little and I told her of my own experience. At last, she thanked me and told me that now, she was feeling better. It made me very happy!

Problems with parents, as described in the quote above, were among the issues that were most often discussed between children and coaches. Nearly all of the families in Bam and its surroundings had lost members and belongings in the earthquake, and for most of them life after the disaster was a daily struggle to make a living. Physical disabilities and mental suffering, high rates of drug consumption, poverty and the unfavourable living conditions in the camps made this struggle even harder and caused problems in the families, from which the children suffered greatly. In a situation like this, the role of the coach as a trusted adult person besides the parents was very important for the children. Not only could the children approach the coaches with their problems and receive support from them in finding solutions, but the coaches also served as role models for the children, providing them with guidance and orientation. One of the coaches reported how the girls of her table tennis and volleyball class often asked her 'whether something is a good thing to do or a bad thing to avoid'. Sport can support the spread of messages such as not to smoke or take drugs, to care about one's body and health, but also messages stressing the importance of reliability, trust and respect for a good team spirit and for friendships in general.

Coaches were also able to serve as a relief for the parents, who were often stressed and helpless in how to assist their children in overcoming their traumatic experiences. This often led to tensions between the parents and their children. For instance the parents often did not understand why their children had such a hard time to concentrate at school and brought home bad grades. Many parents then punished their children by not allowing them to join the sports activities anymore. The coaches were able to act as mediators between parents and children in such situations: they talked to parents and explained to them that weaker school performance could be related to the mental suffering the children had undergone during the earthquake or to their current living conditions, and that participation in sports activities could help them feel better and perform better at school.

Because most parents came to realize that their children liked attending the sports activities very much and that these activities initiated changes in their behaviour, they also respected the coaches in their role as mediators. In particular, the mothers of participants were quick to thank the coaches for their efforts, to watch the training sessions and to invite the coaches to their homes. They also asked them for direct educational support, as they realized that the coaches were highly respected by their children. A coach teaching volleyball and table tennis to girls explained:

> One of the mothers came to me and said that her daughter is coming to the centre right after school, without having her lunch and she was worrying about her health and asked me to talk to her girl, because she would be listening better to me than to her!

On the other hand, due to the fact that the parents had a large amount of respect for the coaches, children tended to ask their coaches to negotiate with their parents to request permission for things they would not have dared to ask themselves.

The fact that the coaches were recruited from the local population was a major advantage for the emergence of such a relationship of mutual trust and respect. As locals, the coaches were more respected by the children and their parents: they knew their situation and shared the same experiences and they could visit each other easily, outside the project activities. It was this personal closeness that allowed the coaches to act as legitimate mediators.

Conclusion

The project in Bam was a pilot project in the field of using sport as an instrument to support the post-disaster psychosocial rehabilitation process of children and youth. Analysing the experiences from the project, it can be concluded that sport and play had a positive impact on the wellbeing and development of the participating children. All parents, coaches and members of the project management team observed significant changes in the children's behaviour and in their group dynamics, which can be taken as indicators for an improvement in their physical and mental wellbeing. Initial aggression and hostility was channelled through sport and play activities into cooperative team play. Through appropriate measures taken by the coaches, weaker or mentally absent participants who were made fun of in the beginning could be integrated into the groups, thereby enhancing their self-confidence and wellbeing. The sport and play activities became an important part of the children's lives, bringing some stability into their shattered lives. Friendships emerged that spread into daily life. The activities were not only very much appreciated by the children themselves, but also by their parents, who were relieved to have educational and mental support for their children, thereby further stabilizing family relationships.

However, the positive effects cannot be isolated to the use of sport alone. Our findings rather suggest that the coaches and their efforts to create a supportive environment play a crucial role in using sport and play as effective instruments for supporting the post-disaster psychosocial rehabilitation process of children and youth. Without coaches who are sensitive to the physical and mental wellbeing of the children in their classes and who are able to take adequate measures in order to build a team spirit – which is based not on competition or individual performance but on respect, tolerance and the inclusion of all children – sport would not have contributed to such positive effects in the aftermath of the Bam earthquake. The coaches are not only responsible for the friendly atmosphere in the sports lesson, but also hold the role as trusted persons for the children and as intermediate agents between them and their parents. Their thorough selection, education and continuing support are therefore crucial factors for the success of the project. Selection and education of the coaches should not focus so much on their experience in sports coaching as on their motivation and ability to fulfil their role as a trusted adult person for the children, who they can turn to with their problems and sorrows, and who can help them to gain more self-confidence and trust in other persons again, experience fun in a group activity and forget their sorrows.

To facilitate a trusted and close relationship with the children and their families, as well as to improve local capacity building and sustainability of the activities, the selected coaches should be recruited from the local population. But precisely due to the high responsibility that the coaches bear for the success of the project, it should not be forgotten that, as locals, they have experienced the traumatizing disaster as well. It is likely that they suffer from its consequences in a similar way as the participating children and their parents do. This adds to their ability to empathize with the children and parents, but also requires continuing support: not only concerning the project activities, but also concerning their own mental state (e.g. through regular exchanges with the other coaches) so that their task does not become too heavy a burden for them to carry. Moreover, the project management should accompany the activities closely through a monitoring system which involves the coaches in a participatory way and provides them with the regular opportunity to talk about possible problems. Solutions can then be sought when problems arise and not only when they have already manifested themselves.

There are certainly many more aspects that could further improve the impact of sport in supporting the post-disaster psychosocial rehabilitation process of children and youth. After having conducted and evaluated the project in Bam, we hope that other organizations will be inspired to make use of the potential of sport and to gain further insights into how it can be best tapped to the benefit of participating children and youth.

Notes

[1] This article is adapted from the SAD report *Sport and Play for Traumatized Children and Youth: An Assessment of a Pilot Project in Bam, Iran* by the author.
[2] See Ehrenreich, *Coping with Disasters*, 5.
[3] ICSSPE, *Sport and Physical Activity*, 62.
[4] Ehrenreich, *Coping with Disasters*, 13.
[5] World Health Organization (WHO), *International Classification of Diseases*, 4.
[6] Luthar, Cicchetti and Becker, 'The Construct of Resilience', 543–62.
[7] ICSSPE, *Sport and Physical Activity*, 75.
[8] Henley, *Helping Children Overcome Disaster Trauma*, 6.
[9] Ibid., 9.
[10] However, it must be noted that psychosocial interventions in the context of a humanitarian crisis often need to be set up quickly and under difficult circumstances. Planning and implementing them in a contextually adapted way is therefore often a big challenge and unfortunately not very well done. See Henley, *Helping Children Overcome Disaster Trauma*, 10.
[11] Henley and Colliard, 'Input Paper', 7.
[12] For an overview of the actors involved in such sport programmes see: Gschwend and Selvaraju, *Psycho-Social Sport Programmes*.
[13] See the publications of Henley, Colliard and ICSSPE in the references.
[14] The evaluations from Colliard of the psychosocial programmes of Terre des Hommes in Bam and Sri Lanka are favourable exceptions (see references).
[15] Quoted passages from the interviews retain the original wording of the local project manager's translation.
[16] The results of this research are not yet published. For an interim report see Meier, *Gender Equity*.
[17] See Ehrenreich, *Coping with Disasters*, 27.

References

Colliard, C. *Well-being and Resilience after the Tsunami – Evaluation of Terre des hommes Psychosocial Programme in Sri Lanka 2005–2007.* Geneva: Center for Humanitarian Psychology, 2007.

Colliard, C. *Evaluating Children's Resilience after the Bam Earthquake – Report for Terre des Hommes (Switzerland)*. Geneva: Center for Humanitarian Psychology, 2005.

Ehrenreich, J.H. *Coping with Disasters: A Guidebook to Psychosocial Intervention*. New York: Mental Health Workers without Borders, 2001.

Gschwend, A., and U. Selvaraju. *Psycho-Social Sport Programmes to Overcome Trauma in Post-Disaster Interventions*. Biel: Swiss Academy for Development, 2007.

Henley, R. *Helping Children Overcome Disaster Trauma through Post-Emergency Psychosocial Sports Programs*. Working Paper. Biel: Swiss Academy for Development, 2005.

Henley, R., and C. Colliard. 'Input Paper for the Break-out Session "Overcoming Trauma through Sport"'. Presented at the 2nd Magglingen Conference on Sport and Development, Magglingen, December 5, 2005, http://www.magglingen2005.org/downloads/02_E_input_trauma.pdf.

International Council of Sport Science and Physical Education (ICSSPE). *Sport and Physical Activity in Post-Disaster Intervention*. 2nd edn. Berlin: ICSSPE, 2008.

Kunz, V. *Sport and Play for Traumatized Children and Youth. An Assessment of a Pilot Project in Bam, Iran*. Working Paper. Biel: Swiss Academy for Development, 2006.

Luthar, S.S., D. Cicchetti, and B. Becker. 'The Construct of Resilience: A Critical Evaluation and Guidelines for Future Work'. *Child Development* 71 (2000): 543–62.

Meier, M. *Gender Equity, Sport and Development*. Biel: Swiss Academy for Development, 2007.

World Health Organization (WHO). 'International Classification of Diseases (ICD – 10)'. Geneva: WHO, 2007. http://www.who.int/classifications/icd/en/.

Esther Phiri and the Moutawakel effect in Zambia: an analysis of the use of female role models in sport-for-development

Marianne Meier[a] and Martha Saavedra[b]

[a]Swiss Academy for Development, Biel, Switzerland; [b]Center for African Studies, University of California, Berkeley, USA

In the burgeoning field of sport and development, 'role models' have been invoked as an important element to increase the participation of girls and women in sport. Grounded in the African sport-in-development experience and in a case study of Zambian women's sports and the boxer, Esther Phiri, this essay examines the discourse around the use of 'role models' and begins to elaborate a theory around the use of this hitherto elusive notion specifically in the experience of sport-in-development projects and programmes which have gender-specific outcomes. We consider how role models may function to encourage and sustain female involvement, as well as to contribute to achieving goals set for sport and development projects, including (positively) altering gender roles and expectations. We conclude with a look towards promising areas of future research as well as a critical reflection on the limits of role models as a tool, especially given real-world intrusions.

Introduction

> The importance of role models for women in sports is undeniable. In fact, one could assert that it is a virtuous circle. The more women take positive, leading roles as athletes, trainers, journalists and decision-makers, the more women will see that gender inequalities can be overcome – not only in sports but in all professions.[1]

On 18 March 2007, in front of 8,000 spectators at the Mulungushi Conference Centre in Lusaka, Esther Phiri, a 23-year-old Zambian single mother, defeated Monika Petrova of Bulgaria in an eight-round unanimous decision to retain the Women's International Boxing Federation Intercontinental Junior Lightweight title. Having achieved already some notoriety in Zambia for her success in the ring, this bout marked her rise to national fame and secured financial backing to continue her pursuit of international boxing triumphs. With numerous accolades, a lucrative endorsement and a savvy manager, she has accumulated status and wealth. Phiri's boxing career and her life more generally are now regular topics in the press, and she has become one of the most well-known personalities in Zambia. In a country with a high level of gender disparity, many see Phiri as a role model for other Zambian women and girls, and point to sport as a way to overcome many of the basic problems women and girls face. Along many dimensions, the story of Esther Phiri is noteworthy. In this essay, using Phiri's story as a backdrop, we specifically will explore how the notion of role models functions within the nexus of gender, sport and development.

In the burgeoning contemporary field of sport and development, advocates (us included) have proffered sport as a means to ameliorate gender inequities and to promote the empowerment of women and girls. If the participation of females in sport has transformative potential for girls and the larger society – a premise we generally endorse but continually and critically evaluate and challenge – a preliminary question concerns how girls and women initially become involved in sport. What encourages them to engage in sport and then to remain involved? What prevents them from participation or causes them to cease such activities? While these questions can be asked equally about males, the questions subsume the notion that historically sport has tended to be a male domain and that for females there are particular obstacles for engagement. In this essay, inspired by observations in the field, we focus on the somewhat elusive notion of 'role models' as a tool within sport and development practice. Coalter notes that 'although there is much talk around the importance of role models in sport, much of this relates to the assertion that elite sports people can have a positive impact on young people's commitment to, and participation in, sport'.[2] Yet, the theory is so far lacking.

With attention to the discourse around this notion, we explore how role models might operate to increase girls' participation in sport, contribute to achieving goals set for sport and development projects, including (positively) altering gender roles and expectations. A major concern is how historical, spatial and cultural contexts affect the nature and efficacy of role models. We review the literature in light of our familiarity with the African context, and offer some preliminary observations based on work in Zambia, but also incorporating perspectives we have gained from fieldwork in South Africa, Senegal and Kenya. Targeted studies testing these ideas on role models have yet to be organized, and it remains to be seen whether there is enough evidence to fully understand how role models influence participation or to extract a set of 'best' practices that can be incorporated into sport and development projects seeking to involve girls. Role models as a tool is invoked often enough though that it is important to begin this closer scrutiny.

The first section provides an overview of Esther Phiri's story and the context for women and sport in Zambia in order to highlight some of the key issues that we want to address. This will be followed by a review of the literature on role models as applicable to what we refer to as the nexus of gender, sport and development, with special attention to African contexts. In the conclusion, we will point to promising areas for further research as well as reflect critically on the limits of role models as a tool, especially given real-world intrusions.

Esther Phiri and the gender sportscape in Zambia

Scholarly literature on the development of sport in Zambia or its interactions with gender is nearly non-existent. Some mention of Zambia is made in Baker and Mangan's 1987 edited volume on sport in Africa, and a year later Andresen *et al.* produced a volume in German about sport structures in Zambia. In 2004, Darby wrote about the 1993 air crash in which the Zambian national football team was killed en route to a World Cup qualifying match. Most recently, in 2007, Peacock-Villada, DeCelles and Banda have analysed Grassroots Soccer sport and development projects, one of which was in Zambia.[3] Zambian scholars such as Banda, Kakuwa, Komakoma and Mwaanga are producing work, but so far most of this is contained in scholarly theses or grey literature.[4] More grey literature is produced by Government ministries and NGOs while the sports pages of local and international media outlets supply the most accessible and updated information. What emerges from a perusal of these sources is a contemporary Zambian sportscape dominated by men's football and perennial hopes for World Cup advancement with significant deficits in infrastructure and programme resources at all levels.

From a historical perspective, as in other locales, colonization – British in Zambia – imposed European sport onto indigenous physical cultures, sport and games.[5] Some indigenous sports and games have been lost entirely, while others such as Mancala or Moruba (stone moving and/or counting 'board' games) continue to be played in Zambia and elsewhere in Southern Africa. During colonization, Western missionaries, teachers, soldiers, administrators and businessmen introduced European and American sports such as football, basketball, netball, tennis and golf.[6] When considering contemporary sport-in-development projects and cooperation, it is critical to recall the instrumental use of sport during the colonial period. Indeed, sport served as a means of 'civilizing' African societies through its disciplining nature, and as a regimen to teach hygiene, cleanliness and self-control.[7] Especially in the British colonies, sport was imbued with values of muscular Christianity that reflected an idealized patriarchal gender order, in which the man is the undisputed head of the family.[8]

Initially, colonial sport in Africa followed the European elitist model. For instance, the first sporting clubs were exclusively European; Africans appeared on the field only as substitutes for absent European players. Outside of these clubs, African athletes especially gravitated towards the sport of football. Since football required minimal equipment, and had relatively straightforward rules, the game attracted the interest of the local population, which soon appropriated the sport and formed their own teams. Especially in African townships, football developed rapidly into an extremely popular sport, often with improvised material, such as home-made balls and rules.[9]

Despite the hegemony of European sports, games and physical activities have a long tradition in Africa and played an important role before the arrival of the Europeans, as the Zambian example shows. The manual, *Zambian Traditional Games and Activities*, developed for the 'Kicking AIDS Out' programme, describes popular traditional sports in Zambia including swimming, martial arts, rock climbing (on trees), steer riding and hiking.[10] Also, in interviews conducted by Meier in Lusaka and Livingstone, women repeatedly reported participating in childhood 'bottle races' (a kind of race with a bottle on the head). These sporting events were held exclusively outdoors and in public places. Reflecting their particular context, these activities varied by area reflecting local conditions and practices. Usually only children and young people participated in sport, with transition into adulthood marking an end to such activities. Although, in principle, both girls and boys participated, the duration of their sportive commitment diverged. Young women over 18 years rarely continued with sport, while young men usually continued until about the age of 21. These differences can be attributed to women marrying at a young age, a trend which continues into the present.[11] Furthermore, having children also meant the end of a sporting activity. For adolescent males, however, physical activity traditionally was important as a preparation for their future roles as defenders and warriors of their clan. Accordingly, young men engaged in the 'tougher' sports, while girls and young women performed in traditional dances.[12]

Several additional factors restrict the sporting activity of girls and women in Zambia today, more so than in earlier periods. The disadvantage of girls and women in access to education and work, as well as the particular burden they bear due to the consequences of poverty and rampant HIV/AIDS pandemic, limits their involvement in sports activities. If a family cannot afford to send all children to school, it is usually the boys who will take precedence. The girls, on the other hand, are often responsible for household chores and the care of dependent family members. They have little personal free time. But even if they can go to school, the possibility of being actively involved in sports is very limited: sport faces severe financial and human resource shortages in most schools, and is considered a luxury compared to other 'more serious' subjects.

On the occasion of the 2nd International 'Next Step' Conference 2005 in Livingstone, Zambia, organized by Norway,[13] the Zambian President, Levy Mwanawasa, promised in his opening remarks that henceforth physical education classes would be made mandatory for all schoolchildren nationwide. Despite this welcomed goodwill gesture, there is still a striking gap between the ideal and the reality, especially given on-going financial restraints. One can only hope that such public endorsements before an international gathering will lead to more support for sport in public education. However, similar public statements about pursuing gender equality in sport, though, suggest achieving such goals is difficult. For instance, in 1980, several heads of state, including Zambia, established the Southern African Development Community (SADC), and drafted a protocol on Culture, Information and Sport. This document aims to strengthen regional cooperation as well as programmes and policies in these areas for the benefit of the entire southern Africa. In addition, this protocol recognizes, *inter alia*, the importance of sport for the regional and national development and also holds that: ' ... member states shall cooperate in ensuring gender equality and equity in the areas of culture, information and sport'.[14] Coordinated action in favour of national sport and culture was agreed upon in Southern Africa in 2001 during a summit in Malawi. Nevertheless, movement towards these goals has been slow in Zambia.

Football, probably the most popular sport on the African continent, dominates the Zambian sportscape, and despite the fact that it has long been exclusively reserved for men, one might expect the popularity of the sport to carry forward the development of the women's side. Organized women's football in Africa emerged only in recent decades. South Africa was a pioneer in the promotion of female football. It was the first African country to create a Women's Football Association (SAWFA) in 1976. The international boycott against the apartheid regime, however, blocked the official recognition of the association. It was only recognized years later as part of the Women's World Conference in October 1992 in Switzerland. After South Africa, Nigeria blazed trails as the first African women's team to participate in a tournament outside the continent, when it went to the 1991 World Cup in China.[15] The official FIFA ranking as of March 2009 lists a total of 156 internationally registered women's teams including 33 squads from Africa, with the numbers and rankings of national African teams continually rising.[16] Up until 2008, the African flagship Nigeria won all previous seven African Championships for Women's Football and ranked as high as 24th worldwide in 2007. With the win by Equatorial Guinea over South Africa, 2-1, in November for the 2008 Championship, a deepening of the African women's game is augured. Nevertheless, Nigeria remains dominant in the worldwide ranking at 29 and is followed by Ghana at 44, South Africa at 54 and Morocco at 62. Zambia occupies the 103rd FIFA ranking position, up from 127 two years ago, but still only 18th among the 21 officially ranked African nations in the FIFA rankings.

These rankings reflect the history of women's football in Zambia, which has been one of starts and stops. According to Dorothy Yamba, general secretary of the ill-fated Zambia Women Football Association (ZWFA), women's football in Zambia started in 1974, with a national team forming in 1976. Yamba recalled that people thought women playing football was 'unusual and obscene', but the players and advocates persisted. Eventually, the game won more supporters.[17] Mwaanga indicates that the Zambia Consolidated Copper Mines, largely owned by the government at that time, was a major sponsor of women's football in the Copperbelt region (north of Lusaka, near the towns of Ndola, Kitwe, etc) in the 1980s (see Figure 1). That ended with the privatization of ZCCM after 1989 such that women's football in the Copperbelt region declined.[18] Women's football

Figure 1. Map of Zambia.
Source: http://www.state.gov/cms_images/zambia_map_2007-worldfactbook.jpg).

picked up again in the capital Lusaka during the 1990s, at least partly with help from external donors, such as the Norwegian aid agency, NORAD. At an inaugural women's football championship in Lusaka in June 1998, William Harrington, the sports minister said, 'The government will do everything possible to ensure that an enabling environment is created'.[19] However, a month later, the ZWFA leadership disbanded the organization in protest, feeling 'neglected, ignored and irrelevant' by the Football Association of Zambia (FAZ).[20] The locus of the woman's game moved to Lusaka with teams sponsored by sport-and-development organizations such as EduSport, and businesses such as Musa Bakery, in a league organized by the Lusaka Province Women Football Association (LPWFA).[21]

Since FIFA started promoting global women's football by supporting the creation of female national teams financially, some national football associations – especially the ones with scarce budgets – became motivated to take bolder or even first steps. Unfortunately, despite claims to support women's football, de facto many female national teams only exist on paper. In June 2006, on the occasion of the 56th FIFA Congress in Munich, a passage in the financial report of 2005 indicated that national football associations are to provide unequivocal support of the women's game:

> The associations are encouraged to invest the funds they receive in high-priority projects. However, as from 2005, they are compelled to at least set aside 10%, in other words USD 25,000, to promote women's football. FIFA believes that women's football will make enormous progress over the next few years as a result of this unequivocal financial commitment.[22]

A search on the FAZ website[23] and elsewhere for recent reports on women's football in Zambia does not reveal an encouraging increase in organizing on the part of FAZ.[24] To be fair there is not much encouraging news either for women's volleyball or netball – particularly the latter where one might expect more efforts being made for women given its standing as a long-established modern sport especially practiced by women. In 2006, the Federation of International Netball Associations suspended the Zambian association for not paying affiliation fees for five years.[25]

While football is the overwhelmingly popular sport, it is not the only sport of note in Zambia. Some Zambians have achieved fame with cricket, golf and rugby, though relatively few Zambians participate in these sports. Zambia has had some international success with two other sports – athletics and boxing. While local enjoyment of sport is valued, international success is particularly important. With the advent of African anti-colonialism and nationalism after the Second World War, sport was of symbolic significance for national cohesion in the ethnically and linguistically heterogeneous newly emerging countries. Sport offered newly independent nations a means to gain and increase international recognition through participation in major international events. Furthermore, sportive successes boosted the national pride and aroused feelings of patriotism.

The Olympic Games are the most hallowed of these events, and unlike the Football World Cup, they offer multiple chances in each staging for a nation to succeed through the performances of many individual athletes and teams. Zambia, formerly known as North Rhodesia, first participated in the Olympics in the 1964 Tokyo Games, but had to wait 20 years to claim its first Olympic medal, one of only two to the present. The sport was boxing: Mwila Keith won a bronze medal in the 1984 Olympic Light Flyweight boxing competition in Los Angeles.[26] The second medal was in athletics, a silver medal won by Samuel Matete in the 400 m hurdles in the 1996 Atlanta games. In the pantheon of Zambian sport heroes, track and field athletes and boxers follow just behind footballers. Women have had some international success in athletics, and a few female athletes have achieved some fame: Lilian Byalya (400 m), Racheal Nachula (200 m, 400 m) and Carol Mokola (60 m, 100 m, 200 m). Indeed, track and field may be where Zambian women have had the largest presence. In April 2009, the IAAF listed the biographies of 57 Zambian women to 62 Zambian men.[27] However, it is the boxing ring where a woman, just one woman, has had the most resounding impact on Zambian public consciousness and has demonstrated the potential to significantly change the national sportscape and prospects for women.

The boxing ring in Zambia, as in most parts of the world, has been an epitome of masculinity. Boxing is body work; its labour value is skilled aggression.[28] Wacquant identifies the bodily labour of Chicago-based fighters as 'fundamentally a work of *engenderment* ... embodying and exemplifying a definite form of masculinity: plebeian, heterosexual and heroic'.[29] Historically, women did box, for example, in eighteenth-century England, and in nineteenth-century United States and France, but practitioners generally came from the lower class, and contemporary social observers greeted their exploits more as titillation than as national achievements.[30] For women to 'display strength, violence and control' through boxing, a disruption of accepted gender boundaries was required.[31] Through much of the mid-twentieth century, laws and codes in many places prevented official matches by women. This began to break down at the millennium and, mirroring changes elsewhere, in 1994 the Zambian sports minister Patrick Kafumukache introduced a bill to allow women to practice boxing and wrestling.[32] This helped to pave the way for Esther Phiri to become the super featherweight boxing world champion of the Women International Boxing Federation (WIBF) in 2007. Journalist Hone Liwanga articulated well the significance to the country of Esther Phiri's March 2007 Women's International Boxing Federation Intercontinental Junior Lightweight title match against Petrova:

> With each blow, one could just imagine how many people watching could never imagine a woman in a boxing ring... With Zambia still failing to attain 30 percent women representation in parliament and other key political positions as required by the Southern African Development Community (SADC), Ms Phiri's success was set to have great meaning to women and girls in Africa and the rest of the world ... The country has a world champion in Ms Phiri, who has proven to be a force to reckon with and an inspiration to other Zambian women that there is power in undertaking challenging things. Young girls watching Ms Phiri must be thinking that if boxing is open to them, then surely any path is theirs for the taking.[33]

In the same article, Liwanga referred to attempts to launch women's football leagues in Lusaka and suggested there was something in the will of Phiri, her management team and the boxing establishment, which was different: 'The Football Association of Zambia has no interest in it. FAZ's action is retrogressive towards the attainment of gender equality in sport and it is not surprising to see women's football being surpassed by boxing.'

Throughout her childhood and most of her adolescence, Esther Phiri lived in poverty. The difficult circumstances reflect the reality of numerous girls and women in Zambia. The United Nations Development Programme's (UNDP) 2008 Gender Development Index, which captures inequalities in development indicators between women and men, rated Zambia 121 out of 157 countries globally, and 32 out 44 Sub-Saharan African countries.[34] The boxer grew up in Mtendere, a disadvantaged area near Lusaka. After the early death of her father from malaria, she had to leave school and earn her own living. She sold food and second-hand clothes on the street. At the age of 16, left on her own, she gave birth to her first child. Like in a movie, the seemingly desperate life of Esther Phiri took a new turn as the NGO 'Africa Directions' launched an AIDS prevention project in her neighbourhood in which health education and sports were combined. Esther was the only female participant in the boxing programme. Luckily, her extraordinary talent was quickly recognized and promoted.

The Zambian women's magazine *Beauty* featured a cover article on Esther Phiri in February 2007 (see Figure 2). The well-known magazine focused on her life outside of the boxing ring. In addition to her hobbies, 'cooking, watching football and dressing up', the magazine hinted at the protective stance of her trainer and manager, Anthony Mwamba, who had discovered her outstanding skills: 'I know she's talented and she can make money from boxing. I advise her not to get married. Once a man gets in her life she could just become a housewife and that talent would go.' This particular set of questions– whether Esther should marry or not, whether anyone but Esther has the right to make that choice and how her decision could affect the country– became a matter of public debate.[35]

After winning the title fight once more in March 2007, the boxer was even officially congratulated on behalf of the Zambian Republic by President Mwanawasa:

> Indeed Esther has made us proud again and continues to lift the Zambian flag higher. It is my sincere hope that she will continue with this spirit and commitment to bringing honour not only to herself but to the country as a whole[36].

President Mwanawasa praised the outstanding achievements of Phiri, but added self-critical general remarks with regard to sport in the political context: 'Congratulations to Esther for demonstrating her capability to succeed regardless of the many challenges and obstacles that are currently prevailing in the area of sport in Zambia.'[37] The best female boxer of Zambia not only received a personal invitation to lunch at the presidential palace, but also was given a K240 million (US$60,420) three-bedroom house by the government, eagerly furnished by several local businesses.[38]

Although it is still a singular occurrence in Zambia, Phiri has successfully managed to enter a men's sport on an international level and has changed many perceptions. Even male sports commentators had to recognize that women's boxing, though still somewhat exotic,

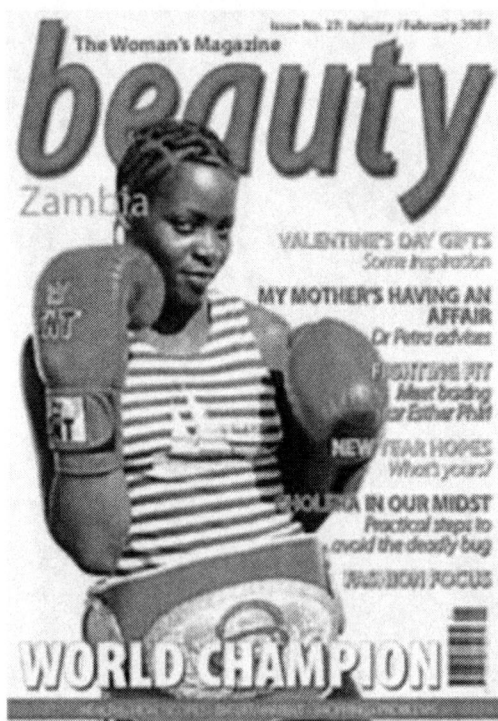

Figure 2.   The 23-year-old boxer Esther Phiri on the cover of the magazine 'Beauty'.

offers a huge imitative potential to attract other females. The journalist Lwandamina wrote accordingly in the *Zambia Times*: 'Phiri is the first ever female boxer fighting for Zambia at international level and her performance tonight will be seen as a source of inspiration to other women in a country where women boxing is still a strange thing.'[39] Besides her role as a model for children and teenagers, Esther Phiri has served to promote the notion that organized recreational activities can influence social behaviour, possibly preventing addiction and other deleterious outcomes. Phiri has spoken out to encourage Zambian adolescent women to engage in sports not only to guard against unplanned pregnancies and sexually transmitted disease, but to become disciplined and focused. 'I would advise my young fellow Zambians to engage in sports as it would take up most of their time which they would spend drinking and engaging in many anti-social vices.'[40]

That Phiri and her management have also made significant money and gained other resources is another factor. The day after Phiri beat Petrova in 2007, Peter Cottan of the National Milling Corporation, a subsidiary of the US company Seaboard Corporation, signed a two year exclusive endorsement deal with Phiri's manager worth about $100,000.[41] Though small compared to deals female boxers elsewhere might be making, this deal helped to propel Phiri to national fame – National Milling Corporation produces *nshima*, a staple made of cornmeal.[42] Phiri's image is everywhere (see Figure 3). By 2008, Barclays also endorsed Phiri and underwrote a training visit to Europe.[43] Her fight against Hondi Hernandez for the Global Boxing Union lightweight title in October 2008 netted her about K400 million ($115,000).[44]

In terms of sport and gender there are enormous gaps in Zambia between the poorer and more conservative rural population and the urban population. People in or near cities and

Figure 3.   Photo of Phiri endorsement by M. Meier.

urban centres do generally have better access to infrastructure, media and so on. Furthermore, seemingly entrenched gender roles and stereotypes are even more persistent in rural settings where ethnically-based traditions and communal practices are still crucial. A 24-year-old male participant of a focus group discussion in Lusaka said: 'Things are changing slowly. But if I send a letter to my parents in my village today, they will find me a wife next month.'

The precise nature of these traditional social structures and practices vary according to different groups and settings. The bride price, for example, is especially anchored in the Tonga culture in which the traditional means of payment are cows.[45] In urban settings, however, such practices are no longer as relevant due to a growing anonymity and the influence of Western cultures. In some cases this means more individual freedom (especially for women), but it can also mean increased danger and misery because of absent or insufficient social structures. On the one hand, male-dominated sportscapes like football and boxing showcase the seemingly insurmountable socio-cultural barriers that are preventing females from getting involved in sports. On the other hand, such examples illustrate the potential of female athletes in a country like Zambia and the changes their efforts might precipitate.

In another part of Africa, Morocco, an individual named Nawal El Moutawakel launched a female sports movement by winning the 400 m hurdles race at the 1984

Olympics. She became the first Arab, African and Muslim woman to win an Olympic gold medal. King Hassan II publicly honoured her for her performance. El Moutawakel opened the door for other North Africa and Arab women's participation and success in later Olympic Games. In 1992 Hassiba Boulmerka of Algeria won the 1,500 meters in Barcelona, and Ghada Shouaa of Syria took the gold in the heptathlon during the Atlanta Olympics of 1996.

In 1993, El Moutawakel organized the first-ever Moroccan women's race through the streets of Casablanca. After a break of seven years between the second and the third event, more than 20,000 women and girls participated in 2001 when the initiative was re-launched. The 'Course Féminine' of 10 km attracted almost 26,000 female runners and walkers of all ages in 2007, and the numbers continue to increase. For more than a decade now, this impressive event takes place annually in May.

> Before the race began, many women running and walking around Casablanca would probably never have dreamed of competing in front of cheering supporters. In a way they have become stars in their own world. This feeling is strengthened by the many husbands, brothers and sons who lined the streets to encourage and support them.[46]

In 2008 El Moutawakel was the first Muslim woman elected to the IOC's powerful executive board. She is currently the only woman on the 15-member board which is responsible for setting the Olympic agenda. The IOC said in 1996 it would aim for a 20% share of women in its overall membership, though it is still far from that target with only 16 women out of 110 members. Furthermore, El Moutawakel, appointed in October 2007, is currently the Moroccan Minister for Youth and Sports. She is a 'role model' and well aware of it: 'I see myself as an ambassador for sport in my country, with the duty to pass on all my hard-earned experience and true values of sport.'[47]

Whereas track and field is nowadays widely recognized (with some exceptions) as an 'acceptable sport' for women and girls, female boxing remains linked to much more controversy and ardent opposition. Even the Executive Committee of the IOC decided unanimously in 2005 to decline women's boxing as an official Olympic discipline for Beijing 2008.[48] Therefore, Esther Phiri, with her popularity and success, has doubly excelled: she is not only the first woman to enter the bastion of elite Zambian sport and celebrity, but has achieved this by performing in a fighting arena that epitomizes male power, privilege and masculinity. A quarter of a century after the 'Moutawakel effect' of the 1980s laid the ground work for the advancement of African female athletes, the 'Phiri effect' may yet lead to new landmarks. As Rotella wrote about the American boxer, Liz McGonigal in 1999:

> That a woman can be a national amateur champion or have an amateur boxing career at all, and that she has prospects for pursuing that career in legitimate professional circles, is a recent development that points to significant changes not only in boxing but in the sexual division of work and play.[49]

Role models: the literature

With Phiri's story in mind, we turn to the concept of role models, seeking to go beyond 'common-sense' intuitions that 'role models are useful'. Our goal is to contribute to a more substantive understanding of the nature and effectiveness of role models, to make explicit what it is that role models can do, and how it is that they can do it. One clear message from the scholarly literature on role models is that the scientifically-validated evidence evaluating their effectiveness in changing behaviour is slim.[50] That said, there are some useful insights to be drawn from the literature.

The immediately recognized function of a role model is to inspire others and to illustrate success. A role model has attained a measure of success presumably desired by others. A role model also has a demonstration effect, achieving that success through a set of choices, behaviours and actions that presumably are within the reach of those who also desire that same success. So the role model operates to illustrate the success of a possible future self and then to demonstrate a strategy to achieve that possible future self.[51] In this way the role model demonstrates to others how to achieve the goal. Role models can be thought of as maps that indicate a distinct destination and a clear route to that destination. The actual goal of the target person may not be exactly the same as the role model's. For instance, Esther Phiri's success may inspire girls to become boxing champions, but it also may inspire them to engage in another sport or physical activity or in any activity that is currently dominated by men or by people from a more advantaged socio-economic status. By exhortation, she may also inspire them to refrain from behaviours and activities that would inhibit them from reaching their goal.

Lockwood *et al.* emphasize that a role model provides an inspiration only if the goal is attainable and if it is within reach. There has to be a reasonable probability that the goal is possible, and that the person has access to the skills, knowledge, resources or networks required. Lockwood *et al.* note how 'superstar' role models might prove to be demoralizing if the goal or strategy demonstrated is not attainable. For example, if the role model is in the same age group as the target, and has achieved a lot of success, the target may believe that the requisite stages for building success have already been forgone and cannot be reclaimed. For athletic success, this may particularly resonate as peak performance in sport seems to reside with youth.[52]

When role models are invoked in the sport and development realm, the assumption is that they are, or need to be, positive. Yet, negative role models also can be very powerful depending on the regulatory focus of the target. Again, Lockwood suggests that, as a role model, someone like Esther Phiri is most likely to resonate with individuals who already are oriented towards promotion goals, i.e. achieving success with additive behaviour (e.g., train daily and you will win the match). Such an individual is seeking to attain an ideal self and is already sensitive to information in the social world which relates to achieving that success.[53] While achieving success would seem to be an obvious universal impulse, it is not the primary impulse for all people, all of the time. For many people, indeed, the main regulatory focus is not one of promotion, but instead of prevention, that is, to avoid negative outcomes or failure. Lockwood suggests that in these cases, negative role models, those who exhibit the consequences of bad behaviours, e.g. no condoms equal pregnancy or HIV and AIDS, are better motivators.[54] Further, in another study, Lockwood, Marshall and Saddler suggest that while one's own individual regulatory focus may vary over time and over goals, there may be cultural factors which could determine the likelihood of one or the other regulatory focus predominating within a community or an individual. The collective group in question may play a role in the efficacy of the particular role model and the message relayed. Hence, one must consider the predisposition or the particular regulatory focus of an individual and community when evaluating the use of role models.[55]

This also suggests another conundrum: is it the success of the communal group or the individual that is most valued? The health, welfare and success of the communal group are not the same as the health, welfare and success of an individual. There may be very powerful social forces that find the success of an individual, especially that of a woman in an atypical occupation in a particular social milieu, threatening to the collective well-being. Hence, for the individual, there are risks at multiple levels. 'Success' in the atypical realm may mean 'failure' to achieve the accepted 'ideal' in the familiar, social sphere.

In other words, what is normally a desirable 'model' for the social group is cast aside for a very different, and transgressive, 'model'.

Thinking carefully about what Phiri and Moutawakel have accomplished, it is clear they stepped into risky spaces. While the outcomes in retrospect are desirable – wealth, fame, power, social impact – they are esteemed as 'role models' precisely because they did something unusual. They were not 'typical' and have taken a path different from the previously accepted 'ideal-type'. The term 'role model' is so often rhetorically invoked when considering how to encourage the entrance of outsiders into a presumed desirable position that has been previously off-limits. Indeed, a word search for 'role model' in the University of California library holdings returns a set of work that focuses on finding, creating, developing or promoting role models largely to encourage girls and women in fields, hitherto predominantly masculine, especially sports and science. While some do exist, there are not many works invoking role models that would, say, encourage boys to become child care workers. Elling focussed her research on the often neglected aspect that, on the one hand, socially dominant groups have more power to (re)construct and convey particular meanings and ideologies (e.g. about sport), but are, on the other hand, less likely to transgress social boundaries to embody the 'other'.[56] Therefore, it seems to be socially more acceptable for girls and women to enter typical male domains (like football, boxing, etc.) than for boys and men to step into female areas like gymnastics or dancing. Stephen Daldry's movie *Billy Elliot* illustrates the story of a boy who wants to pursue ballet, but is forced by his father and social norms to be a boxer. While in the end Billy succeeds, the journey is fraught with violence, and ultimately there is a question mark placed on Billy's heterosexuality, a mark too dangerous for some to contemplate. As the Zambian Vice President George Kunda said in Parliament in March 2009:

> Zambia is a Christian nation and it shall continue to be so because it is part of our constitution. And acts such as homosexuality are not part of the Christian norm. In 2005, this house passed stiff laws against homosexuality. For people having carnal knowledge of each other against the order of nature the punishment is a minimum of 15 years imprisonment. If you have carnal knowledge of an animal you serve a minimum of 25 years.[57]

Much of the discussion around role models suggests that the impact desired is more of a 'ripple effect'. In many ways, role models can have an even deeper and more diffuse impact beyond inspiring an individual to follow along a certain path. For one, a role model or celebrity may change social attitudes which inhibit individual girls and women by raising a topic for public discussion in a way that softens public opinion. This has clearly occurred in the media debate about who controls Phiri's marriage schedule. She insists she does, yet as of 2009 she still has not married her fiancé. There is also the notion of critical mass in the collective imagination: once enough people see a person doing something that was previously unthinkable for someone of that social status or particular group, there is a demonstration effect that simply allows people to think that it can be done and that it might not be such a bad thing. England's Queen Victoria may have had such an effect by buying bicycles for her nieces.

Another impact role models can have is to use their social capital to impact public policy more directly. They may gather and mobilize resources to programmatically seek change. This may be through a grassroots campaign or elite-level lobbying. It may be through bringing in external or foreign resources as a carrot or a stick to change policies and laws that inhibit female participation in sport or to provide new resources to encourage such participation. In this case, the role model becomes a reformer, or even a revolutionary, with more direct impact on change as opposed to the indirect and diffuse impact of changing the choices and behaviours of others who are unknown and distant.

Indeed, activity by women in the political, scientific, military or economic realm was historically, and still is, subject to similar problems as in the realm of sport.

Celebrity sports stars however are notorious for falling off their pedestals, and instead of providing inspiration they may illustrate the cautionary tales of negative role models. Hence, it is not clear that the role model factor is as strong as one may imagine. There are other areas where the role model notion must be questioned. For instance, Cole and Hribar explore the issues around celebratory feminism, where the ideals of a strong woman are used to market products and extend consumer capitalist culture to a new generation of women.[58] Some may view the extension of the neo-liberal market as a positive step on the road of socio-economic development. For others, these strong women are simply marketing tools for large corporations that, in fact, may not be as liberating to the broad swath of women as one might like to think. This is especially true if the global commodity chains involve exploitative labour and materials-sourcing practices. There is the cynical idea that capitalism is just looking for celebrities to make endorsements of products, and then their image is used to market these products in media-saturated cultures.[59]

If we return to the metaphor of a journey and a map, there is still the implicit question of who is driving whom and who is along for the ride. The notion of role model at its heart fits best where an individual is in charge of the journey and is making her own choice, rather than a society making the choices for her. Yet the notion of each individual going alone is not necessarily a universal good. It may be that an individual does not conceive of making choices in determining things on her own. In the United States the influence of peer groups is well known and documented, especially among youth. Hence, one finds the valued use of peer educators in many sport projects. Family and community groups also may have extensive and pervasive influence. Even when an individual is taken into account, the calculus of benefit and risk of undertaking a less common or even prohibited pathway may give significant weight to communal messages.

Another question for advocates of using sport for empowerment is whether role models prove valuable enough such that development entities should systematically create and use role models. With a celebrity role model the success must receive robust media attention to promote the destination as desirable and the route there as charted and feasible. This suggests the value of realistic detailed stories that can be used to teach and reinforce the recommended destination and path. It may be that fictional characters are as useful as real characters.[60] In Zambia, a new generation of schoolbooks with prominent female characters playing sports may in fact be a way of using the power of role models to change attitudes and behaviour. If we know that role models have to have a degree of affinity to the 'target' then we would hypothesize that visits from foreign superstars are less likely to inspire, because they are irrelevant and their success unattainable, whereas Zambian characters in a book or someone like Phiri, who is 'just like us', is much more effective.

Other questions have to do with the exposure to role models. How often is the subject exposed to a particular role model? How often are they provided with new and enhanced goals? How did the goals initially originate? How are they initialized? Regular exposure to the role model would seem to be required to have a lasting effect. In this, we suggest that the most effective role models are actually more like mentors, where there is regular contact and an on-going demonstration of the details required to achieve success customized in situ to address the various challenges and problems as they arise. In this regard, Payne *et al.*'s review of several studies and reports suggest that the effectiveness of role models is embedded in the level of support provided as well as the length and quality of the relationship between the role model and the target. They add that the selection and training of the mentor is a critical factor in success.[61]

Returning to the work of Lockwood, there is the possibility that if the role model and target are too similar, there is a possibility of a negative effect. In other words, if a role model has achieved something outstanding, but has attributes analogous to the target, the target may not be able to discern any characteristic or resource likely to change for her that will get her closer to the goal. She may even feel threatened by the success of the presumed role model. One reaction found in experiments is that subjects may be dismissive of the success of the role model to avoid demoralization. Lockwood *et al.* suggest that individuals have a lot of protective comparative measures that they deploy to minimize the negative effects of a close role model. However, given that these studies where all done in Western settings, we would want to retain the possibility of significant cultural differences affecting outcomes.

There may also be uncomfortable moments when the role model will disappoint or heroines will fall – and not necessarily because of their own doing. People who are trailblazers may encounter significant, costly and painful retributions for stepping too far out of line. It is difficult to control the message if the role models are real people, because real life is messy, contradictory and incoherent. The lessons may be that it is dangerous to pursue this line. For example, Hassiba Boulmerka felt that she had to leave her home, Algeria, because of the threats on her life after her Olympic achievements. Does this diminish her value as a role model to girls in Algeria or others beyond? Do they take home the idea that change is not possible for them? Or that the path includes leaving the country, a difficult, but necessary sacrifice for one's own integrity, safety or self-realization? A more chilling example is that of Eudy Simelane. A former star mid-fielder with the South African national women's team, Banyana Banyana, she was training to be the first female referee at the 2010 World Cup. In April 2008, she was accosted on her way home, dragged to a ditch, brutally beaten, gang raped and stabbed to death. Her attackers targeted her in what has been called a 'corrective rape', classified by others as a hate crime for she was a 'voracious equality rights campaigner and one of the first women to live openly as a lesbian' in her community of Kwa Thema.[62]

One of the hushed, but potent, issues underlying female participation in sport is the perception that it not only masculinizes women, but somehow is a cover for lesbianism. While a horrifying number of women of all sexualities have suffered sexual violence, being targeted because one is a lesbian signifies one of the strongest expressions of prohibition for women's participation in sport. The fact that Simelane's case has galvanized media attention and advocacy within and outside of South Africa, and the trial has produced the first convictions for a 'corrective rape', may mean that Simelane made the ultimate sacrifice to be a pioneer. And girls may yet be dissuaded from participating in football for fear of the lesbian label and the threat of violence that accompanies it.[63]

Conclusion

As Coalter suggests, an important first step towards more effective programmes using role models in gender sport and development is to better explicate the programme theory. He concedes that measuring outcome may be extremely difficult, but suggests being clearer on the underlying theory of change helps to maximize the possibilities of achieving a particular outcome.[64]

Sport and development organizations may find that role models who have many affinities to the target population will be the most effective role models. They may also find that developing role models really means developing mentors, where there is an ongoing sustained link between the role model and the subject, and the role models have a strong base of support and training.[65] Indeed, it is an educative process. Nevertheless controlling the message is still an issue – negative messages may still be received, despite the best intentions of the programme. The social milieu may offer powerful alternative messages as to the safest, least risky path that will maximize a known, and relatively proven, set of individual desires. Social practices are both malleable and resilient.

While the topic 'role models' as it relates to gender, sport and development is generic, we have structured this inquiry around the Zambian boxer Esther Phiri, and the prospects for women's sport in Zambia. Ultimately, it is important to be very specific about how 'sport and development' projects could use 'role models' as a tool or a focusing device for staff and participants as individuals will not necessarily be most receptive to a positive role model, which requires a path of individual risk. Further, the larger culture can impact on how an individual will interpret a 'role model'. Beyond the theory of role models, there is the larger frame of sport and society, especially the material and the political. The term 'role model' is invoked with a presumption that role models are 'good' and are necessary to inspire and motivate those not represented in desirable professions and places. 'Role models' though are usually outliers. Furthermore, theoretically, the process of role modelling is always operative for everyone at least at some point in their lives; we are always getting messages from our social surrounding and network about viable (or probable) life pathways. Messages about options, risks and pay-offs are constantly being shared. In essence, this is really about on-going processes of socialization, social communication and education. Further work in specific settings over a period of time may help to reveal in what ways and under what circumstances sport and development can use role models for social change, but the casual assumption that role models are an important part of progress must still be tested.

Notes

1   ILO, 'Women in Sports', 30.
2   Coalter, 'Sport-in-Development', 63.
3   The few academic works include Baker and Mangan, *Sport in Africa*; Darby, 'A Context of Vulnerability'; Andresen *et al.*, *Sportstrukturen in Afrika*; Peacock-Villada, DeCelles and Banda, 'Grassroot Soccer Resiliency Pilot Program'.
4   Komakoma, 'An Investigation Into Fan Identity'; Mwaanga, 'HIV/Aids at Risk Adolescent Girls' Empowerment'; Kakuwa, *Zambian Traditional Games*; Banda, 'Evaluating the Role of Sport Orientated Non-Government Organisations'; Banda, 'Linking Teaching and Research'.
5   Scholarly work on the history of sport in Africa is limited, but more is coming into circulation. In addition to other work mentioned here see, Alegi, *Laduma!*; Darby, *Africa, Football, and FIFA*; Nauright, *Sport, Cultures, and Identities*; Fair, 'Kickin' it'; Jones, 'Women and Sport in South Africa'. There are numerous unpublished doctoral and masters theses in African university libraries that have programmes in sports education such as at INSEPS (Institut National Supérieur de l'Education Populaire et du Sport) in Dakar.
6   'Introduced' suggests that the sports were fully formed in Europe and then disseminated. Rather, nationalism, colonialism, imperialism, the neo-liberal state and globalization all influenced and continue to influence the development of modern sport. As such, sport experiences in the colonies themselves feed back into what is understood as 'modern sport'.
7   See Deville-Danthu, *Le sport en noir et blanc*.
8   Saavedra, 'Sport'.
9   See Giulianotti and Armstrong, 'Drama, Fields and Metaphors'. This cursory overview of the general history of modern sport and especially football in Africa is provided with the recognition that in fact there were multiple trajectories for the introduction and reinvention of various sporting codes and physical cultures throughout the continent.
10   Kakuwa, *Zambian Traditional Games*.

11 'Early Marriages Disappoint Headteacher'. *Zambia News and Information Services*, April 8 2009, (Kazungula). http://www.zanis.org.zm/index.php?option=com_content&task=view&id=3429&Itemid=70.
12 Kakuwa, *Zambian Traditional Games*.
13 Specifically by the Norwegian Olympic and Paralympic Committee and Confederation of Sports.
14 SADC, 'Article 9, Gender'.
15 Saavedra, 'Football Feminine'; Meier, *Zarte Füsschen am harten Leder*.
16 These are the rankings from 27 March 2009 found on the FIFA website: for all women's teams: http://www.fifa.com/worldfootball/ranking/lastranking/gender=f/fullranking.html. For African teams: http://www.fifa.com/worldfootball/ranking/lastranking/gender=f/fullranking.html#confederation=23913&rank=525. Of the 33 African nations listed in the FIFA rankings, only 21 are considered official, with the rest being provisional rankings. Only teams that have played five matches against teams with official rankings are deemed official. M. Saavedra is working on an analysis of the rankings of African women's national football teams over the years.
17 H. Chilufya, 'Zambia: Women Suffer Another Gender Discrimination'. *Panafrican News Agency*, July 30, 1998. http://allafrica.com/stories/199807300044.html.
18 Mwaanga, 'HIV/Aids at Risk Adolescent Girls' Empowerment'.
19 M. Muyumba, 'Women's Soccer Wins Govt Support'. *The Post*, June 30, 1998 (Lusaka). http://allafrica.com/stories/199806300162.html.
20 'Women Soccer Body Disbands'. *Times of Zambia*, June 15, 1998 (Ndola). http://allafrica.com/stories/199806150142.html.
21 'Support Women's Football, Lusaka Traders Challenged'. *Times of Zambia*, February 3, 2003 (Ndola). http://www.times.co.zm/news/viewnews.cgi?category=all&id=104430 1803.
22 FIFA, *FIFA Financial Report 2005*, 35.
23 http://www.fazambia.com/ and http://www.faz.org.zm/.
24 For instance, Recreational Sport Soccer Statistics Foundations (RSSSF) statistics for Zambian women's football shows results, sketchy at that, only from 2002, 2003, 2005, 2006 and 2007 with the note on the latter that 'FAZ hopes to start a national tournament 2008'. See http://www.rsssf.com/tablesz/zamb-wom07.html.
25 'FINA Kicks Zambia Out of International Netball'. *Times of Zambia*, March 8, 2006, (Ndola). http://www.times.co.zm/news/viewnews.cgi?category=all&id=1141843792.
26 He actually shared the bronze with José Bolivar of Venezuela.
27 http://www.iaaf.org/athletes/biographies/country=zam/index.html.
28 Rotella, 'Good with Her Hands'.
29 Wacquant, 'Pugs at Work', 90.
30 Park, 'From "Genteel Diversions" to "Bruising Peg"'; Hargreaves, 'Women's Boxing and Related Activities'; Guttmann, *Women's Sports*. Some refer even in the present moment to the near pornographic treatment of some women's boxing. This issue deserves more attention, but is beyond the scope of this essay.
31 Mennesson, '"Hard" Women and "Soft" Women', 22.
32 Women Boxing Archive Network, 'Boxing Trivia'.
33 H. Liwanga, 'Zambia's Female Boxing Star Challenges Stereotypes'. *Afrol News/Gender Links*, March 28, 2007. http://www.afrol.com/articles/24897.
34 UNDP, *2008 Statistical Update – Zambia*.
35 See P. Banda, 'Esther Phiri: To Marry or Not to Marry' 'Zambian Famous Female Boxer'. *Zambia Daily Mail*, August 7, 2008. http://www.daily-mail.co.zm/media/news/viewnews.cgi?category=19&id=1218091351.
36 Republic of Zambia. 'Levy Congratulates Esther for Retaining Title'. http://web.archive.org/web/20070810204539.
37 Ibid.
38 '…As Business Community Weighs in with Flurry of Donations'. *Times of Zambia*, April 5, 2007 (Ndola). http://www.times.co.zm/news/viewnews.cgi?category=all&id=1175760684.
39 George Lwandamina, 'Phiri to Battle it out Against Keli Cofer'. *Times of Zambia*, December 2, 2006 (Ndola). http://www.times.co.zm/news/viewnews.cgi?category=all&id=1165048836.
40 'Esther Phiri Receives World Recognition for her Boxing Talents'. *Lusaka Times*, February 25, 2007. http://www.lusakatimes.com/?p=193.
41 J.J. Schatz, 'Esther Phiri Rises to Prominence Despite Limited Sponsorship Avenues in Southern Africa'. *Wall Street Journal*, August 4, 2008.

[42] This is the Zambian equivalent of General Mills, the American company, putting star athletes on their Wheaties™ breakfast-of-champions cereal boxes.

[43] Caple, 'Fists of Phiri'; 'Levy Congratulates Esther Phiri'. *Lusaka Times*, April 28, 2008. http://www.lusakatimes.com/?p=2690.

[44] Caple, 'Fists of Phiri'.

[45] Taylor, *Culture and Customs of Zambia*.

[46] Nawal El Moutawakel, cited in Van Kempen Consultancy, *Creating Support for Change*.

[47] 'Role Model: Nawal El Moutawakel'. Olympic Review, 'Role Model', http://www.multimedia. olympic.org/pdf/en_report_792.pdf.

[48] On 13, August 2009, the IOC Executive Board approved the addition of women's boxing, beginning at the 2010 London Olympics. http://www.olympic.org/uk/news/media_centre/press_release_uk.asp?id=3092.

[49] Rotella, 'Good with Her Hands', 583.

[50] Speizer, 'Role Models'; Payne *et al.*, *Sports Role Models*; Vescio, Wilde and Crosswhite, 'Profiling Sport Role Models'; Lockwood *et al.*, 'To Do or Not to Do'; Lockwood *et al.*, 'Promoting Success or Preventing Failure'; Lockwood and Kunda, 'Superstars and Me'.

[51] Lockwood and Kunda, 'Superstars and Me'.

[52] Lockwood *et al.*, 'To Do or Not to Do'; Lockwood and Kunda, 'Superstars and Me'.

[53] Lockwood *et al.*, 'To Do or Not to Do'.

[54] Ibid.

[55] Lockwood, Marshall and Sadler, 'Promoting Success or Preventing Failure'.

[56] Elling, '"They (Don't) Have the Right Build for It"'.

[57] E. Chanda, 'Kunda Warns Homosexuals'. *Sunday Post* (reported by *Behind the Mask*), March 24, 2009. http://www.mask.org.za/article.php?cat=zambia&id=2074.

[58] Cole and Hribar, 'Celebrity Feminism'.

[59] Rail, *Sport and Postmodern Times*.

[60] One of the authors, Marianne Meier, collected such textbooks in Zambia in 2008.

[61] Payne *et al.*, *Sports Role Models*.

[62] S. Ahmed, '"Corrective Rape" in South Africa'; Kelly, 'Raped and Killed for being a Lesbian'. *Channel 4 News*, March 12, 2009 (UK). http://www.channel4.com/news/articles/world/africa/corrective+rape+in+south+africa+/3027797.

[63] We should note that in Martha Saavedra's hometown of Richmond, California, in December 2008 there was a gang rape of a woman just outside of her home allegedly because she was a lesbian. AP, 'Woman Possibly Targeted in Richmond Gang Rape'. *CBS 5 Crime Watch*, December 22, 2008 (Richmond, CA). http://cbs5.com/crime/richmond.gang.rape.2.893338.html.

[64] Coalter, 'Sport-in-Development'.

[65] Payne *et al.*, *Sports Role Models*.

References

Alegi, P. *Laduma!: Soccer, Politics and Society in South Africa*. Scottsville: University of KwaZulu-Natal Press, 2004.

Andresen, R., C. Kröger, P. Olango, and R. Andresen. *Sportstrukturen in Afrika: Sambia und Uganda* [Sport structures in Africa: Zambia and Uganda. Development cooperation and sport]. Entwicklungszusammenarbeit im Sport, 3. Ahrensburg: I. Czwalina, 1988.

Baker, W.J., and J.A. Mangan. *Sport in Africa: Essays in Social History*. New York: Africana Pub. Co., 1987.

Banda, D. 'Evaluating the Role of Sport Orientated Non-Government Organisations in the Fight against HIV/AIDS'. MA diss., Institute of Sport and Leisure Policy, Loughborough University, 2003.

Banda, D. 'Linking Teaching and Research through International Development Student Placements on HIV/Aids Projects in Africa'. Paper presented at the International Studies Association Annual Convention, New York, February 2009.

Caple, J. 'Fists of Phiri'. *ESPN Outside the Lines*, September 26, 2008. http://sports.espn.go.com/espn/eticket/story?page=phiri.

Coalter, F. 'Sport-in-Development: Accountability or Development?' In *Sport and International Development*, edited by R. Levermore and A. Beacom, 55–75. Houndsmills: Palgrave MacMillan, 2009.

Cole, C.L., and A. Hribar. 'Celebrity Feminism – Nike Style Post-Fordism, Transcendence, and Consumer Power'. *Sociology of Sport Journal* 12 (1995): 347–60.

Darby, P. *Africa, Football, and FIFA: Politics, Colonialism, and Resistance*. London: Frank Cass, 2002.

Darby, P. 'A Context of Vulnerability: The Zambian Air Disaster, 1993'. *Soccer and Society* 5, no. 2 (2004): 248–64.

Deville-Danthu, B. *Le sport en noir et blanc: du sport colonial au sport africain dans les anciens territoires français d'Afrique occidentale (1920–1965)* [Sport in black and white: from colonial sport to African sport in the former French territories in Western Africa (1920-1965)]. Paris: L'Harmattan, 1997.

Elling, A. '"They (Don't) Have the Right Build For It": Social Constructions of Gender and Sport'. In *Geschlechterforschung im Sport. Differenz und/oder Gleichheit* [Gender studies and sport. Difference and or equity], edited by C. Kugelmann, G. Pfister, and C. Zipprich, 21–34. Hamburg: Czwalina, 2004.

Fair, L. 'Kickin' it: Leisure, Politics and Football in Colonial Zanzibar, 1900s–1950s'. *Africa* 67, no. 2 (1997): 224–51.

FIFA. *FIFA Financial Report 2005*. Munich: FIFA, 2006.

Giulianotti, R., and G. Armstrong. 'Drama, Fields and Metaphors: An Introduction to Football in Africa'. In *Football in Africa: Conflict, Conciliation and Community*, edited by R. Giulianotti and G. Armstrong, 1–25. Basingstoke: Palgrave MacMillan, 2004.

Guttmann, A. *Women's Sports: A History*. New York: Columbia University Press, 1991.

Hargreaves, J. 'Women's Boxing and Related Activities: Introducing Images and Meanings'. *Body Society* 3, no. 4 (1997): 33–49.

ILO. 'Women in Sports: How Level is the Playing Field'. *World of Work: The Magazine of the ILO* 56 (2006): 27–30.

Jones, D.E.M. 'Women and Sport in South Africa: Shaped by History and Shaping Sporting History'. In *Sport and Women: Social Issues in International Perspective*, edited by I. Hartmann-Tews and G. Pfister, 130–44. London and New York: Routledge, 2003.

Kakuwa, M. *Zambian Traditional Games and Activities. A Kicking AIDS Out Resource Book*. Lusaka, Zambia: Kicking AIDS Out, 2005.

Kelly, A. 'Raped and Killed for Being a Lesbian: South Africa Ignores "Corrective" Attacks'. *The Guardian*, March 12, 2009 (UK). http://www.guardian.co.uk/world/2009/mar/12/eudy-simelane-corrective-rape-south-africa.

Komakoma, L. 'An Investigation into Fan Identity Among Supporters of the English Soccer Premier League in Lusaka, Zambia'. MA diss., Rhodes University, 2005.

Lockwood, P., and Z. Kunda. 'Superstars and Me: Predicting the Impact of Role Models on the Self'. *Journal of Personality and Social Psychology* 73, no. 1 (1997): 91–103.

Lockwood, P., T.C. Marshall, and P. Sadler. 'Promoting Success or Preventing Failure: Cultural Differences in Motivation by Positive and Negative Role Models'. *Personality and Social Psychology Bulletin* 31, no. 3 (2005): 379–92.

Lockwood, P., P. Sadler, K. Fyman, and S. Tuck. 'To Do or Not to Do: Using Positive and Negative Role Models to Harness Motivation'. *Social Cognition* 22, no. 4 (2004): 422–50.

Meier, M. *Zarte Füsschen am harten Leder: Frauenfussball in der Schweiz 1970–1999* [Tender feet kicking hard leather: women's soccer in Switzerland 1970-1999]. Frauenfeld, Stuttgart & Wien: Verlag Huber, 2004.

Mennesson, C. '"Hard" Women and "Soft" Women: The Social Construction of Identities among Female Boxers'. *International Review for the Sociology of Sport* 35, no. 1 (2000): 21–33.

Mwaanga, O. 'HIV/Aids at Risk Adolescent Girls' Empowerment through Participation in Top Level Football and Edusport in Zambia'. MA diss., Norwegian University of Sport and Physical Education, 2003.

Nauright, J. *Sport, Cultures, and Identities in South Africa*. Cape Town: David Philip, 1998.

Olympic Review. 'Role Model: Nawal El Moutawakel' *Focus: Women in Sport* (2004). http://www.multimedia.olympic.org/pdf/en_report_792.pdf.

Park, R.J. 'From "Genteel Diversions" to "Bruising Peg": Active Pastimes, Exercise, and Sports for Females in late 17th- and 18th- Century Europe'. In *Women and Sport: Interdisciplinary Perspectives*, edited by D.M. Costa and S.R. Guthrie, 27–43. Champaign, IL: Human Kinetics, 1994.

Payne, W., M. Reynolds, S. Brown, and A. Fleming. *Sports Role Models and their Impact on Participation in Physical Activity: A Literature Review*. Melbourne: Victorian Health Promotion Foundation, 2003.

Peacock-Villada, P., J. DeCelles, and P.S. Banda. 'Grassroot Soccer Resiliency Pilot Program: Building Resiliency through Sport-based Education in Zambia and South Africa'. *New Directions for Youth Development* 116 (2007): 141–54.

Rail, G. *Sport and Postmodern Times*. Albany, NY: SUNY Press, 1998.

Rotella, C. 'Good with Her Hands: Women, Boxing, and Work'. *Critical Inquiry* 25, no. 3 (1999): 566–98.

Saavedra, M. 'Football Feminine – Development of the African Game: Senegal, Nigeria and South Africa'. *Soccer and Society* 4, no. 2 (2003): 225–53.

Saavedra, M. 'Sport'. In *A Companion to Gender Studies*, edited by P. Essed, A. Kobayashi, and D.T. Goldberg, 437–54. London: Blackwell, 2005.

Southern African Development Community (SADC). 'Article 9, Gender'. In *Protocol on Culture, Information and Sport*. Blantyre, Malawi: 2000.

Speizer, J.J. 'Role Models, Mentors, and Sponsors: The Elusive Concepts'. *Signs: Journal of Women in Culture and Society* 6, no. 4 (1981): 692–712.

Taylor, S.D. *Culture and Customs of Zambia*. Westport, CT: Greenwood Press, 2006.

UNDP. *2008 Statistical Update – Zambia: The Human Development Index – going beyond income*. 2008. http://hdrstats.undp.org/en/2008/countries/country_fact_sheets/cty_fs_ZMB.html.

Van Kempen Consultancy. *Creating Support for Change: How to Empower Women through Sport? Make the Case – Attract Funders & Partners – Results of the Conference 'Gender Equity in Sport for Social Change'*. Casablanca: NCDO/Amsterdam, 2008, 1–44. www.toolkitsportdevelopment. org/html/resources/E6/E6DC0A9D-BE30-42F5-B15A-A28C7F13EBE2/Report_Casablanca_ 2008.pdf.

Vescio, J., K. Wilde, and J.J. Crosswhite. 'Profiling Sport Role Models to Enhance Initiatives for Adolescent Girls in Physical Education and Sport'. *European Physical Education Review* 11, no. 2 (2005): 153–70.

Wacquant, L.J.D. 'Pugs at Work: Bodily Capital and Bodily Labour among Professional Boxers'. *Body Society* 1, no. 1 (1995): 65–93.

Women Boxing Archive Network. 'Boxing Trivia: Zambia Decides to Introduce Bill to Allow Women to Boxing and Wrestle – November 1994'. http://www.womenboxing.com/Trivia.htm.

'Zambian Famous Female Boxer Differs on Marriage with Sponsor'. *The Post (cited by Xinhua)*, July 31, 2008. http://news.xinhuanet.com/english/2008-07/31/content_8875483.htm.

Developing through sport: evidencing sport impacts on young people

Tess Kay

Institute of Youth Sport, Loughborough University, Loughborough, UK

The use of sport in pursuit of international development goals is broadening, with widespread policy support for sports-based programmes that promote social, educational and health goals. Academic assessment has however been more critical, posing searching questions about the paucity of evidence that justifies the use of sport in these roles. Recent growth in evaluation studies has increased the evidence-base but carries some risks of privileging positivist forms of knowledge and fails to engage with issues surrounding decolonization of research.[1] This essay suggests that reflexive qualitative studies that capture authentic local knowledge can help address both of these issues, illustrating this through an exploratory study conducted with young women and adult sport workers involved in a 'successful' community-based sports programme in Delhi, India (n = 38). It is argued that the form of data obtained can enhance academic understanding and assist in the process of decolonization of sport-in-development research.

Introduction

This essay has a dual purpose. Its first function is to report on empirical data on the social impact of sport, obtained during a series of research visits to sport-in-development programmes in Recife (Brazil), Delhi (India) and Lusaka (Zambia) undertaken between 2006 and 2008. This work yielded a volume of qualitative data which contains some very explicit statements, from participants and professional and volunteer workers, about the value of sport and it would seem useful for these local voices to be heard within the emerging literature addressing the use of sport for development. We must stay vigilant about the modest scale of this particular evidence base, however, and ensure that reporting of this data is proportionate and does not over-reach. The second function of the essay is therefore to reflect on the contribution that qualitative work may make within sport-in-development research.

This line of argument raises a number of issues about sport-in-development research, itself in a formative stage. The rapid expansion in the use of sport in development work has been accompanied by a concomitant rise in research-based evaluation and monitoring. This has catapulted researchers into an area of activity in which the already complex issues surrounding assessment of the social impact of sport exponentially increase. It is particularly challenging for (mainly) western researchers to address such complex phenomena in (mainly) non-western cultural settings. This raises fundamental issues about the cultural underpinnings of the research process. Although the sport-in-development research community is an encouragingly self-critical one, the latter issues have not yet been prominent within its debates, and this essay therefore introduces these considerations.

To fulfil its two functions the essay is organized into three main sections. The first section overviews the current debate surrounding the complexities of researching the social impact of sport in development contexts and considers the contribution of qualitative study to a field that can easily become dominated by the requirements of policy for 'hard facts'. The second section then provides a case study of data obtained through qualitative approaches in which participants and deliverers articulate their views of the benefits of sports experiences. Many of the statements appear powerful and the third section reflects on this, arguing that while the case study indicates the potential value of reflexive approaches that express authentic local voices, it also raises more fundamental issues about research processes which need to become part of current debates on improving quality in sport in development research.

Critiques of research into sport-in-development

We are becoming very familiar with the arguments surrounding the problems of evidencing the social impact of sport. It is widely recognized and extensively repeated that:

- There is a widespread and historically long-standing[2] assumption that sport can provide social benefit beyond the immediate experience of participation;
- Contemporary rhetoric and policy have raised the profile of sport in these roles, often expressing very high expectations of the instrumental role sport may play.[3] The use of sport in international development contexts is a rapidly expanding application of this;[4]
- The claimed benefits attributed to sport over-reach the research base as the evidence of sports' social impacts is unsatisfactory.[5] This holds in all contexts, not just international development ones;
- The absence of robust data does not in itself disprove the actual or potential value of sport.[6]

These debates therefore address two issues – a question of actuality and a question of evidence. Researchers are not only uncertain about the potential social impacts of sport but also about the capacity of research to uncover these, and in the last decade much attention has focussed on this latter issue. In the United Kingdom from the late 1990s the debate had two stimuli: the renewed prominence given to sport across a wide range of policy agendas under the New Labour government's commitment to 'joined-up' approaches to social policy; and its parallel embracing of 'evidence-based policy', positing that research can find out 'what works' and that appropriate evaluation can tell us if, and why, it has. The result was a growth in sports-based programmes addressing a range of social policy goals, and a growth in research into them.

In this climate Collins *et al.* were amongst the first commissioned to evaluate existing evidence on what might be achieved through sport, and they, like many other contemporary and subsequent analysts, noted that these political drivers might lead to research quantity but not necessarily quality. They reported that there were 'a growing number of studies that describe ... short term outputs/throughputs in anecdotal/descriptive or even quantified forms', but observed that 'few of these looked at longer term outcomes, because of the difficulty of measuring these, or of having the data or resources over a long enough period to make a rigorous assessment'. The weaknesses identified included lack of clarity in planning and specifying outcomes; lack of baseline data; short-termism, in projects and evaluations; conceptual difficulties in defining measures for outcomes; practical difficulties in operationalizing measures; and difficult in deconstructing and attributing causality. They concluded that in most cases, 'evaluation is tentative, indicative and anecdotal, because insufficient (human and financial) resources are given to it, and insufficient intellectual attention in most cases is expended to identify outcomes and gather the necessary evidence to demonstrate them'.[7] These concerns persist, as subsequent commentaries have shown.[8]

Over the last decade these issues have continued to concern agencies who have invested in sport in support of wider policy agendas. There has been further growth in monitoring and evaluation activity as research has been commissioned to provide appropriate assessments of the impact of programmes. Alongside this, a body of work has also emerged to guide organizations in establishing their own systems for evaluating their activities.[9] The emphasis has been on providing data that can inform organizational processes – as for example in Coalter's (2006) manual for monitoring and evaluating sport-in-development initiatives, commissioned by UK Sport in partnership with UNICEF and Magic Bus and written to 'provide guidance and assistance to develop sustainable and effective sporting organisations that also have a broader social purpose'.[10] Much research into how individuals experience the 'social outcomes' of sport has thus been framed by, and undertaken within, research programmes that have a primary purpose of informing management and policy. It does not detract from this significant body of work to suggest that we might look to extend and diversify our research approaches.

Developing sport-in-development research

There are a number of implications for research when it is undertaken to meet the requirements of policy and organizations. Laws, Harper and Marcus, writing specifically about research for development, identify the key concerns that influence those researching 'for' policy: 'Who needs to have confidence in the findings of your research? What are their values, and ideas about what is valid evidence? Are they interested in community members' views? Or do they only recognise traditional "scientific" approaches?'[11] The last question captures a familiar challenge for social scientists: that in its need for 'hard facts', policy-oriented research traditionally privileges quantitative, positivist approaches over qualitative, social constructivist approaches.[12] The enthusiastic embracing of evidence-based policy has accentuated this: at an organizational level the requirement for accountability encourages an emphasis on methods that can help 'measure'. Alongside this, the use of qualitative approaches is limited by difficulties in resourcing more intensive forms of data collection at the level required to achieve credibility. This poses problems when the object of study is complex forms of human behaviour, and these difficulties multiple exponentially when researchers operate in very different cultural contexts in international development settings.

The process through which research influences policy is however fluid and political and is affected by factors beyond the intrinsic quality and rigour of the research itself.[13] Assumptions that policy will be influenced by simply presenting robust 'factual' evidence are therefore unrealistic and naive – and so too are preconceptions about what constitutes 'evidence' in the first place. Despite the undoubted predominance of positivist approaches, qualitative research is also extensively used to inform policy.[14] Laws, Harper and Marcus have therefore advised researchers that they should not always take at face value 'what people say about the kind of research they trust', observing that 'a strong case study which explores relevant themes in a convincing way' can be as influential as 'hard' statistics.[15] In the move to improve the quality of research into the social impact of sport, this stance allows us to adopt a wide approach and address the unresolved challenge of deepening our understanding of the potential outcomes of sport.

At a generic level qualitative approaches can secure rich descriptions that capture individuals' points of view, locate their experience within the constraints of everyday life.[16] In the sport-in-development context the particular value in securing accounts of this type is that they provide a mechanism for addressing the complex social phenomena with which we are concerned. They allow us to use a wide lens, reaching beyond the sports programme to broader social context of family and community. They also offer a research process which, while undoubtedly continuing to privilege the researcher, employs tools which facilitate reflexivity and can offer a first step towards democratizing the research relationship.

It is in this context that this essay now presents findings from recent work undertaken in India, acknowledging from the outset that small-scale, qualitative, exploratory studies of this type have limited application. Nonetheless, even short-duration projects can capture insights that have value in themselves, can inform other elements of a wider programme of research, and are especially important for their reflexive representation of local knowledge.[17] The work presented here is therefore offered as exemplifying possible strategies for reconciling the tension between fulfilling the demand for 'robust' research and valuing authentic local voices and knowledge.[18] It seeks to demonstrate that the inclusion of individuals' accounts of their sports experiences is, at the very least, a legitimate and important component in assessments of the 'impact' of sport; alternatively and more ambitiously, they are a voice without which such work is incomplete.

The research

The case study presented here is from research undertaken in Delhi, India, in May 2008. This investigation was one of a series which were undertaken in Brazil, India and Zambia between 2006 and 2008 on the social impact of sport on young people. The specific contractual and funding context for each study differed but the purpose of each was to obtain data on the benefits young people obtained from participating in sports programmes. The projects which participated were using sport to work with young people in acutely disadvantaged communities in three diverse cities. None of these projects were staffed only, or even predominantly, by sports personnel. All were led by (and worked widely in partnership with) professionals from education and community services who had become convinced from their experience of working with young people over many years that sport had a special role to play in their work.

The research was not examining whether sport provides benefits to young people: it was working with projects that were already deemed 'successful' in engaging and benefitting young people. We were not assessing programme impact or evaluating planning, implementation or delivery. Our focus was on the nature of the outcomes in situations in which sport was believed to be benefitting young people: what types of benefits were being gained? And how did those who were closest to this experience – the young people themselves, and those who worked with them – feel that sport itself contributed to this process?

Across the three countries data was obtained from 130 young people and 48 adult interviewees. The methods used were individual in-depth interviews, small-group/paired interviews, and focus group discussions. Additional material was obtained by recording (with consent) several of the informal discussions which took place between the research team, project personnel and other local stakeholders. All data was transcribed in full on return to the United Kingdom.

The young people interviewed represented a wide range of participants, aged from 8 to 20, who had participated in the projects for varied periods of time. They offered a rich diversity of experience, ranging in their level of sports involvement and skill from those who had never previously played sport to those who had participated in national competitions. The adults' accounts included extensive information from staff from local education and community services who had worked with young people for many years and had detailed knowledge and understanding of the issues confronting them. In addition to classroom teachers and community workers, interviewees included several more senior staff (e.g. head teachers and senior community project managers) with professional experience and knowledge of the local social context.

In all three countries the focus of the data collection was upon the young people's experiences of sport as described in their own words and through the commentary of adults who worked with them. Throughout the research the emphasis was on experiential accounts rather than speculative views about sport's 'potential' benefits. Children and young people were questioned about their own participation in the projects, while adult interviewees were asked for specific examples from their experience of using sport in work with young people.

Young women's education and empowerment through sport in Delhi, India

The research undertaken in Delhi was conducted with the GOAL project operated by the Naz Foundation (India) Trust, a New Delhi based NGO which has been working on HIV/AIDS and Sexual Health since 1994. GOAL is a relatively recent addition to the Trust's range of programmes and is a small-scale intensive sports-led intervention that aims to empower women to become leaders and social activists in their communities. Netball is used as a medium through which young women aged 13–19 can be reached, with the focus on sustained, intense support and education with relatively small, close-knit groups of young women.

At the time of the research visit, the GOAL project had been working for around 15 months with approximately 45 participants in Deepalaya and Aali Gaon, two impoverished neighbourhoods within the city boundaries. Most of the young women at Aali Gaon had had very little school education whereas those at Deepalaya were currently attending school or taking part in other forms of education. This distinction underpinned differences in the roles that the young women from each community were expected to take in their families and the extent of their activity outside the home. Young women at Aali Gaon were expected to help extensively in the domestic sphere and stay mainly within it whereas the young women at Deepalaya were able to spend some time outside it. None of the young women had however participated played netball before.

In both locations the project ran twice-weekly netball sessions supplemented by educational modules. The modules covered personal issues such as hygiene, health and communication; social issues including the environment; and economic issues such as micro-finance and computing. The modules were intended to complement the health and well-being, teamwork and leadership promoted through the netball sessions.

The research entailed a programme of meetings with staff and participants of the GOAL project, and field visits to both sites at which the project operated. In total, 38 individuals participated in the research. Interviews were undertaken with four GOAL staff responsible for the delivery of the programme (one administrator, one manager and two coaches), and with three other professional workers with involvement: a very experienced and long-standing Community Coordinator at Aali Gaon, and the School Principal and Community Co-ordinator at Deepalaya. Discussion groups were held with participants, with 19 young women participating at Aali Gaon and 12 at Deepalaya. Individual interviews were also conducted with two participants at Aali Gaon and three former participants at Deepalaya who now assisted with coaching at that site. Interviews with the GOAL staff and some other adult workers were conducted in English, with the project manager in attendance to translate if required. Focus groups and individual interviews with the young women were translated through the project manager, although those with stronger English chose to give some answers in English.

The data identified a very wide array of reported benefits from the young women's participation in the GOAL programme. It also offered rich accounts of how these benefits occurred and how they were located within the young women's broader life experience. The capacity of qualitative data to capture accounts of social processes in this way can be particularly valuable in sport-in-development research, and the report below focuses especially on this. Following Denzin and Lincoln (above), it aims to provide rich descriptions that capture individuals' points of view and locate their experience within the constraints of their everyday life. The data is presented under three themes:

- What are the 'problems' that the project is attempting to address? How are nationally recognized policy priorities articulated at local level by participants, project staff and other involved parties?
- What benefits did the project offer? Again, how were these articulated by the participants themselves and by those who worked with them and knew them?
- How are the benefits obtained through experiences on the programme? What specific role, if any, did the sport play in these processes?

For the purpose of this essay, the account below has been narrowed to focus primarily on benefits relating to education and knowledge. As the data will show, this is a somewhat artificial division as the array of benefits are closely interwoven. It is used here simply as a device to keep the analysis within the necessary limits for this essay.

The challenge: local views on the situation of young women

The GOAL project was established in a strongly patriarchal society to empower young women and equip them to challenge constraints on their lives. These issues are recognized internationally, for example through the Millennium Development Goals, and in India through policies to address a range of oppressive practices (e.g. female infanticide; forced marriage) and empower females. The priority policy areas include education, seen as a pivotal strategy to address gender inequity through female empowerment, and health. Health concerns include fertility and sexual health, including HIV/AIDS education.

The research obtained several accounts of how inequitable gendered relations were directly experienced in the day-to-day lives of the young women in Aali Gaon and Deepalaya. Prior to taking part in GOAL, young women had little life outside the home:

> The only place I used to go was to school, come back from school to home, that was the only journey I used to do on my own, the rest I used to stay in the home, so there was not much movement for me. [Aali Gaon girl B]

There were very limited expectations about women's lives:

> Before I started the programme, my father had told me that you will study till class 7 or 8 and I will get you married off, and you will be happy, in a married, happy life. [Deepalaya girl D]

It was difficult in any case for young women to oppose or resist these expectations. Their views were neither sought nor valued:

> The background of the children is [that] they come from first generation learners and young women are not given that much... importance and their views are not given adequate weighting. [School Principal, Deepalaya]

> Nobody would even listen to what the young women have to say. [GOAL Project Manager]

The young women's constrained lifestyles also did not equip them to articulate any opposition:

> We never had the opportunity to go out, and when you don't go out, you hardly speak. [Aali Gaon girl K]

> I used to tremor or shiver when it came to talking to somebody, I would just hide myself behind a wall or just run away. [Deepalaya girl K]

Young women' position was compounded by their limited access to education. The young women in Aali Gaon had little formal education and had found time spent in school unproductive:

> I used to go to a government school where the teachers were horrible, they would just bunk classes, they were there just for the namesake. [Aali Gaon girl A]

> When we have to ask a question to a teacher I am scared to ask because she might just refute us back and scream and shout and scold me back for no reason. [Aali Gaon girl B]

For the young women in Deepalaya, social conventions meant that even at school they received limited information on issues of central importance to their well-being. They discussed this especially in relation to fertility and sexual health:

> The science teacher was explaining the body chart, the organs of the body, and when it came to the sexual organ, she flipped the page, she didn't even try to do it, because she thought it was a sensitive issue. So there is no medium where we can talk about it. And even if we asked questions, they would always shout at us or scold us or cut us or no response. [Deepalaya girl E]

> I never even encountered the word sex in my life till the time I joined this [GOAL] programme. [Deepalaya girl L]

The school principle confirmed these problems: 'Teachers in classroom have certain inhibitions, they do not want to speak openly, they do not know how to go about it' [School Principal, Deepalaya].

On a day-to-day basis the young women' lack of education left them unequipped to safeguard their own health and wellbeing and manage their lives effectively, and also gave them few skills for changing their situation. The GOAL programme was using sport to address both of these issues – as a basis for imparting information and knowledge through educational modules, but also to create a process of empowerment that would enable the young women to use that knowledge in their lives.

The benefits gained from the participation in GOAL

This section mainly focuses on accounts given of two broad types of benefits: acquiring knowledge and education, and empowerment.

Acquiring knowledge and information

One of the key benefits obtained by the young women was knowledge about factors of importance to their own lives, especially those relating to health and reproduction:

> I know my own body now, I know which part is functioning how and where, which I had no idea. Even though the body is mine, I was absolutely unaware of my own body. [Aali Gaon girl K]

> My biggest learning was something about a killer disease like AIDS. I had no idea about it, and now I know what it is, and I can stand against it, because I have the knowledge, and probably this knowledge would also help me to help the people around me. [Aali Gaon girl D]

The information the young women obtained was passed to others, especially family members:

> Our mothers encourage us to go and play and once we get back home, they also look forward to us coming back home because we go home with a lot of information, which we share with them. [Aali Gaon girl H]

The importance of communicating what had been learnt was mentioned very frequently and is in keeping with the collectivist nature of Indic cultures. The young women displayed a strong general consciousness of how this process of sharing knowledge might engender social change:

> Whatever I learn here I go and teach it to my brother and sister, so it's like passing on of knowledge, that itself is a learning. [Aali Gaon girl C]

> If god wishes, if I have children, I'll at least try to pass [what I have learnt] on to them, and they'll pass on, and that's how it goes on. [Aali Gaon girl I]

> We would like to become people like you [GOAL Project Manager], spreading the knowledge, and creating the chain, you know, the way you have. We want to create the ripple. [Aali Gaon girl H]

In the above quotations the young women not only report the benefit of acquiring new knowledge, but also demonstrate critical reflection on the significance of such information for themselves and their communities.

Empowerment

The young women gave detailed accounts of how taking part in GOAL built their personal confidence, giving them greater status in others' eyes (especially family members'), raising their aspirations and giving them experience of collaboration which could foster collective action. Multiple reports were given of the young women's new-found ability to express themselves:

> Before I was a part of this, I always used to be very shy, even talking to the people with whom I live every day, like my father, my mother, my brother. I was so uncomfortable even talking to them, I used to shy away. But now it's not like that. I am like a confident girl … And the fear, the factors like fear, or negativity, or you know, 'I won't be able to face a crowd', has gone. [Aali Gaon girl J]

> I have changed overall, like the way I talk, the way I present myself … now I can face people, when I coordinate in a team in the field and the sessions I have become much more confident, I can face the world … today, in class 9, one of our teachers came and said, have you seen the class 7 girls, they are so good at football, and if you have a match with them, I'm sure you guys would lose it. And I felt sure, it was such a different feeling inside me, and I actually ended up telling my teacher 'just give us a chance and you will see who wins and who loses'. It's not the matter of winning, or losing, it's the matter of having the confidence of going and playing there and I know at this point I can do it. [Deepalaya girl I]

This confidence affected how young women were viewed within their families:

> Initially it was that they [family] would just make fun of us. 'What will you do, you can't do anything except cooking and cleaning.' And now they said that you can really go ahead, move, keep moving. And I feel so empowered, cos initially they never used to respect us. And now we all get the respect. [Aali Gaon girl K]

> Now the scenario has changed, because they have seen the changes in me, the way I talk, I am active, my laziness has gone. And now my father says, 'Don't worry I will not get you married off. Go ahead.' [Deepalaya girl F]

Several of the young women made strong statements about the impact of the project on their aspirations:

> The programme has caused me to think on a different line that I really want to prove certain things, I don't have a dream as of now, I don't know where I will end up, but one thing is for sure that I want to do something. [Deepalaya girl E]

> People, families, when the sport came up, and the programme was here, they said 'clean, cook, and that's your life'. And there was this line that was drawn that we could never cross. But now that line is going backwards. And we are just, you know, coming out, we have crossed it. And now we have realised that our life is not just limited to washing clothes, washing utensils, or cooking. And now we think that when we do everything we have done, this is the time we have for ourselves, and we don't want to compromise on that. [Aali Gaon girl C]

In each location a very experienced adult worker (the School Principal at Deepalaya, and the long-standing Community Coordinator at Aali Gaon) also highlighted the significance of the young women' experiences for the wider benefit of families and communities:

> (Now) they know how to assert their rights, they know how to speak within their family and be heard which I think is a step in the right direction. They can be very active decision makers in the long run in the families. [School Principal, Deepalaya]

> ... these young women have learnt that we need a team spirit, we need a group relationship, we must be united, we must have a group who has relations with another group, so this idea, if they start fighting for any issue, regarding their life, regarding their goal, as women, they can fight. [Community Coordinator, Aali Gaon]

The quotations above – a small selection from many – recount multiple benefits of the programme. They show the value of relating benefits to their context, as in the descriptions of how family members are responding to the young women's involvement in the programme.

Accounts of process: how GOAL delivered benefits

This third section presents data extracts which give indications of *process*: how participation in the programme resulted in benefits for the young women. One way in which GOAL provided the young women with the opportunity to develop more assertive identities was by giving them the chance to remove themselves from domestic responsibilities, and also from the home as a physical space:

> This girl says she is always smiling, all the time, and she thinks that's the biggest learning for her. When she is at home, she doesn't get that moment when she can openly laugh, because all the time there is this pressure on her. This in the only place where she comes and she can laugh. That's why she keeps laughing. And that's one of her learnings, freedom. [GOAL Project Manager]

The programme accustomed the young women and their families to the idea that they could go outside their homes:

> Initially before we were part of this programme we couldn't have even thought of, dreamt of stepping out of home, but now just because of the game, we can move out, we can come out,

to the [netball] field, to this ground at least. Initially it was not possible, without the game, so we love and respect the game. [Aali Gaon girl E]

Now we walk down from our villages to the [netball] place, we play, walk and go back. And now also because of this independence, our parents let us go out, so even if someone has to buy a vegetable, we walk out and get the vegetable. [Aali Gaon girl B]

Some young women explained how their growing self-confidence derived from increased body confidence, leading to more fundamental changes in how they expressed themselves and behaved:

It's all about the energy, when you feel nice, and you have the nice figure, and you don't have the fat, hanging around, you can run better, you have more energy, and you are more confident. [Deepalaya girl D]

One of the major changes is I have lost a tremendous amount of weight, I used to be fat, and now I have lost it … I have lost a lot of weight, which has made me feel a lot more comfortable, and now, once I have come here, my personality has developed in the sense, now you can see me talking, I never used to talk like this, so that itself is a development in my personality. [Aali Gaon girl A]

Several of the young women and adult workers highlighted the fact that netball made a specific contribution to this process because it was a team sport which engendered communication skills and developed collaborative working:

I have learnt a new game, and also because of the team activity that goes on, I have started, I have learnt how to interact, which I would never have done before. [Aali Gaon girl C]

One thing which is very important, these young women, during their sessions of the sports, they have developed team spirit, which is a very big thing for them. They will play a game, but team spirit is very, very important for their lives. As a team they can fight for their locality, as a team they can fight for any personal issues, now they know, that single person cannot do it, anything, you have to unite, to fight. [Community Coordinator, Deepalaya]

Several young women talked about how their experiences on the programme had allowed them to become clearer about their own views, and more able to make decisions:

You can see the confidence in these young women, I mean the leadership quality and their communication skills and now they like, they will listen and understand and try and make analytical understanding and then take the right decision which is very important for the children. [School Principal, Deepalaya]

This quality was judged important by the School Principal:

One of the best changes that has ever happened in my life is that I can take my decisions now. Initially what happened for every decision, usually it's left or right, but we always used to be in the middle, and going from here and there and finally not knowing what to do. But now the situation is we know either left or right, so it becomes much easier for us to carry on a conversation or explain to our parents what we actually want, put them across, that is one thing. [Deepalaya girl A]

The gains of the programme were underpinned by relationships. The relationships the young women formed with each other were important to this:

I never knew about anything. I used to go to school for the sake of going to school, there was no proper knowledge that was being imparted. And staying at home I never used to interact with anybody because there is very less interaction with family members. But the moment I started coming to this medium I have started talking to people, and once you talk to people you share knowledge, that is one important change, development in me. [Aali Gaon girl H]

Relationships with GOAL staff were referred to frequently and enthusiastically. It was clearly important that these were democratic and that the approach to imparting information was informal and reflexive. The young women felt that they could raise any issue they wanted:

> I love them [GOAL staff], we all love them like crazy, they are always there to care about us, they make us feel special all the time ... and above all they are not like our teachers or our leaders, they are like our best friends ... It's a very close, it's a friendly relationship, because there is no apprehension in this relationship. [Aali Gaon girl B]

> ... the coaches, most importantly they don't scare us, they don't scold us. Nothing is right or wrong, it's like a forum where you can come and discuss, ask your questions, share your doubts. So that makes it much easier. [Deepalaya girl K]

GOAL staff deliberately fostered a structure in which giving and receiving information was a regular feature of the sessions, and was integrated with the netball activities:

> What we do is we talk, there are a lot of interactions, and then there are questions when they go back home and reflect. So the next netball session we have is a group discussion, and when we are playing, someone will say 'you said this yesterday' ... they will ask questions, everybody gets to learn. Even though one person asks the question, the answer is shared by everybody. [GOAL Project Manager]

Sport was important in the process of relationship-building and in establishing a relaxed, enjoyable environment conducive to learning:

> What I actually think when I do my coaching, I make it more interesting, by pulling their legs, and changing the position, like GS to GK, GK to centre, centre to GS, then they have to move around ... laughing with them, small, small things, and, playing lots of different activities, these kind of things. They are comfortable, they do really talk about anything, they can talk about HIV, they do talk about HIV, about condoms, about self-development, fitness and all. [Coach A]

> We are so much more comfortable with everything, parents have always been very supportive of us going ahead, but issues like sex and sexuality, HIV/Aids, boys and girls being friends, like love, was a big thing for us but now it's just so normal for us and we are so comfortable with it. [Deepalaya girl A]

Sport was also helpful in school settings in reducing barriers between participants and teachers that often inhibited learning;

> Once you are doing sport you are free, like you are mobbing around speaking, even the teacher comes out from their own kind of shell and kind of mixes with the students so the gap between the student and the teacher is different, yes. [School Principal, Deepalaya]

> [Sport] plays a very important role; one factor is getting across the bridge between the teacher and the student. Then it makes the learning also fun, yes, because it is not very structured like in a classroom setting so we definitely see children learn better also, because in school it's not just sport you are learning, leadership and all the qualities that are being taught through sport the team activities, everything is coming through netball. [School Principal, Deepalaya]

The quotations above provide participant and adult worker perspectives on the process through which young women experienced multiple benefits from taking part in GOAL. Sport was considered to be instrumental in this process and the examples provide interviewees' own explanations of how sport directly or indirectly facilitated learning and change.

Emerging issues of research and understanding

The example of sport-in-development research above illustrates some of the contributions qualitative study can offer to our understanding of the social impact of sport in development contexts. The young women's narratives describe in detail how the programme impacted positively on their own behaviour and self-perception, and also affected how others viewed and treated them. Equivalent observations were made by the adults who worked with the young women, two of whom drew on more than two decades of experience in educational and community capacities. There is notable consistency across the different categories of interviewee, and the outcomes of the study overall concur with theoretical and empirically based analyses which attribute sport with the potential to contribute to positive social outcomes.

Qualitative investigations may therefore help capture the complex and multi-faceted process through which individuals experience beneficial social outcomes from sport. This means that it is important that concern with 'rigour' in sport-in-development research does not lead to too narrow a concentration on positivist methods that deliver the 'hard facts' beloved of policymakers. We must be cautious about privileging positivist forms of knowledge by valuing research primarily for its contribution to policy and organization effectiveness. Efforts to understand the social impact of sport are unnecessarily limited if we study human behaviour (e.g. behavioural and attitudinal change) only *as a product of policy implementation*. This leads to limited consideration of broader contextual influences.

More fundamentally, qualitative methodologies are needed to help address a neglected issue within sport in development research – the need to subvert enduring 'colonial' power relationships. Researching the social impact of sport in an international development context requires more than tactical adaptations of approaches researchers employ in western contexts. A research model derived from the structures and values of western sports systems is culturally specific.[19] We need to look critically into what currently shapes sport-in-development research: on the one hand, what is required of researchers by their funding agencies and on the other, what is appropriate to the phenomena under study. This means engaging with debates surrounding 'decolonising' methodology and knowledge[20] which feature prominently in development studies.

Figure 1 provides a simple representation of how researchers are positioned at the interface of, on the one hand, the required 'product' of their research, and on the other, the 'object' of study. In non-western contexts, this also positions researchers between contrasting thought systems – the embedded Cartesian rationality of western scientific thought, and the alternative ontologies and epistemologies of non-western cultures.

Researchers themselves are of course not value-free. The non-indigenous researchers who dominate sport-in-development research are embedded in the western thought system.

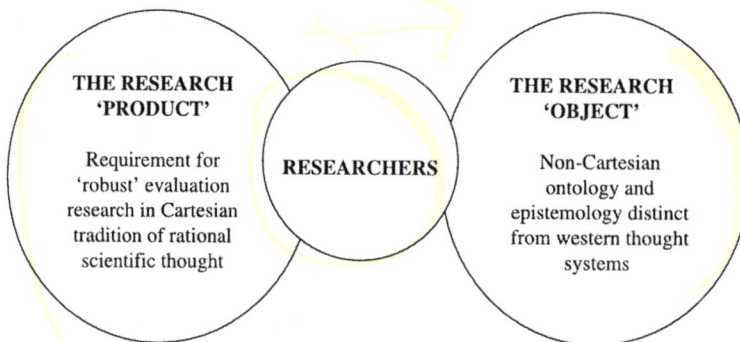

THE RESEARCH 'PRODUCT'	RESEARCHERS	THE RESEARCH 'OBJECT'
Requirement for 'robust' evaluation research in Cartesian tradition of rational scientific thought		Non-Cartesian ontology and epistemology distinct from western thought systems

Figure 1.   The research relationship.

More specifically, much of the current critique of sport-in-development research derives from assessments that were initially undertaken, not for international sport-in-development research, but for research into the social impact of sport in western settings. In some cases the intellectual legacy is very explicit: texts vary minimally. While the central challenge of assessing 'social impact' is certainly common to both contexts, it does not justify an uncritical assumption about the universality of methodology and its epistemological and ontological underpinnings. Basing research inquiry on an implicit model of western scientific rationality carries the danger of dismissing – and perhaps just missing – authentic local voices.

Is it realistic to aspire to an alternative approach which focuses on being more responsive to the characteristics of the object of study and emphasizes reflexivity? To some extent this may be construed as simply a reproduction of the familiar tension between positivist and social constructivist standpoints epitomized in the feminist challenge to methodology. Of more significance however are issues surrounding methodology and the production of knowledge that are specific to cross-national research development contexts and especially heightened in development contexts. These pertain to the (de)colonization of methodology and knowledge, epitomized in the work of Tuhiwai Smith, and Apffel-Marglin and Marglin.[21] Tuhiwai Smith is unequivocal in her rebuttal of 'western' research:

> From the vantage point of the colonized, a position from which I write, and choose to privilege, the term 'research' is inextricably linked to European imperialism and colonialism. The word itself, 'research', is probably one of the dirtiest words in the indigenous world's vocabulary... It galls us that Western researchers and intellectuals can assume to know all that is possible to know of us, on the basis of their brief encounters with some of us.[22]

Of particular significance is the challenge Tuhiwai Smith offers to the ontological and epistemological underpinning of western research and its positivist empiricist roots:

> Many critiques of research have centred around the theory of knowledge known as empiricism and the scientific paradigm of positivism which is derived from empiricism ... From an indigenous perspective Western research is more than just research that is located in a positivist tradition. It is research which brings to bear, on any study of indigenous peoples, a cultural orientation, a set of values, a different conceptualisation of such things as time, space and subjectivity, different and competing theories of knowledge, highly specialised forms of language, and structures of power.[23]

Apffel-Marglin and Marglin are particularly concerned to illuminate the cultural specificity of Cartesian rationality that underpins western knowledge. Descartes' 'utter separation between the mind and matter left the world and the body empty of meaning and thoroughly subjectivized the mind. This subjectivization of mind, this radical separation between mind and the world, placed human beings in a position external to the body and the world, with an instrumental stance towards them'. For 'modern persons' the separation between the human mind or spirit and the world is therefore absolute. Other cultures do not make this separation: in Indic civilizations (Hindu, Buddhist, and Jain), for example, 'the Cartesian separation between mind and the world does not exist'.[24] There is therefore a 'radical contrast... between Indic epistemology and ontology and the modern Western one' and a need for western researchers to be alert to 'the cultural specificity of the Western ontological cleft between the human mind and the rest of the world'.[25]

Sports researchers have generally not engaged with issues surrounding the decolonization of research. These are important considerations that should be incorporated in the debates surrounding how we evaluate the worth of different types of research knowledge within the sport in development context. Discussions surrounding what constitutes 'good' research into the social impact of sport reflect only western thought systems.

To uncritically 'export' these approaches is to perpetuate the process of colonization through research about which Tuhiwai Smith and others are so critical.

This essay does not suggest that qualitative methodologies magically transform and democratize underlying power relationships between researchers and the researched. They clearly do not, and especially do not when implemented by western non-indigenous researchers. It does argue, however, that reflexive forms of research provide a mechanism for the expression of local understandings and knowledge that are crucial to the assessment of the 'social impact' of sport in development contexts.

Notes

1 Tuhiwai Smith, *Decolonizing Methodologies.*
2 Coalter, Long and Duffield, *Recreational Welfare*; Holt, *Sport and the British*; Collins *et al.,* *Sport and Social Exclusion.*
3 E.g. in the UK, Department for Media Culture and Sport (DCMS), *A Sporting Future for All* and *Game Plan*; also Policy Action Team 10, *The Contribution of Sport and the Arts.*
4 E.g. Sport for Development and Peace International Working Group (SDP IWG), *Literature Reviews.*
5 E.g. Blackshaw and Long, 'What's the Big Idea?'; Coalter, Allison and Taylor, *The Role of Sport*; Coalter, *A Wider Social Role*; Crabbe, 'Avoiding the Numbers Game'; Donnelly *et al.,* 'The Use of Sport'; Kay, Houlihan and Welford, *Guide to Education and Sport*; Long *et al., Count me in.*
6 E.g. Coalter, Allison and Taylor, *The Role of Sport*; Kay and Bradbury, 'Youth Sport Volunteering'; Long *et al., Count me in.*
7 Collins *et al., Sport and Social Exclusion*, 8.
8 E.g. Bailey, 'Physical Education'; Coalter, Allison and Taylor, *The Role of Sport*; Coalter, *Sport and Community Development*; Coalter, *A Wider Social Role*; Long *et al., Count me in*; Long and Sanderson, 'Community Benefits from Sport?'; SDP IWG, *Literature Reviews.*
9 E.g. Coalter, *Sport and Community Development*; Almond *et al., New Opportunities.*
10 Coalter, *Sport-in-Development*, 2.
11 Laws, Harper and Marcus, *Research for Development*, 273.
12 Brown and Strega, *Research as Resistance*; Denzin and Lincoln, *The Landscape of Qualitative Research*; Weiss, 'Where Politics and Evaluation Meet' and 'How Can Theory-based Evaluation'.
13 Coalter, *A Wider Social Role*, 41–5; following Weiss, 'Where Politics and Evaluation Meet' and 'How Can Theory-based Evaluation', and Pawson, *Evidence-Based Policy.*
14 Spencer *et al., Quality in Qualitative Evaluation.*
15 Laws, Harper and Marcus, *Research for Development*, 273.
16 Denzin and Lincoln, *The Landscape of Qualitative Research*, 16.
17 Ibid.; Laws, Harper and Marcus, *Research for Development.*
18 Tuhiwai Smith, *Decolonizing Methodologies.*
19 E.g. Martinez *et al.,* 'Culturally Appropriate Research'.
20 Tuhiwai Smith, *Decolonizing Methodologies*; Apffel-Marglin and Marglin, *Decolonizing Knowledge.*
21 Tuhiwai Smith, *Decolonizing Methodologies*; Apffel-Marglin and Marglin, *Decolonizing Knowledge.*
22 Tuhiwai Smith, *Decolonizing Methodologies*, 1.
23 Ibid., 42.
24 Apffel-Marglin and Marglin, *Decolonizing Knowledge*, 9.
25 Ibid., 7, 9.

References

Almond, L., C.L.J. Mason, S. Simkin, I. Lindsey, K. Armour, B.M.J. Houlihan, and M. Nevill. *New Opportunities for PE and Sport Self Evaluation Handbook.* Loughborough: Loughborough University, 2004.
Apffel-Marglin, F., and S. Marglin. *Decolonizing Knowledge: From Development to Dialogue.* Oxford: Clarendon Press, 1996.

Bailey, R. 'Physical Education and Sport in Schools: A Review of Benefits and Outcomes'. *Journal of School Health* 76 (2006): 397–401.

Blackshaw, T., and J. Long. 'What's the Big Idea? A Critical Exploration of the Concept of Social Capital and its Incorporation into Leisure Policy Discourse'. *Leisure Studies* 24 (2005): 239–58.

Brown, L., and S. Strega. *Research as Resistance*. Toronto: Canada Scholar's Press/Women's Press, 2005.

Coalter, F. *Sport and Community Development: A Manual*. Edinburgh: sportscotland, 2002.

Coalter, F. *Sport-in-Development: A Monitoring and Evaluation Manual*. London: UK Sport, 2006.

Coalter, F. *A Wider Social Role for Sport*. London: Routledge, 2007.

Coalter, F., M. Allison, and J. Taylor. *The Role of Sport in Regenerating Deprived Areas*. Edinburgh: SECRU, 2000.

Coalter, F., J. Long, and B. Duffield. *Recreational Welfare: The Rationale for Public Leisure Policy*. London: Routledge, 1988.

Collins, M., I. Henry, B. Houlihan, and J. Buller. *Sport and Social Exclusion*. Loughborough: Loughborough University, 1999.

Crabbe, T. 'Avoiding the Numbers Game: Social Theory Policy and Sport's Role in the Art of Relationship Building'. In *Sport and Social Capital*, edited by M. Nicholson and R. Hoye, 21–37. Oxford: Elsevier Butterworth-Heinemann, 2008.

Denzin, N., and Y. Lincoln. *The Landscape of Qualitative Research*. 3rd edn. Thousand Oaks, CA: Sage, 2008.

Department for Culture, Media and Sport (DCMS). *A Sporting Future for All*. London: DCMS, 2000.

Department for Culture, Media and Sport/Strategy Unit. *Game Plan: A Strategy for Delivering Government's Sport and Physical Activity Objectives*. London: DCMS/Strategy Unit, 2002.

Donnelly, P., with S. Darnell, S. Wells, and J. Coakley. 'The Use of Sport to Foster Child and Youth Development and Education'. In *Literature Reviews on Sport for Development and Peace*, edited by Sport for Development and Peace International Working Group, 7–47. Toronto: University of Toronto, 2007.

Holt, R. *Sport and the British*. Oxford: Oxford University Press, 1989.

Kay, T., and S. Bradbury. 'Youth Sport Volunteering: Developing Social Capital?' *Sport, Education and Society*, 14 (2009): 121–40.

Kay, T., with B. Houlihan, and J. Welford. *Guide to Education and Sport: Report to British Council*. Loughborough: Institute of Youth Sport, 2008.

Laws, S., with C. Harper, and R. Marcus. *Research for Development*. London: Sage, 2003.

Long, J., M. Welch, P. Bramham, K. Hylton, J. Butterfield, and E. Lloyd. *Count me in: The Dimensions of Social Inclusion through Culture and Sport*. Leeds: Leeds Metropolitan University, 2002.

Long, J., and I. Sanderson. 'Community Benefits from Sport?' *The Regional Review* (2002): 7–8.

Martinez, S., E. Arredondo, G. Ayala, and J. Elder. 'Culturally Appropriate Research and Interventions'. In *Youth Physical Activity and Sedentary Behavior: Challenges and solutions*, edited by A. Smith and S. Biddle, 453–77. Champaign, IL: Human Kinetics, 2008.

Pawson, R. *Evidence-based Policy, a Realist Perspective*. London: Sage, 2006.

Policy Action Team (PAT) 10. *National Strategy for Neighbourhood Renewal: Policy Action Team Audit: Report of the Policy Action Team 10: The Contribution of Sport and the Arts*. London: DCMS, 1999.

Spencer, L., J. Ritchie, J. Lewis, and L. Dillon. *Quality in Qualitative Evaluation: a Framework for Assessing Research Evidence*. London: Government Chief Social Researcher's Office, 2003.

Sport for Development and Peace International Working Group (SDP IWG). *Literature Reviews on Sport for Development and Peace*. Toronto: University of Toronto, 2007.

Tuhiwai Smith, L. *Decolonizing Methodologies: Research and Indigenous People*. Dunedin: University of Otago Press, 1999.

Weiss, C. 'Where Politics and Evaluation Meet'. *Evaluation Practice*, 14 (1993): 93–106.

Weiss, C. 'How Can Theory-based Evaluation Make Greater Headway?' *Evaluation Review* 21 (1997): 501–24.

Engaging sport-for-development for social impact in the South African context

Cora Burnett

Department of Sport and Movement Studies, University of Johannesburg, Johannesburg, South Africa

The politics of development ideology and global leadership set the scene for sport (for) development in South Africa. Academic inquiry followed in an ad hoc way, mostly in the wake of contracted and/or externally and diverse disciplinary infused research paradigms. Diverse research agenda and donor requirements set the scene for Participatory Action Research as an enabling tool for researchers, funders and research participants whereby indigenous knowledge systems can be accessed and enriched in a collaborative venture of knowledge production. Four case studies of sport-for-development projects in the South African context explain the evolving architecture in this field. A discussion of three distinct and interrelated models, based on the rationale of Mintzberg (2006), affords insights within a social capital framework of a top-down, bottom-up and outside-in approach in various integrated formats. It is apparent that social impact and networking evolved around strategic alliance formation and development agendas of major stakeholders.

Introduction

Sport-for-development has received overnight global status and international legitimacy through the adoption of resolution 58/5 by the General Assembly of the United Nations in November 2003, entitled 'Sport as a means to promote education, health, development and peace'.[1] This motion propelled sport into the realm of universal development strategies with assumed anecdotal powers to address the many ills of populations entrenched in conflict, chronic poverty and its multi-faceted manifestations.[2] By declaring 2005 the International Year of Sport and Physical Education and producing a report on 'Sport for Development and Peace: Towards Achieving the Millennium Development Goals', the United Nations[3] and UNICEF elicited widespread support from governments, NGOs and powerful transnational corporations that found a profitable partnership with key stakeholders through their Corporate Social Investment.

Kidd remarked on such major initiatives and the mass mobilization to 'Making Poverty History' by reflecting on the historical development of the Sport for Development and Peace (SDP) movement,[4] which has grown in leaps and bounds in a very uncoordinated and donor-infused way. Global networks are being established, such as in the case of the Swiss Academy for Development, where 166 organizations are listed on The International Platform on Sport for Development.

Substantial resourcing and innovative schemes and initiatives flooded the market. Not only did governments invest millions in sport-for-development programmes, but companies have made major investments, such as Nike, which has invested $100 million in the last two years, pledging another $315 million to community-based sport initiatives worldwide.[5] International stakeholder clusters such as the Commonwealth, International Olympic Committee (IOC), FIFA (Football for Hope), UNICEF in partnership with UK Sport and the British Council (International Inspirations) and a myriad of foundations capitalized on the 'sportification of social investment' sparking a post-modern figuration. This also set the scene for the formation of strategic partnerships, social engineering, entrepreneurship and alliance seeking to deliver on a sport-for-development agenda within an ever changing landscape.

It is inevitable that African countries where populations are subjected to severe poverty (living on less that $1 per day), gender inequality, a high prevalence of HIV/Aids, environmental erosion and neglect, conflict zones, high mortality rates and relatively low levels of literacy would be targeted for delivering on the Millennium Development Goals by 2015.[6] As South Africa will be the host nation for the FIFA World Cup in 2010, the first country in Africa to do so, it has been targeted as a gateway for international agencies to explore and export their sport development initiatives into the rest of the African continent.

These market-related forces and the need for academic inquiry through monitoring, evaluation and impact assessments underpin most scholarly contributions since early 2000.[7] As academics from diverse scientific fields are increasingly being drawn to this field of study, it is to be expected that the complexity of development dynamics, the absence of longitudinal research results, methodological limitations and contextual realities would translate into the lack of guiding theories. It is against this background that the essay will explore conceptual frameworks and reflect on four sport-for-development programmes in South Africa. Two of the programmes are funded by Sport and Recreation South Africa (SRSA) and refer to the national mass participation programmes implemented in the community (Siyadlala) and school (School Sport Mass Participation Programme). The third programme discussed as a case study refers to the Active Community Clubs' Programme implemented in the Eastern Cape Province under the auspices of the Australian Sports Commission. The fourth case study entails Youth Development through Football as a joint initiative of the German Development Corporation (Gesellschaft für Technische Zusammenarbeit, GTZ) and the European Union (EU).

Sport-for-development

Sport-for-development is a contested social construct which encapsulates a wide range of movement phenomena and activities that present various degrees of institutionalization, reflecting unique individualized and cultural meanings as it finds expression in diverse social contexts. Hylton *et al.* argue that social change is inherent in the in-field application of sports development,[8] where sport is instrumental to the change in whatever form of focus it might have. Change represents a process that could have positive or negative consequences. Development is reflected in the notion of progress for the recipients earmarked for development by a multiplicity of agencies seeking accountability for their 'development work' in the form of tangible evidence – a result-driven focus where the product, rather than the process, is the focus of development.[9] Monitoring and evaluation thus becomes part of a Participatory Action Research framework where the development focuses on people engaged in the co-shaping of their own destiny, being central to a scenario of interchange and co-existence.[10]

The multilevel manifestations of development dynamics and interrelatedness of different components of sport activities and/or programmes necessitate a multidisciplinary and/or integrated theoretical approach.[11] Academics further pose methodological challenges for quantitative and qualitative approaches that will provide the empirical validation and descriptive narrative of contextual explanation.[12]

Conceptual frameworks

The sport-for-development discourse is informed by multidisciplinary frameworks evidenced by diverse disciplinary and research foci within the field of social development. It is mostly directed towards disenfranchised collectives within the wider population. Girls and women (gender), people with disabilities (ability), ethnic minorities (race), senior citizens or children (age), people suffering from diseases of stigma (HIV/Aids) and/or class distinction (socio-economic vulnerability) fit this category of relative marginalization. Broad theories of change,[13] generic theories of attitudinal and behaviour change and social learning theories underpin a critical mass of development studies.[14] Academic inquiries followed, tapping into existing disciplinary frameworks with inductive approaches setting the scene for the generation of grounded theory.

Cultural dynamics, in-group values and sport subculture formation are informed by cultural resource theory[15] and social constructionist frameworks.[16] Intergroup conflicts are explained by the conflict model of social theory.[17] Deviant behaviour and the measuring of 'crime reduction interventions' through different sports programmes, pose multidimensional analytical features inclusive of resource-based pragmatism that would provide insights for programme design, management and delivery. Exploring the factors and conditions that shape pro- and anti-social behaviour, a multidimensional model is also utilized.[18]

In the field of social psychology, the research themes relate to interpersonal relationships, friendships and the development of the social self,[19] the socialization influences of significant others as social agents and role models,[20] whilst holistic approaches tap into the social cognitive theory, self-efficacy theory and social context frameworks.[21] These micro-level interventional effects have spin-offs at the institutional level (e.g. a school) as reported by Langbein and Bess[22] in terms of pro-social behaviour and the occurrence of related disturbances. Primary foci relate to meso-level analysis of social institutions and collectives (e.g. volunteers), and on the impact of programmes on community well-being.[23]

Development work and studies are mostly undertaken in smaller geographical areas where people are subjected to socio-economic marginalization. The concept of community is contested, as may be imagined, or realized in terms of locality. Hylton and Totten explain:

> Community implies some notion of collectivity, commonality, a sense of belonging or of something shared. A community can be self-determined by its members or it can be a label externally constructed and defined by some statutory agency. Either way, community can be imagined as much as it can be realised.[24]

Community development is closely associated with concepts of 'social transformation', 'community regeneration', the development of citizenship through sport-based volunteering,[25] multi-stakeholder involvement and networking.[26] Building bridges and forging relationships of care and 'peaceful coexistence' are particularly challenging in conflict areas where hatred is entrenched in national values such as in the case of the Football for Peace initiative in Israel and Palestine.[27]

A critical mass of academic work has recently been published utilizing the concept of 'social capital'. Coalter[28] and Burnett[29] have drawn on the conceptual frameworks of Bourdieu's neo-classical capital theory, Coleman's rational choice theory, network theory, Putnam's framework of civil engagement and Verweel's multilevel analysis in discussing the bonding, bridging and linking of social capital generated by the Active Community Clubs' Initiative in the Eastern Province of South Africa. The formation of strategic partnerships for the delivery of sport development (identifying and nurturing athletic talent) and promoting the development agenda in developing countries are particularly rife in the spheres of government and the NGO fraternity as entrepreneurial agents facilitating participation and ensuring a pathway for individual and collective development.[30]

Sport-for-development programmes

There seems to be an influx of donor funding channelled to sport-for-development projects as first world countries have set a target of spending 0.7% GDP for Overseas Development Assistance (ODA). Foreign powers seek justification for their investments and development agendas of their notion of humanitarian work which is often 'conducted and planned with missionary zeal'.[31] In the field of sport-for-development, many agencies, especially NGOs, are advocating an 'evangelist' approach offering 'sport' as an antidote to many illnesses of society. It is within this context of network formation that Mintzberg critically reflected on three distinct development approaches, namely i) the top-down government planning approach, ii) the inside-up indigenous development approach, and iii) the outside-in 'globalization' approach.[32]

The top-down development approach mainly refers to a pre-designed programme that is implemented in different contexts. Most often pilot work is carried out prior to the roll-out and implementation in a new context or community. Such an approach is based on the notion that the recipients will benefit in 'prescribed' ways as signalled by the outcomes or success indicators stipulated by the developers. It is assumed that co-ownership will develop over time and that the preconceived outcomes will be reached. Often government programmes are developed and implemented according to such an approach where it might be aimed at broadening the base of participation, talent development and/or addressing inequalities within the sport and recreation participation sector.

The 'inside-out' development refers to widespread community consultation in the structuring and implementation of a programme. The focus is to address local needs in a bottom-up approach of a programme that is community-driven as opposed to being merely community-based. The 'outside-in' approach in sport-for-development encapsulates networking and the formation of strategic partnerships for delivering on a pre-conceived (often global) agenda such as youth and/or gender empowerment, as well as on 'combating HIV Aids' and disease profiles as stipulated by international agencies such as UNICEF and the United Nations (see the Millennium Development Goals).

The four case studies have been chosen to illustrate the development dynamics of such models in the South African context of poverty where individuals (developing athletes), collectives (schools, clusters and organizations) and communities have been targeted for sports-related development. A critical standpoint will be explored, as posed by Mintzberg, to reflect on the nature of intervention and its ideological underpinnings. Social impact will inevitably relate to the approach, foci of investigations and developing agendas. Given the context of chronic poverty and unequal socio-economic conditions, the research was participatory and an 'empowering' experience focussed towards the building of capacity (human capital) as an asset to 'leave behind' once a programme has matured beyond the 'delivery phase'.[33]

The South African context

Poverty is multidimensional and has unique manifestations at all levels of human existence. It represents a dynamic and complex process whereby vulnerable populations such as women and children are exposed through interlocking factors that deny them relative access to available resources.[34] Poverty thus manifests itself in a recognizable lack of income and assets at the individual and community level,[35] displays specific disease profiles such as malnutrition, HIV/Aids and tuberculoses and is synonymous with fragmented family lives.[36] Low literacy levels, high incidences of violence, high school drop-out rates, teenage pregnancies, gang formation, physical neglect, psychological scars and a 'live-for-the-moment' mentality exemplify a life of chronic poverty. The poor mostly have low skill and literacy levels, and are often denied access to stable employment and turn to low-paid self-employment.[37]

Government-sponsored feeding schemes only provide the bare minimum of subsistence needs, and parents or guardians are unable to carry any additional cost of sport participation, despite the fact that 'free education' (introduced by the Education Laws Amendment Act of 2005) has been delivered to about five million learners in 13,856 schools across South Africa.[38] The lack of school and community sport facilities restricts sport participation and soccer is often the only sport offered at community level.[39] Limited access to resources fostered a culture of interdependency; however, extreme poverty eroded networks of cooperation, undermining the social fabric and, in 2008, flared up as xenophobic-inspired violence targeting immigrant minorities from other African countries (e.g. Zimbabwe), which swept through major townships.[40]

It is against this background of poverty that Sport and Recreation South Africa (SRSA) funded and implemented mass participation programmes and external developing agencies became involved, each with its own approach and product.

Sport-for-development: case studies

The Participatory Action Research approach was followed for all four programmes, focusing on building various degrees of empowerment in monitoring and evaluation. All agencies were interested in the deliverables, but equally committed to have process information revealing intended and unintended consequences by tracking change according to a pre-post comparative design. For the Youth Development through Football Programme and the School Sport Mass Participation Programme only baseline data currently exists, reflecting mostly on perceptions, expectations and experiences reported as quantitative (structured questionnaires) and qualitative methods (focus groups and interviews with stakeholders), implanted for triangulation purposes and to provide empirical data integrated with a cultural narrative of contextual lived realities.[41]

Methodology

A pre-post designed impact study was followed to trace change regarding delivery and 'uptake' at all levels of programme delivery and engagement. The S·DIAT (Sport-in-development Impact Assessment Tool) was utilized, ensuring a synthesis and the triangulation of quantitative and qualitative data according to, and directed by, two main indicator bands (Programme Management and Delivery, as well as Human and Social Development) and the related indicator fields.[42]

Siyadlala

Siyadlala, the national community-based Mass Participation Programme, was introduced nationwide with the aim of promoting mass participation in selected sport and structured physical activities in the most disadvantaged communities in South Africa. In 2004, seven sporting codes were introduced for optimal participation across gender and age categories. The codes were indigenous games, general gymnastics (including gymnastrada events), aerobics, street ball games (soccer, basketball and handball), and 'fun run and big walk' (athletics). In 2005, nine additional sporting codes were introduced from which provinces and local Hub Coordinators could make a selection according to the interest in their particular communities. Most popular channels of delivery included schools or community clubs which were structured, or with which Activity Coordinators cooperated to offer regular sports participation to 'out-of-school youth', and absorbed learners for participation beyond the school sports programme. In addition to the broadened base for sport participation and feeding 'talent' through to competitive sporting structures (at the school, community and those linked to National Sports Federations), Siyadlala also aimed at delivering on national development priorities, especially those aligned with the Millennium Development Goals.[43]

Results indicated that two models emerged in the different contexts, with especially urban hubs developing according to a competitive framework, particularly in the North West Province and Free State where political powers influenced an 'event-driven' programme to such an extent that the regular programme delivery and community-based 'development' were compromised. In hubs where local municipalities and local stakeholders bought into the Programme, networks developed and regular activities and local events addressed multi-stakeholder needs at different levels of implementation and participation.

The drastic increase in participation (406.1% growth of participants who regularly attend practices) meant that the gaining of access to facilities became a challenge, especially for young boys and girls, as community and school facilities were mostly dominated by older boys. Indigenous games as newly introduced sports code was the most popular among all the participants, inclusive of adult participants. The fact that players received regional, provincial and national colours for the first time was highly acclaimed. Despite the focus on including 'out-of-school youth', 80.9% of all participants were school children making the school the most ideal channel for delivery. All categories of participants showed a marked increase in numbers, post recruitment, whilst local volunteers increasingly attached themselves to the programme (showing an increase of 3,740%, from 5 to 192 in the selected hubs or communities over the two-year period) in search of a possible career pathway in and/or through the programme.[44]

As a gender equitable representation was established among the coordinators, more girls (59.4%) participated, whereas more men (65.6%) than women became volunteers on the Programme. This could be explained in terms of recruitment targets, type of activity favouring girls' participation (e.g. aerobics, general gymnastics and indigenous games), and men volunteering due to a background in sport, low skill levels that limited their entry into formal employment, and having an interest in sports coaching.[45]

The lack of resources and unsatisfactory delivery impacted negatively on the social indicators. Only five hubs established partnerships with health organizations, providing access to programmes and services. The over-utilization of physical resources, poor quality of school-based facilities and material deprivation limited access to the poorest of the poor. The stipend of R1,200 (€97) for Activity Coordinators contributed to the survival of 54 households (42.7%), whilst the majority valued the education and training component. Trusting relations developed between Activity Coordinators and participants resulting in a heightened sense of self-worth, sense of belonging and empowerment for being valued as a coach in the community.[46]

School Sport Mass Participation

The School Sport Mass Participation Programme was introduced in all nine provinces of South Africa in 2006, following the community-based Siyadlala Programme. SRSA signed a Memorandum of Understanding with the Minister of Education for the delivery of the Programme at schools within a cluster context in impoverished areas of the country. Prior to the baseline study that was conducted in 2008, 76 fieldworkers were trained in the collection of data according to pre-designed methods of the S·DIAT. Data from 161 schools in 18 clusters selected for the baseline study provided in-context pre-impact data on different indicator fields for post-impact comparisons.

Local stakeholders and recipients participated in identifying contextual priorities to be addressed by the Programme against such social realities as a high teenage pregnancy rate of an average of 9.4 per annum for secondary school girls, and 1.2 for primary school girls. The manifestations of poverty are recognizable in poor health, criminality, deviant behaviour, low literacy levels and economic dependency of school sport assistants on the stipend of R1,200 per month, of whom 48.4% are breadwinners and 30.3% are essential contributors towards the survival of households.[47]

The baseline study identified increased opportunities in 'new' sporting codes such as rugby, cricket and volleyball, in addition to more traditional codes such as athletics, netball and soccer. Other benefits included participation in festivals, inter-school and inter-class competitions that stimulated sustained participation and the development of a 'sporting culture' among the majority of participants and in their schools.

Despite 'start up' equipment and contracted school sport assistants, main challenges remain the lack of physical resources, replacement of damaged equipment, non-credit bearing and skill-appropriate training. The decline of participation over time (from 63% to 10% in the secondary school, and from 71% to 31% in the primary school, with an average of 3.5% of girls' participation at grade 12) can partially be accounted for by the delivery of traditionally male sports, the lack of ID documents, budget constraints and lack of monitoring, evaluation and feedback.[48]

Active Community Clubs

The Active Community Clubs' Initiative is funded by the Australian Agency for International Development (AusAID) and delivered by the Australian Sports Commission. An impact assessment was conducted in 2003 on two clubs in the Eastern Cape Province and another one in 2006 in Keiskammahoek (also in the Eastern Cape Province). This was followed by baseline studies in 2008 in KwaZulu-Natal (a province in South Africa), Swaziland and Botswana under an outreach programme (ASOP) where partnerships were established between researchers from South Africa, Swaziland and Botswana. This programme is based on recruitment, training and building partnerships with local stakeholders through inclusive community consultation and the needs-based, community-driven structuring of a club.

The impact study of 2003 illustrated this outside-in and bottom-up approach where a central component of the Active Community Club (ACC) was the delivery of a sport programme (rugby, netball and cricket) to local schools. Other activities that were developed under club leadership included a gardening project (in Tshabo) and a health programme (HIV/Aids education and training).[49] Some of these programmes experienced a decline in participation as community leadership changed and new priorities emerged. The gardening project of 2003, in which about 12 individuals participated, is now operated by a teacher and her husband who just produce enough vegetables for the pre-school where she is the teacher, and for their own use. On the other hand, the more institutionalized sport programme is still being delivered to the local schools, and some volunteers have been with the programme for more than eight years. There is an overwhelming belief that volunteering will enhance unemployed youths' opportunities to obtain employment by gaining relevant experience, and learning job-related skills and values. The following continuum illustrates a belief system of relative helplessness in avoiding the poverty trap and as such offering a way 'out of the streets' (Figure 1).

The initial social value of the increase in social trust between coaches and participants, reduction of social distance between children and parents, increased self-esteem and a sense of self-worth for the unemployed volunteers are highly valued consequences within the context of extreme poverty and psycho-social destitution and neglect.[50] The dependency on the 'external' provision of resources for programme implementation and events, timely education and training, dependency on leadership for strengthening institutional capacity and a competitive environment to forge meaningful relationships beyond the social realm of the community, are indicative of the relative delicateness of sustaining bridging and linking ties. However, widely acclaimed exposure and the flagship status of this programme opened up opportunities for a possible partnership with Siyadlala, as the top-down model has been met with mixed success after the initial few years of implementation due to the fact that it lacks community uptake and shared ownership.

Youth Development through Football (YDF)

Youth Development through Football (YDF) is an initiative established in July 2007 by the GTZ that envisaged involvement in development work in Africa until March 2011. The European Union became a main partner in March 2009 with an extended mandate to also support initiatives and/or programmes for mass participation and youth development through different sporting codes and youth development initiatives. The main focus would however remain on the YDF programme, tapping into the hype of the FIFA World Cup of 2010 as 'belonging to Africa'. By utilizing the popularity of football, youth and community development will be promoted in economically disadvantaged communities to afford boys and girls the opportunity to education and capacity building. Through the Youth Development through Football programme GTZ and the European Union have become major partners with Sport and Recreation South Africa with a representative to drive a 'Legacy Programme' in commemoration of the FIFA World Cup that will be presented in South Africa in 2010.[51] The YDF programme follows an outside-in approach as they forge partnerships with different NGOs and the government sector, with which it will collaborate to ensure sustainable social development through sport, and particularly football-for-development initiatives. The focus of the programme is on building a

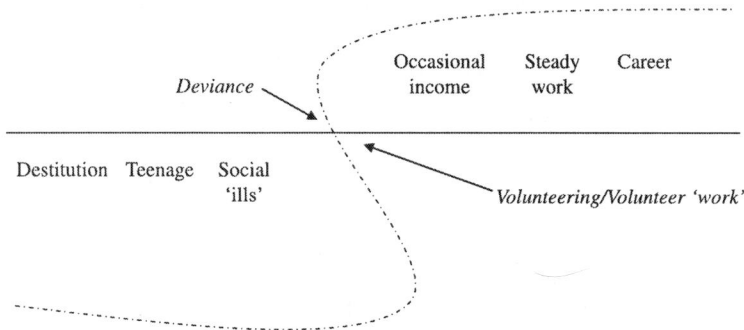

Figure 1.   The perceived role of volunteering towards responsible citizenship and employment.

conceptual framework on football-for-development work. There is also a drive to provide leadership, develop material and build capacity through education, training and consultancy within their network of partners. The Nike Network, different NGOs, the sports fraternity and government departments are major partners for supporting programmes and delivering services whereby a 'development philosophy' will be spread, and their partnerships strengthened and showcased.

The following diagram (Figure 2) is reflective of their framework of operation and directive in forming a network and collaborative service delivery that will ensure a lasting footprint for football for development work.

In the first instance, the Youth Development through Football initiative is focused on identifying major country-based stakeholders and partners within the youth and sport development domains, taking cognizance of existing programmes, government and existing GTZ operatives, operations and priorities. Often, country operations are structured according to local and multi-stakeholder needs, and aligned with strategic objectives without necessarily focusing on establishing a network and creating a synthesis between a myriad of service providers. This represents an outside-in approach with a top-down dynamics when a partnership with government programmes such as Siyadlala is forged, yet a bottom-up approach prevailing when a partnership with the Active Community Clubs' Initiative is formed. Both partners have been recruited for collaborative ventures with the most recent including the placement of German volunteers in the Eastern Cape where the collaboration between Siyadlala and the Active Community Clubs' Initiative is in the early stages. In Figure 3, the South African-based parent organization for driving a compatible development agenda has been identified.

In such multilevel and diverse stakeholder collaboration, the ties will be relatively weak and in need of seeking to deliver on mutual outcomes. The delivery and success of the corporation will largely be met by the partnerships, and within the diversity of partnerships, YDF brand and donor-inspired expectations will transpire. The success of collaborative work will inevitably lie in the collective association and goal achievement within a particular network of partners.

Conclusion

The top-down approach of Siyadlala and the School Sport Mass Participation Programme allowed for the introduction and resourcing of sport activities and structured programmes that are to provide a broad base of participation to deliver on national

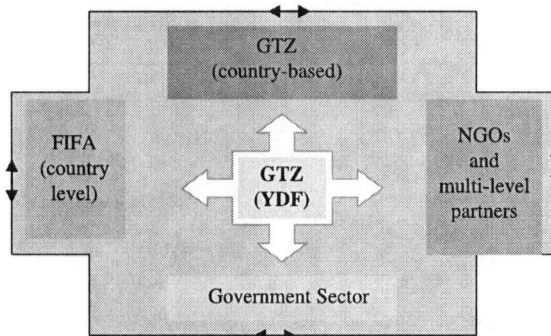

Figure 2.   Youth-development-through-football framework.[52]

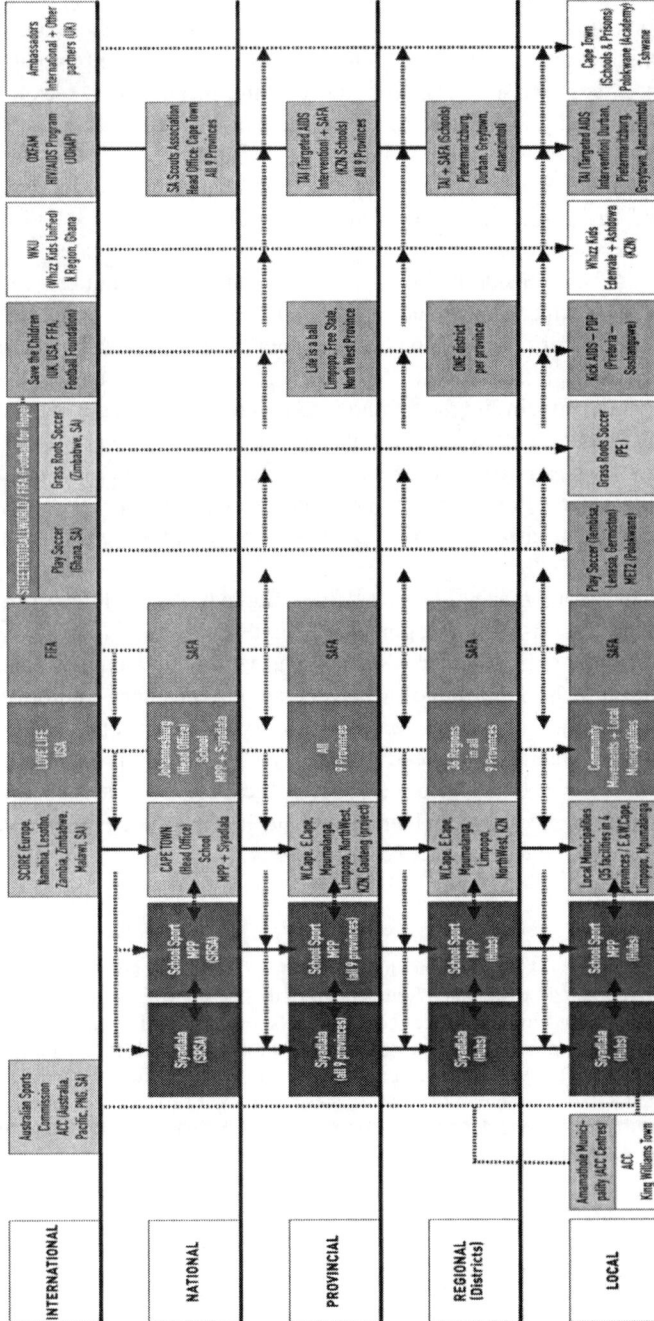

Figure 3. Multilevel sport-for-development programmes in South Africa.[53]

priorities of sporting excellence and a framework of development aligned with the Millennium Development Goals.[54] Inter-departmental collaboration is challenging, especially at the level of implementation where the relatively undereducated school sport assistants and teachers have a strained relationship. This top-down approach and unequal power relations at all levels of implementation have direct implications for gender and class divisions, demonstrating the significance of local leadership, contextual priorities and appropriate needs-based education and training to address the expectations of the (current and potentially future) unemployed by creating career pathways or enhancing the employability status of vulnerable populations.

Initiated by outside agencies such as the Australian Sports Commission, the Active Community Clubs' Initiative was implemented in the Eastern Cape and KwaZulu-Natal provinces to address issues of community development and regeneration in selected rural and urban areas. The 'outside-in factor' is minimized as communities structure their own clubs – first by introduction and later by request – around community needs where sport participation at primary school level is a 'given'. Strategies and structures follow an 'Australian model' interwoven with local dynamics for uptake and ownership. Linking and bridging ties remain fragile,[55] and needs-based sustainable development seems feasible through collaboration, mutual reflection and reflective learning.[56] The mobilizing of local networks and strategic partners may counter the external influence to be absorbed and given 'life' in the local vernacular. Volunteering provides the context for social learning[57] and active citizenship in the need to seek mutual ground for delivery and collective impact.

The 'outside-in' approach of GTZ is demonstrated by the building of partnerships and co-delivering on a sport-for-development agenda through existing delivery channels, yet focusing on alignment and inclusion of partners that would support the Youth Development through Sport philosophy and targets. In such multilevel and diverse stakeholder collaboration, the delivery and success of the cooperation will largely be determined by the quality and effectiveness of partnerships, and within the diversity of partnerships will run a donor-inspired process and product – a post-2010 legacy. The success of collaborative work will inevitably lie in the collective association and goal achievement within a particular network of partners.

Acknowledgements

The two national Mass Participation studies (Siyadlala and School Sport Mass Participation Programme) were funded by Sport and Recreation South Africa. Seventy-six School Sport Assistants were trained and assisted in data collection. Principals, teachers and learners in different 'hubs' or 'clusters', as well as community members, leaders and local stakeholders meaningfully contributed towards the research. The Active Community Clubs' Initiative was funded by the Australian Sports Commission and AusAID, and elicited the services of national coordinators, employees, volunteers and community-based stakeholders for the research. The GTZ baseline study was funded by GTZ's YDF programme through its head office in Pretoria.

Notes

[1] United Nations, *Sport as a Means to Promote Education.*
[2] Levine, *Girls Count*, 2.
[3] United Nations, *Sport for Development and Peace*, 4.
[4] Kidd, 'A New Social Movement', 370.
[5] Nike, 'Let Me Play'. http://www.nikeresponsibility.com.
[6] United Nations, *Sport for Development and Peace*, 5.
[7] Girginov, *Management of Sports Development*, xi.

8 Hylton *et al.*, *Sports Development*, cited in Griginov, *Management of Sports Development*, 17.
9 Powell, 'Culture: Intervention or Solidarity', 196.
10 Cunningham and Beneforti, 'Investigating Indicators', 96.
11 Hartmann and Massoglia, 'Reassessing the Relationship', 485.
12 Burnett, 'Building Social Capital', 286.
13 Scott Porter Research and Marketing Ltd., 'Sport and Ethnic Minority Communities', 15.
14 Blinde and Taub, 'Personal Empowerment through Sport', 181.
15 Miller et al., 'Sports, Sexual Behaviour', 366.
16 Glover, 'The "Community" Center', 65.
17 Shuttleworth and Wan-Ka, 'Youth Sport Education', 37.
18 Hartmann and Massoglia, 'Reassessing the Relationship.'
19 Hills, 'Friendship, Physicality and Physical Education', 335.
20 Green, 'Sport as an Agent', 131.
21 Fraser-Thomas, Côté and Deakin, 'Youth Sport Programs', 22.
22 Langbein and Bess, 'Sports in School', 436.
23 Arai and Pedlar, 'Moving Beyond Individualism', 185.
24 Hylton and Totten, 'Community Sports Development', 81.
25 Eley and Kirk, 'Developing Citizenship through Sport', 151.
26 Misener and Mason, Creating Community Networks', 39.
27 Sugden, 'Teaching and Playing Sport', 221.
28 Coalter, 'Sport Clubs', 537.
29 Burnett, 'Building Social Capital', 283.
30 Green, 'Sport as an Agent', 131.
31 Kidd, 'A New Social Movement', 370.
32 Mintzberg, 'Developing Leaders?', 7.
33 Burnett, 'Siyadlala's Contribution', 3.
34 Narayan *et al.*, *Voices from the Poor*, 4–5.
35 Kane-Berman, ed., *South Africa Survey*, 317.
36 May, *Experience and Perceptions of Poverty*, 61, 118.
37 Dimant, Lebone and MacFarlane, 'Business and Employment', 141.
38 Botsis, Cronje and MacFarlane, 'Education', 259.
39 Burnett and Hollander, 'Post-impact Report', 134.
40 Burnett and Hollander, 'Baseline Study', 43.
41 Burnett and Hollander, 'An Impact Study', 3.
42 Burnett and Hollander, 'Post-impact Report', 9.
43 Burnett, 'Siyadlala's Contribution', 131.
44 Burnett and Hollander, 'Post-impact Report', vi.
45 Ibid.
46 Ibid., 57.
47 Ibid., ix.
48 Burnett and Hollander, 'Baseline Study', 85–6.
49 Burnett, 'Building Social Capital', 283.
50 Ibid., 283.
51 Burnett, 'Baseline Study of YDF', 1.
52 Burnett, 'Siyadlala's Contribution', 131.
53 Ibid., 131.
54 Burnett, 'Baseline Study of YDF', 26.
55 Coalter, 'Sports Clubs', 537.
56 Cunningham and Beneforti, 'Investigating Indicators', 89.
57 Green, 'Sport as an Agent', 131.

References

Arai, S., and A. Pedlar. 'Moving Beyond Individualism in Leisure Theory: A Critical Analysis of Concepts of Community and Social Engagement'. *Leisure Studies* 22, no. 3 (2003): 185–202.
Blinde, E.M., and D.E. Taub. 'Personal Empowerment through Sport and Physical Fitness Activity: Perspectives from Male College Students with Physical and Sensory Disabilities'. *Journal of Sport Behavior* 22, no. 1 (1999): 181–202.

Botsis, H., F. Cronje, and M. MacFarlane. 'Education'. In *South Africa Survey 2006/2007*, edited by J. Kane-Berman, 141–258. Johannesburg: South African Institute of Race Relations, 2007.

Burnett, C. 'Building Social Capital through an Active Community Club'. *International Review for the Sociology of Sport* 41, no. 3 (2006): 283–94.

Burnett, C. 'Siyadlala's Contribution Towards Reaching the Millennium Development Goals'. *African Journal for Physical, Health Education, Recreation and Dance* (June 2007): 136–48.

Burnett, C. 'Baseline Study of YDF (Youth Development through Football) Networks in South Africa.' Report prepared for the Gesellschaft für Technische Zusammenarbeit. Department of Sport and Movement Studies, University of Johannesburg, 2008.

Burnett, C., and W.J. Hollander. 'An Impact Study on Australia Africa AA 2006. Sport Development Programme's Active Community Clubs' Initiative.' Report prepared for the Australian Sports Commission. Department of Sport and Movement Studies, Rand Afrikaans University, Johannesburg, 2003.

Burnett, C., and W.J. Hollander. 'Post-Impact Report of the Mass Participation Projects of Sport and Recreation South Africa'. Report prepared for SRSA. Department of Sport and Movement Studies, University of Johannesburg, 2006.

Burnett, C., and W.J. Hollander. 'Baseline Study of the School Sport Mass Participation Programme'. Report prepared for SRSA. Department of Sport and Movement Studies, University of Johannesburg, 2008.

Coalter, F. 'Sports Clubs, Social Capital and Social Regeneration: "Ill-Defined Interventions with Hard to Follow Outcomes"?'. *Sport in Society* 10, no. 4 (2007): 537–59.

Cunningham, J., and M. Beneforti. 'Investigating Indicators for Measuring the Health and Social Impact of Sport and Recreation Programs in Australian Indigenous Communities'. *International Review for the Sociology of Sport* 40, no. 1 (2005): 89–98.

Dimant, T., K. Lebone, and M. MacFarlane. 'Business and Employment'. In *South African Survey 2006/2007*, edited by J. Kane-Berman, 141–258. Johannesburg: South African Institute of Race Relations, 2007.

Eley, D., and D. Kirk. 'Developing Citizenship through Sport: The Impact of a Sport-Based Volunteer Programme on Young Leaders'. *Sport, Education and Society* 7, no. 2 (2002): 151–66.

Fraser-Thomas, J., J. Côté, and J. Deakin. 'Youth Sport Programs: An Avenue to Foster Positive Youth Development'. *Physical Education and Sport Pedagogy* 10, no. 1 (2005): 19–40.

Girginov, V., ed. *Management of Sports Development*. Oxford: Elsevier, 2008.

Glover, T.D. 'The "Community" Center and the Social Construction of Citizenship'. *Leisure Sciences* 26 (2004): 63–83.

Green, C. 'Sport as an Agent for Social and Personal Change'. In *Management of Sports Development*, edited by V. Girginov, 129–45. Oxford: Elsevier, 2008.

Hartmann, D., and M. Massoglia. 'Reassessing the Relationship between High School Sports Participation and Deviance: Evidence of Enduring, Bifurcated Effects'. *The Sociological Quarterly* 48 (2007): 485–505.

Hills, L. 'Friendship, Physicality and Physical Education: An Exploration of the Social and Embodied Dynamics of Girls' Physical Education Experiences'. *Sport, Education and Society* 12, no. 3 (2007): 335.

Hylton, K., P. Bramham, D. Jackson, and M. Nesti. *Sports Development: Policy, Process and Practice*. London: Routledge, 2007.

Hylton, K., and M. Totten. 'Community Sports Development'. In *Sports Development*, edited by K. Hylton and P. Bramham, 77–117. London: Routledge, 2007.

Kane-Berman, J., ed. *South Africa Survey 2006/2007*. Johannesburg: South African Institute of Race Relations, 2007.

Kidd, B. 'A New Social Movement: Sport for Development and Peace'. *Sport in Society* 11, no. 4 (2008): 370–80.

Langbein, L., and R. Bess. 'Sports in School: Source of Amity or Antipathy?'. *Social Science Quarterly* 83, no. 2 (2002): 436–54.

Levine, R., C. Lloyd, M. Greene, and C. Grown. *Girls Count. A Global Investment and Action Agenda*. Washington, DC: Center for Global Development, 2008.

May, J. *Experience and Perceptions of Poverty in South Africa*. Durban: Proxis Publishing, 1998.

Miller, K.E., D.F. Sabo, M.P. Farrell, G.M. Barnes, and M.J. Melnick. 'Sports, Sexual Behavior, Contraceptive Use, and Pregnancy among Female and Male High School Students: Testing Cultural Resource Theory'. *Sociology of Sport Journal* 16 (1999): 366–87.

Mintzberg, H. 'Developing Leaders? Developing Countries?'. *Development in Practice* 16, no. 1 (2006): 4–14.

Misener, L., and D.S. Mason. 'Creating Community Networks: Can Sporting Events Offer Meaningful Sources of Social Capital?'. *Managing Leisure* 11, no. 1 (2006): 39–56.

Narayan, D., R. Patel, K. Schafft, A. Rademacher, and S. Koch-Schulle. *Voices from the Poor: Can Anyone Hear Us?* New York: Oxford University Press, 2000.

Powell, M. 'Culture: Intervention or Solidarity'. *Development in Practice* 5, no. 3 (1995): 196–206.

Scott Porter Research and Marketing Ltd. 'Sport and Minority Ethnic Communities: Aiming at Social Inclusion. Summary'. *Research Digest* 58 (2000): 1–15.

Shuttleworth, J., and Wan-Ka, C. 'Youth Sport Education and Development in Hong Kong: A Conflict Model Social Impact Assessment'. *Sport, Education and Society* 3, no. 1 (1998): 37–58.

Sugden, J. 'Teaching and Playing Sport for Conflict Resolution and Co-existence in Israel'. *International Review for the Sociology of Sport* 41, no. 2 (2006): 221–40.

United Nations. *Sport as a Means to Promote Education, Health, Development and Peace. General Assembly Resolution 58/5.* New York: United Nations, 2003.

Participation in sport: bonding and bridging as identity work

Jeroen Vermeulen and Paul Verweel

Utrecht School of Governance, Utrecht University, the Netherlands

Nowadays sport is assigned a crucial role in solving social problems, especially those relating to social cohesion. Participation in sport is assumed to build relevant bonding and bridging social capital that generates reciprocal contacts and trust in others. In this essay we will present findings of two, mainly qualitative studies on participation in sport in the Netherlands. We argue that while sport indeed makes contributions to the development of social capital, bonding and bridging are much more complex and differentiated processes than is usually assumed in both social policies and social capital theory. An argument is made to view bonding and bridging as identity work.

Introduction

Sport as social policy tool is high on the agenda, in the Netherlands as elsewhere. Although research on the subject shows that positive social effects of sport are difficult to prove, the social value of sport in itself is being affirmed.[1] One of the reasons that the social effects of sport are hard to establish lies in the vagueness and elusiveness of the concepts that are being used in social policies. This goes especially for the concept of social capital that is central in circles of government and theorists of sport alike. Moreover, as Blackshaw and Long[2] argue, the concept of social capital in the popular sense of Putnam[3] is based on communitarian assumptions of equality, engaged citizenship and inclusion that underscore the positive connotations surrounding sport. As an illustration, read Etzioni who noted that society can be made more 'community friendly by the provision of sport and leisure facilities to satisfy the need for social connectedness'.[4] This leads to unwarranted high expectations of the social impact of sport. While we subscribe to the importance of sport in society, we will argue here that sport is as much a divider as an integrator. Moreover, we agree with Coakley[5] and others that sport is embedded in a social world where inequality is a structural phenomenon. The challenge we face is to consider the social impact of sport from the perspective of cultural and social diversity and from the perspective of local processes of inclusion and exclusion.

In this essay we will present findings from two studies on sport and social participation in the context of ethnic diversity in the Netherlands: one on sport clubs in the Netherlands, and another study on community sport in playgrounds in Dutch multicultural urban neighbourhoods. We will discuss our findings in the light of the concepts of 'bonding' and 'bridging' that are central in the theory of social capital. We will argue that while sport indeed may make important contributions to the development of social capital in terms of useful and reciprocal relations and trust in others, bonding and bridging are much more complex and differentiated processes than usually assumed. From this we will propose to understand bonding and bridging processes in terms of identity: participation in sport is to be regarded as identity work.

In the next section we will contextualize both studies from the perspective of the relation between social policies and sport, emphasizing the concept of social capital. The section that follows will be devoted to the presentation of the findings of our studies on participation and sport. In the final section we will make some concluding remarks on bonding and bridging in sport from the perspective of identity work.

Social policy and sport

Over the past ten or so years there has been an increasing interest from Dutch policy-makers in sport.[6] The social value of sport has been widely recognized, up to the point that sport is now considered as a major instrument in social policies. Sport is seen as potentially contributing to a wide array of social issues, including to social integration and participation, to reducing antisocial behaviour of youths, to restraining violence and enhancing security (community safety) in urban areas and to reducing gender inequality. Following its policy statement, 'Time for Sport: Moving, Participating and Achieving' from 2005,[7] in the last few years the Dutch Ministry of Health, Welfare and Sport (VWS) has initiated various measures that aim to provide a stimulating role for sport, such as in the projects called 'Neighbourhood, Education and Sport' (*Buurt onderwijs sport*), 'Participation Non-autochthonous Youth' (*Meedoen allochtone jeugd*), 'Stimulating Community Schools' (*Impuls brede scholen*) and 'Sport and Culture' (*Sport en cultuur*).[8] Consider, as an illustration of the rhetoric accompanying the interest in sport for social issues, the following excerpt from a recent policy document on sport from the Dutch Ministry of Health, Welfare and Sport, entitled 'The Power of Sport':

> The Cabinet supports sport primarily because it promotes social values. Because of its social function, sport is a highly desirable and effective way of achieving key government objectives, in the fields of prevention and health, youth policy, education, values and standards, integration, communities, safety and international policy.[9]

Sport seems to have been embraced by Dutch government and policy-makers as a panacea for all social issues. On the one hand, the increased interest can surely be seen as a positive development for practitioners as well as scholars in the field of sport, as recognition of their work. As a result, governmental, public as well as private organizations made more financial means available. The increased funding has over the past few years generated a proliferation of (new) sport organizations and projects as well as organized sport activities in the Netherlands. On the level of local communities, a growing number of people are being stimulated to participate in informal and formal sport activities. On the other hand, though, increasing demands are being made of providers and professionals of sport activities to live up to the expectations of local and central policy-makers.[10] Results of sport projects have to be accounted for, need to be monitored, evaluated and benchmarked. This translates, for instance, into an increasing pressure toward professionalization of voluntary sport organizations.[11] But the same goes for informal volunteer-run organizations as well, as Sharpe describes in his study on 'grassroots recreation organisations'.[12] He points to 'increasingly complex administrative demands' that need 'professional competencies'. Skinner, Zakus and Cowell report on the issue of development through sport for disadvantaged communities.[13] They uncover the political agenda behind these policy initiatives and agree with Craig[14] about the dangers in cases where these initiatives are being made top-down without assessment of local needs.

Social capital

There is undoubtedly an overly optimistic tone to be heard from policy-makers when estimating the effects of sport for social issues. Much of the conceptual thinking moves around the concept of social capital, mainly in the sense of Putnam's work.[15] Although the concept remains largely elusive,[16] contested and ideology-driven,[17] social capital became the cornerstone of policies on sport and social issues. As theorists of policy implementation[18] as well as discourse analysts[19] have argued, the elusiveness and vagueness hardly counts as a disqualification, and can be said to be characteristic for most policy language and concepts.[20] At the same time, this also means that the relation between policy aims, implementation and effects will always be ambiguous and contested.

Let us briefly discuss the concept.[21] Social capital exists in social networks and refers to the gains that derive from social networks such as useful mutual contacts, development of civic norms of reciprocity and generation of mutual trust.[22] Social capital for Putnam is a measure of social cohesion: communities or societies that produce more or less social capital show, as a consequence, more or less social cohesion. Putnam argues that social capital is developed best through participation in shared activities; these can be performed in formal (civic organizations, sport clubs), as well as informal (neighbours, personal relations), networks. In general, Putnam distinguishes between two types of social capital: bonding capital, the ties and relations between people that share similar socio-economic and ethnic backgrounds; and bridging capital, the ties and relations between people from different groups.

From the perspective of strengthening social cohesion, Putnam's line of thought is that for individuals and society at large bridging capital is more profitable than bonding capital as the former type is indicative for cohesive ties between individuals and groups. Blackshaw and Long argue that 'the appeal of social capital' for policy makers lies in the (Putnamian) insight that, 'Leisure, whether sport, arts or socialising, does not have to be valued only because it can create employment, generate income or improve health, but because it brings different people together'.[23] Bourdieu, however, in his own work on social capital, argued that the positive assets that come with membership of civic associations and social networks are not available to everybody, due to existing political-economic constraints.[24] Moreover, those who do profit from social networks and indeed build social capital 'do so precisely because others are excluded'.[25] In short, while both Putnam and Bourdieu would agree on the value of social capital for enhancing social cohesion and while both emphasize the importance of participation in formal and informal community activities, they disagree on the point of achieving equal possibilities of access to profitable social capital.

Sport, participation and identity

The centrality of the concept of social capital in social policies concerning sport leads to a focus on issues of in- and exclusion, social integration and social cohesion.[26] As Bailey puts it: 'A uniting theme for ... social capital theorists is that of "social cohesion", which is addressed through creating or strengthening the physical, social and cultural infrastructures of communities'.[27] A relevant and central question is therefore: does sport contribute to participation and social inclusion? But further questions are: in what way does sport contribute to social inclusion and with what consequences in terms of the exclusion of others?

In this section we will discuss two of our studies that addressed these questions. First we will present the results of a study on participation and the development of social capital by non-autochthonous Dutch sportsmen and sportswomen in mixed and separate sport clubs in the Netherlands. Next, we will discuss some findings from a study on participation in sport at public playgrounds in multi-ethnic neighbourhoods in Dutch cities. Based on the results we will make three points regarding the role of sport in processes of participation and social inclusion, in terms of bonding and bridging. First, in both mixed and separate sport clubs bonding as well as bridging capital is developed, and instances of both bonding and bridging are found in practices of sport on public playgrounds. We conclude that sport indeed makes contributions to the development of social capital. Having said this, we found, secondly, that bonding and bridging are much more complex and differentiated processes than is assumed usually in both social policies and social capital theory (i.e. Putnam's approach). Following from this second point, our third point is to propose to analyse bonding and bridging processes in terms of identity: participation in sport is to be regarded as identity work,[28] as dynamic social (inter)actions of both inclusion and exclusion.

The contribution of sport clubs to social capital

Verweel and Janssens' study on social capital in sport focused on possible differences in the development of social capital between non-autochthonous people participating in 'mixed' (*gemengd*) sport clubs versus those participating in 'separate' (*eigen*) clubs.[29] The 'ethnic' or separate sport clubs have come under heavy fire in the current Dutch debate on multiculturalism that is dominated by the discourse of assimilation. So one of the underlying questions that guided the research was whether separate sport clubs form indeed barriers for non-autochthonous members to social integration and to the development of social capital. The study was based on a mixed qualitative/quantitative research design. The qualitative part consisted of 10 male researchers participating in sport clubs that had many or almost exclusively non-autochthonous members, during one sport season. The quantitative part of the research consisted of a survey among 900 respondents. The respondents were active sportsmen at their sport clubs.

We found that one third of the respondents said that they generated their social networks, their self-esteem and trust in others primarily through sport.[30] One third confirmed that sport contributed to these three profits of social capital mentioned above next to other spheres of life. And only one third responded that sport did not have any influence on their development of social capital. These figures were almost similar for both autochthonous and non-autochthonous sportsmen (mainly of Turkish, Moroccan, Antillean or Surinamese origin).

Another interesting finding was that 30% of the respondents changed their images and opinions of other ethnic groups through their participation in sport: for 26% the change was positive; only 4% changed their opinions in a negative way. The following quote came from a Moroccan player in a mixed football club:

> At first I didn't feel the need to start playing football at a club. But on a certain moment my father asked the father of a boy next door, who was member of the board of a football club, if I could be a member too... There I saw that parents put much of their time and effort in making their children happy on a voluntary basis. Sometimes they do so even if their own children are not present. I like that very much, that you do things not only for getting something back, but just to make other people happy. That's why I became sports leader at the club too. Even in the past I felt like training and coaching a few of these kids.

Ramsahai, in a study on the development of social capital in separate football clubs, or 'immigrant football clubs' as he calls them, confirms our results on this point: 'In the process of winning and losing, teasing and pleasing they [i.e. members of immigrant clubs] have increased their attitude to accept each other in a more positive manner.'[31]

The commonly held assumption that non-autochthonous members of separate clubs mainly build 'bonding' social capital and that non-autochthonous members of mixed clubs build 'bridging' capital needs to be nuanced at least, according to our study. Both qualitative and quantitative data suggested that sporting in mixed clubs does not result exclusively in bridging, but, on the contrary, in many cases, to more bonding. On the other hand, participation in separate clubs leads to bonding as well as bridging.

Bonding, though, is important for members of separate clubs. Non-autochthonous members of separate sport clubs indicated that they spent a relatively large amount of time at their clubs (more than autochthonous members of mixed clubs). The sport clubs for them seems to fulfil a broader function than is the case for regular (mixed) sport clubs. The club is an important place to meet and to interact; for some, meeting others may even be more important than the sport itself, as demonstrated in the following remark made by the president of a Surinamese football club when asked about the necessary traits that a new president of the club needs to have: 'Most importantly, he needs to be a good cook'. While said laughingly, his remark is indicative for the importance that non-autochthonous members attach to sociability.

In general, we were able to conclude that both separate and mixed sport clubs created contexts for the formation of social networks, for the development of norms of reciprocity and the generation of social trust. In that sense, sport clubs are fertile grounds for developing social capital, for autochthonous as well as non-autochthonous sportsmen.[32] These findings were affirmed in a recent study on social capital in separate football clubs in the Netherlands.[33]

Differentiation within bonding ties

We found that separate sport clubs usually are quite mixed in terms of their members. Moroccan, Turkish, Surinamese and Antillean clubs are rarely homogeneous. The separate clubs that were part of our research were characterized by diversity, in contrast to the 'mixed' clubs. However, autochthonous Dutch people mostly were absent in ethnic minority sport clubs. On the other hand, in regular (mixed) sport clubs we noticed that separation along the line of autochthonous–non-autochthonous is common. At regular places and moments where decisions had to be made of dividing groups, such as when using separate dressing rooms, or making teams, or assigning places in cars that drive to away games, often the division was made visible. The following observation may serve as an example:

> Remarkable is the clear ethnic divide between dressing room 1 and 2. In dressing room 1 the Dutch boys are sitting, aged between 20 to 30 years. In dressing room 2 are mostly boys of Moroccan origin: seven to be precise, in the age between 20 to 25 years old. Here also W. is sitting, half Dutch and half Indo, and C. who is from Surinam.

We may suppose that interethnic experiences and contact outside sport will have a great impact on the building of trust between groups, as our results mentioned earlier indeed indicated. Results of the survey showed that ethnic minority members of separate sport clubs on average share the same educational level and salaries with autochthonous members of the mixed clubs. Moreover, they do not live in deprived areas more often and do not have less frequent contacts with autochthonous people than do autochthonous members of mixed clubs. These findings are supported by a recent Dutch study on the social networks of non-autochhonous sportsmen outside the domain of sport.[34]

So, we may conclude that what is commonly labelled as 'bonding' ties, especially when talking about ethnic minorities, are in fact characterized by differentiation when examined more closely. So called 'separate' clubs are much more 'mixed' internally in terms of their members as well as in terms of the social ties that their individual members maintain outside the domain of sport. We thus do agree with Blackshaw and Long who claim:

> The 'like us/unlike us' presumption that lies at the heart of the distinction between bonding and bridging is hard to appreciate given the multi-dimensionality of any individual (sex, age, class, occupation, ethnicity, sexual orientation, political belief, abilities, interests).[35]

Blackshaw and Long point to the relevance of taking into account that individuals have multiple identities. More precisely: there are multiple dimensions along which relevant distinctions between individuals and groups can be made. In actual interactions, these distinctions may be used dynamically by individuals as markers of their identity and as markers of the identity of others. In the context of skateboarding, Anthonissen and Sterkenburg show how skaters creatively identify themselves and others along lines of ethnicity, gender and class.[36] We need to recognize the differentiation within bonding networks by zooming in on processes of (self-) identification and identity work in the context of sport and sport clubs in order to gain better insight in the social effects of participation.

Participation through sport as identity work

Membership of a sport club as well as participation in sport activities are related to matters of identity, in separate and mixed sport clubs alike. Membership of a sport club, in general, is also a demonstration of an identity, of belonging to a group. De Ruijter[37] compares sport clubs to arenas, where two types of fights are happening simultaneously: one is to win the match and the other is to demonstrate one's identity. Concrete processes of participation in activities of sport, and related ones connected to sport clubs (like drinking a beer together after the match), always deal with dividing between those who are 'in' and those who are 'out', in other words, drawing boundaries that define identities. Sport and sport clubs provide symbolic resources that are used to mark and display different identities: evidently, the sport matches themselves with two teams competing against each other defines identities; skills in playing are part of identity work, but also age and gender and even artefacts such as outfit, food and – as mentioned earlier – the separation of dressing rooms. All kinds of identities may be constructed, in principle, in very context-dependent ways. Relational identities meaningful for direct participation in on-going events are being expressed by means of symbolic resources. At the same relational identities may refer to (sub) groups within and across sport clubs and to identities on a larger scale, like ethnicity or class.[38]

Sport and identity in public playgrounds

Some issues of identity work concerning ethnicity come to the fore in our research on participation of youths in sport activities at public playgrounds in multi-ethnic urban neighbourhoods in the Netherlands. Six playgrounds in various Dutch cities were being studied ethnographically over a period of two years.[39] Playgrounds are public places where many activities occur simultaneously: the playgrounds that we studied are places specifically designed and equipped for doing sport (mainly for football, basketball and tennis[40]) but the places are also used for hanging around, for talking, for eating, for fighting. All these activities, not only sport, could be seen as 'acts of identity', as ways for youths to express, emphasize and work out their self and their belongingness to a group. The public nature of the playground adds to the multi-functionality of the playgrounds, for these playgrounds in principle belong to 'everybody' and to 'nobody'. Their location and free accessibility define them as part of the neighbourhood and the street. The users of the playgrounds, together with their way of using the playgrounds, define the place.[41] Ownership is a matter of relevance here. Those who 'own' the place will have the power to determine what happens, how and with whom. Playgrounds thus become territories: not only functional places for doing sport but also symbolic places for identity constructions. We did not observe any physical territorial fighting between users or visitors of the playgrounds. But we frequently experienced 'symbolic' fights, like in the following observation:

> Three boys are walking across the field holding their bikes, without saying or looking. There is no contact between those on the field and these three boys, while one of them is passing a boy on the field very closely. They don't look at each other.

Participation in sport (which remains its 'core business') at playgrounds always is explicitly and visibly concerned with making distinctions between those who belong and those who do not – albeit often only temporarily during the sporting activity. In that sense the interactions on the playgrounds are identity works.

Dominance of bonding ties

The majority of the youngsters that make use of the sporting facilities at the playgrounds have ethnic backgrounds other than Dutch. The ethnic origins of the youths, however, are rather diversified: Turkish, Moroccan, Somali, Angolan, Antillean and Surinamese. There are differences per playground. In general, greater numbers of non-autochthonous youths seem to play in public places than autochthonous youth.[42] Friendship is omnipresent at playgrounds.[43] However, the playgrounds are not so much places where new friendships are made as meeting points for existing friendships.[44]

Next to friends, playgrounds attract many youngsters that maintain family ties: sisters and brothers, nephews and nieces. And lastly, most users live in the areas directly surrounding the playgrounds. Many told us that they know each other from their neighbourhood or from school. All in all, the kinds of relationships that are prevalent between youngsters using the playgrounds indicate that bonding seems to be dominant. By this, we mean that in free play (i.e. not organized by third parties) boys and girls that already know each other usually participate in sport together.

However, the youngsters in the playgrounds do not form closed and homogeneous networks. Ties between youths do overlap sometimes, as for instance small groups of boys and girls are sometimes connected through family ties. We found that participation in sport activities in public playgrounds is the result of situational processes of in- and exclusion along lines of age, gender, family or friendship relations, ethnicity and skill in sport. These are resources of identity constructions that interact in complex and often situational ways. We discerned patterns in these interactions that may point to more general processes: gender overrules ethnicity, mostly when ethnicity is combined with age; only younger boys and girls (of different ages) do play together. Another pattern we found is that ethnicity may be overruled by skill in playing.

We found that ethnicity as a marker of (group) identity was never without meaning, to put it negatively. However, we encountered instances where ethnic differences were overcome in the process of participation, i.e. for playing together, for example:

A group of Angolan boys comes to the playgrounds to play basketball. They tell us that they come there regularly, about three times a week. When we ask if they sometimes play with other boys not from their group, one of them said: 'Yeah, sure, if some Dutch boys come here and they know how to play a bit of ball, they just join us, yes.'

Although ethnicity as an explicit marker of social identity is mentioned even here, in the practice of doing sport, ethnicity may be bracketed or postponed as a dividing line. What counts more in such situations is the technical skill to play well. In that sense, sport provides a way to neutralize ethnicity.[45]

On the other hand, we found interesting instances of the use of sport as a regulating 'tool' of ethnic divides where ethnicity is not so much neutralized but rather emphasized. Van der Meij, in one of the case studies of the research project, describes a situation on the playground where tension is building up between two small groups of youngsters, Dutch and Moroccan.[46] At one moment one of the Moroccan boys invites the Dutch to play a match. One of the Moroccan boys screams 'we are enemies on the pitch', emphasizing the 'us versus them'. The Dutch appear the far better side and they beat the Moroccan team, on their home ground. After 45 minutes the Dutch end the game and go away without saying anything. Other Moroccans appear on the field and a new game starts.

Here we see a complex situation of bridging and bonding at the same time. The two groups are playing together but at the same time they remain separate. Nevertheless, they were able to bridge their differences through (the rules of) sport.

Inclusion and exclusion

In order for youths to be included and/or to participate in sport activities in playgrounds they must be recognized and respected, identified as someone who belongs. To belong to a group in terms of ethnicity is not enough to obtain access to participation in sports activities: gender, age and measure of skill in playing are at least some dimensions that potentially preclude participation. On the other hand, having the same ethnicity is not an absolute condition for participation in sport activities. Skill in playing may rank higher situationally, next to the necessity to play against others.

Although 'bonding' relations are dominant in public playgrounds, the interplay of various potential dividing lines again show that the concept of 'bonding' is too rough for describing and understanding the complexity of identity work that takes place in concrete occasions of participation in sport at playgrounds. Youths have multiple identities that all can be relevant in different ways and in different situations for getting access to sport activities in playgrounds. Yet, the identity work on playgrounds to be performed in order to participate in sport is hardly a volatile process. Rather, the process is structured in the sense that participation in spontaneous sport activities is related to, amongst others, the dominance of adolescent boys, past experiences with 'outsiders' ('did he or she join us before?'), skill and kind of sport (football being dominant). As we found, a regular programme of organized activities under supervision of local sport leaders, in general, can function as an important tool to reach those groups that would be excluded easily under the 'laws of the street': youngsters and girls, but also the less talented. In those cases, access to the playground and to sport activities is being regulated.

Discussion and conclusion

Active sportsmen participating in activities of sport and sport clubs seem to prefer bonding relations. At least, our studies into sport clubs and community sport at public playgrounds seem to indicate that this is the case. It is more fun and it feels safer and more familiar to spend one's leisure time with people that one knows and feels comfortable with. The aims of both social policies on contributions of sport to social integration and research projects that look for empirical evidence for relations between those 'entities' are at odds with people's motives to join sport clubs or to participate in sport activities on the playground around the corner. Ties with similar people add to the sociability and pleasure of doing sport. In that sense, participation in sport is an act of identity, in both the senses of expressing a self and of displaying membership of a group.

With respect to the latter, doing sport is a means of building relational identities that are direct, flexible but also ephemeral. At the same time these relational identities do refer to identities on the macro-level, that are more enduring, such as ethnicity or class.[47] These identities, and the resources – also in sport – out of which these are being constructed, give meaning and sense to individuals. Sport provides possibilities and resources for identity work in bonding as well as in bridging interactions. From the perspective of local processes and accounts of participation in sport activities, bonding and bridging appear to be differentiated and complex even up to the point where the difference between bonding and bridging may not be clear at all. Bonding ties in sport do not, as is assumed in policy and theory, form closed and homogeneous networks. Members of sport clubs have multiple identities and flexible identifications. In that sense, bonding ties are as much pre-existing resources for identities as emergent products of interactions and sport practices.

Our findings would subscribe to the positive role that participation in sport potentially has for meeting others, i.e. 'other' than members of the well-known social circles. Note that we take some pains in choosing words for describing 'other': in order to analyse identity work at the level of concrete interactions in sport activities it is important not to use ethnicity or culture as existing and relevant a priori. The differentiation within bonding and bridging relations indicates that individuals participating in sport activities have 'multiple belongings'.[48] In our perspective, any approach to studying bonding and bridging processes in sport that reduces individuals to one dimension will not be able to fully understand what it means that sport has *potential* in meeting others and crossing structural boundaries of groups. There is hardly any room for naive optimism when it comes to sport participation being able to fix structural social problems of stigmatization, discrimination and inequality. The social potential of sport lies rather in the opportunities that sport activities (both organized and spontaneous, although both in different ways) provide to individuals to construct their identities and find out their positions towards others in the processes of both in- and exclusion.

In a sense we agree with Krouwel *et al.* who, in an article on interethnic contact through sport participation in the context of the Netherlands, 'warn against the rosy picture that is sometimes sketched about sport activities, and their ability to integrate new groups and overcome inter-ethnic tensions in other spheres'.[49] But we do not subscribe to their strongly stated conclusion that, 'the potential bridging capacity of sport is... almost nullified by the influence of tensions brought from outside sport'[50]. We will raise three points of criticism on their study, which simultaneously allow us to explain in more detail our own position on the issue of the social impact of sport. Firstly, we would like to reiterate that our findings show that bonding ties are multi-dimensional and constructive in nature. Krouwel *et al.*, on the contrary, argue:

> Sport activities seem to perform a strong function in the reinforcement of existing (ethnic) identities, rather than in new identity formation. However, this longing to be among one's fellows in leisure time activities should be understood in a broader, structural perspective. For ethnic minority groups, sport activities are particularly useful to temporarily get away from

social spheres with tense relations (the neighbourhood, the school, the workplace) and to seek 'shelter' among members with similar ethnic and cultural backgrounds.[51]

Indeed, sport participation tends to favour interaction among identical people – as we stated above – but we would disagree that this is characteristic for ethnic minorities only. Autochthonous sportsmen also would rather play sport with and among 'identicals', and it would seem quite odd to call their sport clubs 'shelters', as though they were hiding from tensions in other social spheres. It is quite debatable whether the distinction between autochtonous and non-autochthonous sportsmen – and, hence, the category of ethnicity – is at stake here. Krouwel *et al.* take ethnicity as a pre-existing category only and, moreover, as a dominant feature of bonding ties in sport. Their point of departure leads them to explain their findings in exactly the same terms that actually require explanation.

Our second point is related to the first and has to do with their normative stance toward interethnic contact and the role of sport. Their 'structural' argument seems to be a disguise for normativeness. Several phrases in their article seem to imply that inter-ethnic contact in sport – in the default case – is imbued with positive associations. In case these positive associations cannot be confirmed by research findings, the explanation is sought in structural 'tensions brought from outside sport'. We read: 'In soccer the result of inter-ethnic encounters is *not always a peaceful and meaningful* exchange';[52] 'when [inter-ethnic] sporting encounters occur, they are *not always friendly and positive*';[53] 'we found that if ethnic groups meet each other within the context of a mixed competition, these *shelters easily transform into an arena*'[54] (italics added). We consider sport participation always to be about both inclusion and exclusion, about both cooperation and competition. That means that the domain of sport is best viewed in terms of an arena, where meanings of sport, identity and culture are contested and are put to the test. Our focus then would be on the specific contexts in which the encounters take place and on understanding the situational processes that lead to the outcomes.

Our third point of criticism, then, concerns the methodology of the studies by Krouwel *et al.* into ethnic identity and sport participation. As we saw above, the authors write about the relation between sport and identity in rather deterministic, structural terms: 'Sport activities seem to perform a strong function in the reinforcement of existing (ethnic) identities, rather than in new identity formation'. And they conclude that 'tensions and discrimination in other societal spheres appear to cause the most marginalized ethnic minorities … to prefer to be part of ethnically homogeneous teams'.[55] Their conclusions may well be derived from the methodological perspective used. The focus was on questionnaires and other quantifiable data that intrinsically orient toward consistency and generalizability. Evidently, the choice for quantitative measures is legitimate (we did use them in our own studies). But at the same time we would strongly recommend using qualitative methods, at least as complementary to quantitative methods, when processes of identity formation are concerned. Studying identity processes demands research methods that allow for fine-grained analyses of daily interactions and accounts from an inside perspective of the people studied. This goes especially for complex multi-ethnic societies like the Netherlands, where personal identity and group membership are hardly ever one-dimensional, but rather multiple as well as ambiguous and layered.

Overseeing the discussion we would make the claim to approach bonding processes in terms of identity. Put differently and more concisely, bonding is identity work. Following Bucholtz and Hall,[56] we would like to point to three relevant characteristics of identity work here. First, identities are brought about by social action and are not simply reflections of (self) categorizations. The property of *doing* identity work does not rule out that resources for identity constructions are structural. Second, different dimensions of identity usually occur simultaneously during concrete interactions. Third, for individuals or groups to be judged or seen as alike 'they need not be identical, but must merely be understood as sufficiently similar for current interactional purposes'.[57] These three properties of identity work suggest that participation in sport is a much more subtle and complex process than the dichotomous terms of bonding and bridging would indicate. The terms themselves may still be useful, but only when taken as processes. From the perspective of real-life, day-to-day identity work then, sport may indeed be seen as providing specific and important resources for constructing bonding and bridging ties.

Participation in and through sport can help individuals to develop competence in the sometimes subtle and situational processes of inclusion and exclusion; and to learn that where someone is included, others are excluded. As Bourdieu pointed out, developing social capital is also a matter of distinction, being seen and recognized by others. Sport does provide ways to be included, and to attain (self) recognition and self-esteem (in short, an identity) by being recognized as skilful in sport for instance.

Another matter is whether or how this kind of social capital in sport can be transformed into other forms of capital. The proposition that sport is embedded in societal structures[58] suggests that transformation, at least potentially, can be successful. But an identity that is constructed through sport is not simply a kind of commodity that can be 'handed over' to other domains of life. As Blommaert argues with regard to identity in different domains: 'Society is full of niches in which highly particular identities can and need to be performed, using resources that have no such positive identity-performing values elsewhere.'[59] So, work has to be done and conditions are to be created in order to be included in other domains than sport. The contribution of sport to social capital and social integration is not to be assessed (nor to be achieved) by putting these concepts in causal chains, but by gaining insight in the intricacies and complexities of bonding and bridging through sport as identity work.

Notes

1. Breedveld, Kamphuis and Tiessen-Raaphorst, *Rapportage sport*; Verweel, Janssens and Roques, 'Kleurrijke zuilen'; Bailey, 'Evaluating the Relationship'.
2. Blackshaw and Long, 'What's the Big Idea?'
3. Putnam, *Bowling Alone*.
4. Etzioni, *The Spirit of Community*, 128.
5. Coakley, *Sports in Society*, 21ff.
6. Cf. Elling, De Knop and Knoppers, 'The Social Integrative Meaning of Sport'.
7. Dutch Ministry of Health, Welfare and Sport, *Time for Sport*.
8. Breedveld, Kamphuis and Tiessen-Raaphorst, *Rapportage sport*.
9. Dutch Ministry of Health, Welfare and Sport, *Time for Sport*.
10. Cf. Coalter, 'Sport Clubs'; Crabbe, 'Reaching the "Hard to Reach"'.
11. See for instance, Boessenkool, Van Eekeren and Lucassen, 'Moderniseringsambities'. The authors describe their study of sport clubs in transition in the Netherlands.
12. Sharpe, 'Resources at the Grassroots of Recreation'.
13. Skinner, Zakus and Cowell, 'Development through Sport'.
14. Craig, 'Community Capacity-Building', 340.
15. E.g. Putnam, *Bowling Alone*.
16. See Morrow, 'Conceptualising Social Capital'.
17. See Blackshaw and Long, 'What's the Big Idea?'
18. E.g. Yanow, *How does a Policy Mean?*; Stone, *Policy Paradox*.
19. E.g. Blommaert and Verschueren, *Debating Diversity*; Blommaert, *Discourse*.
20. Blommaert, *Discourse*, 185–201. Read the author's analysis of the concept of 'integration' in policy texts.

[21] For extensive and critical reviews of the concept of social capital see, for instance, Portes, 'Social Capital'; Morrow, 'Conceptualising Social Capital'; and in the context of sport and leisure studies, Blackshaw and Long, 'What's the Big Idea?'
[22] Cf. Putnam, *Bowling Alone*; Bailey, 'Evaluating the Relationship'.
[23] Blackshaw and Long, 'What's the Big Idea?', 244.
[24] For instance, Bourdieu, 'The Forms of Capital'.
[25] DeFilippis, 'The Myth of Social Capital', 790.
[26] Cf. Skinner, Zakus and Cowell, 'Development through Sport'; Elling and Claringbould, 'Mechanisms of Inclusion'.
[27] Bailey, 'Evaluating the Relationship', 76.
[28] Cf. Blommaert, *Discourse*; Bucholtz and Hall, 'Identity and Interaction'.
[29] Cf. Verweel, Janssens and Roques, 'Kleurrijke zuilen'.
[30] Cf. Breedveld and van der Meulen, 'Vertrouwen in de sport'.
[31] Ramsahai, *Thuiswedstrijd in een vreemd land*, 201.
[32] Verweel, Janssens and Roques, 'Kleurrijke zuilen'.
[33] Ramsahai, *Thuiswedstrijd in een vreemd land*.
[34] Ibid.
[35] Blackshaw and Long, 'What's the Big Idea?', 245.
[36] Anthonissen and Sterkenburg, *Battles om aanzien en respect*.
[37] De Ruijter, *De multiculturele arena*.
[38] Walseth, 'Young Muslim Women and Sport'. The author analysed the identity work of young immigrant Muslims in Norwegian sport clubs.
[39] Vermeulen, *Het kapitaal van de playground*; Verweel, *Respect in en door sport*.
[40] The playgrounds in our research are established, designed and maintained in cooperation with the Richard Krajicek Foundation, see www.krajicek.nl.
[41] Blommaert, Collins and Slembrouck, 'Polycentricity and Interactional Regimes'.
[42] For similar findings, see Cevaal *et al.*, *Mijn favoriete plek in de wijk*; Bakker *et al.*, *Playground van de toekomst*.
[43] Verweel, *Respect in en door sport*.
[44] See Cevaal *et al.*, *Mijn favoriete plek in de wijk*.
[45] Cf. Verweel, *Respect in en door sport*, 36ff.
[46] Van der Meij, *Buitenspel*.
[47] See also Blommaert, *Discourse*, 209.
[48] Ibid., 75.
[49] Krouwel *et al.*, 'A Good Sport?', 177.
[50] Ibid., 176.
[51] Ibid.
[52] Ibid., 173.
[53] Ibid.
[54] Ibid., 176.
[55] Ibid.
[56] Bucholtz and Hall, 'Identity and Interaction'.
[57] Ibid., 15. The authors use the term 'adequation' here.
[58] Cf. Coakley, *Sports in Society*.
[59] Blommaert, *Discourse*, 209.

References

Anthonissen, A., and J. van Sterkenburg. *Battles om aanzien en respect. Een studie naar identificaties van skaters met hun hobby.* [Battles for recognition and respect. A study into identifications of skaters with their sport.] Amsterdam: SWP, 2006.

Bailey, R. 'Evaluating the Relationship between Physical Education Sport and Social Inclusion'. *Educational Review* 57, no. 1 (2005): 71–90.

Bakker, I., S.I. Vries, C.M.H. van den Boogaard, W.J.E.M. van Hirten, J.P. Joore, and M.W.A. Jongert. *Playground van de toekomst. Succesvolle speelplekken voor basisscholieren.* [Playground of the future. Successful playgrounds for school children.] Leiden: TNO, 2008.

Blackshaw, T., and J. Long. 'What's the Big Idea? A Critical Exploration of the Concept of Social Capital and its Incorporation into Leisure Policy Discourse'. *Leisure Studies* 24, no. 3 (2005): 239–58.

Blommaert, J. *Discourse: A Critical Introduction*. Cambridge: Cambridge University Press, 2005.
Blommaert, J., and J. Verschueren. *Debating Diversity: Analysing the Rhetoric of Tolerance*. London: Routledge, 1998.
Blommaert, J., J. Collins, and S. Slembrouck. 'Polycentricity and Interactional Regimes in "Global Neighborhoods"'. *Ethnography* 6, no. 2 (2005): 205–35.
Boessenkool, J., F. Van Eekeren, and J. Lucassen. 'Moderniseringsambities voor sportverenigingen gaan aan behoeften van driekwart van clubs voorbij.' [Ambitions for modernising sportclubs go beyond the needs of most of the clubs.] http://www.sportknowhowxl.nl/index.php?pageid=inleiding&catid=alleen-op-de-wereld&cntid=1722.
Bourdieu, P. 'The Forms of Capital'. In *Handbook of Theory and Research for the Sociology of Education*, edited by J. Richardson, 241–58. New York: Greenwood Press, 1986.
Breedveld, K., C. Kamphuis, and A. Tiessen-Raaphorst. *Rapportage sport*. Den Haag: SCP & Mulier Institute, 2008.
Breedveld, K., and R. van der Meulen. 'Vertrouwen in de sport. Een empirische analyse van de relatie tussen sportdeelname en sociaal kapitaal'. [Trust in sport. An empirical analysis of the relation between participation in sport and social capital.] *Vrijetijdstudies* 20, no. 2 (2003): 37–49.
Bucholtz, M., and K. Hall. 'Identity and Interaction: A Sociocultural Linguistic Approach'. *Discourse Studies* 7, nos. 4–5 (2005): 585–614.
Cevaal, A., R. van der Meulen, D. Romijn, and K. Breedveld. *Mijn favoriete plek in de wijk. twee jaar ervaringen met het Cruyff Court NEC veld*. [My favourite spot in the area. Two years of experiences with the Cruyff Court NEC sport field.] Den Bosch: W.J.H. Mulier Institute, 2009.
Coakley, J. *Sports in Society. Issues and Controversies*. 10th ed. Boston, MA: McGraw Hill, 2009.
Coalter, F. 'Sports Clubs, Social Capital and Social Regeneration: "Ill-Defined Interventions with Hard to Follow Outcomes"?' *Sport in Society* 10, no. 4 (2007): 537–59.
Crabbe, T. 'Reaching the "Hard to Reach": Engagement, Relationship Building and Social Control in Sport Based Social Inclusion Work'. *International Journal of Sport Management and Marketing* 2, nos. 1–2 (2007): 27–40.
Craig, G. 'Community Capacity-Building: Something Old Something New...?'. *Critical Social Policy* 27, no. 3 (2007): 335–59.
DeFilippis, J. 'The Myth of Social Capital in Community Development'. *Housing Policy Debate* 12, no. 4 (2001): 781–806.
Dutch Ministry of Health, Welfare and Sport. *Time for Sport*. The Hague, Netherlands: Ministry of Health, Welfare and Sport, 2005.
Elling, A., and I. Claringbould. 'Mechanisms of Inclusion and Exclusion in the Dutch Sports Landscape: Who Can and Wants to Belong?'. *Sociology of Sport Journal* 22, no. 4 (2005): 498–515.
Elling, A., P. De Knop, and A. Knoppers. 'The Social Integrative Meaning of Sport: A Critical and Comparative Analysis of Policy and Practice in the Netherlands'. *Sociology of Sport Journal* 18, no. 4 (2001): 414–34.
Etzioni, A. *The Spirit of Community*. London: Fontana, 1993.
Krouwel, A., N. Boonstra, J.W. Duyvendak, and L. Veldboer. 'A Good Sport? Research into the Capacity of Recreational Sport to Integrate Dutch Minorities'. *International Review for the Sociology of Sport* 41, no. 2 (2006): 165–80.
Morrow, V. 'Conceptualising Social Capital in Relation to the Well-Being of Children and Young People: A Critical Review'. *Sociological Review* 47, no. 4 (1999): 744–66.
Portes, A. 'Social Capital: Its Origins and Applications in Modern Sociology'. *Annual Review of Sociology* 24 (1998): 1–24.
Putnam, R.D. *Bowling Alone: The Collapse and Revival of American Community*. New York: Simon & Schuster, 2000.
Ramsahai, S. *Thuiswedstrijd in een vreemd land*. [Home match in a foreign country.] PhD diss., Utrecht University 2008.
Ruijter, A. de. *De multiculturele arena*. [The multicultural arena.] Tilburg: Tilburg University Press, 2000.
Sharpe, E.K. 'Resources at the Grassroots of Recreation: Organizational Capacity and Quality of Experience in a Community Sport Organization'. *Leisure Sciences* 28 (2006): 385–401.
Skinner, J., D.H. Zakus, and J. Cowell. 'Development through Sport: Building Social Capital in Disadvantaged Communities'. *Sport Management Review* 11, no. 3 (2008): 253–75.

Stone, D. *Policy Paradox: the Art of Political Decision Making*. 3rd ed. New York: W.W.Norton & Co, 2001.

Van der Meij, N. *Buitenspel. Over jeugdparticipatie op de playground*. [Off side. About youth participation on the playground.] MA diss., Utrecht University 2008.

Vermeulen, J. *Het kapitaal van de playground*. [Social capital on playgrounds.] Utrecht: Utrecht University, 2008.

Verweel, P. *Respect in en door sport*. [Respect in and through sport.] Amsterdam: SWP, 2007.

Verweel, P., J. Janssens, and C. Roques. 'Kleurrijke zuilen. Over de ontwikkeling van sociaal kapitaal door allochtonen in eigen en gemengde sportverenigingen'. [Colourful pillars. On the development of social capital by non-autochthonous people in separate and mixed sport clubs]. *Vrijetijdstudies* 23, no. 4 (2005): 7–21.

Walseth, K. 'Young Muslim Women and Sport: The Impact of Identity Work'. *Leisure Studies* 25, no. 1 (2006): 75–94.

Yanow, D. *How Does a Policy Mean? Interpreting Policy and Organizational Actions*. Washington, DC: Georgetown University Press, 1996.

Race relations, Indigenous Australia and the social impact of professional Australian football

Chris Hallinan and Barry Judd

Centre for Australian Indigenous Studies, Monash University, Australia

We consider how Indigenous athletes have become symbols of what is perceived by white Australia to be progressive race relations. In particular, the men's professional sports of Australian football and Rugby League draw the most heavily mediated attention as well as significant numbers of Indigenous players. We draw upon the narratives of key advocates of Indigenous participation and performance in professional Australian football: journalists and recruiting managers. The emergent theme of white privilege is used to examine how their advocacy of Indigenous performance masks shortcomings in access and opportunity beyond playing roles. We conclude with the idea that race relations progress fulfils the needs of white Australia but fails to sufficiently deliver genuine opportunity for Indigenous Australian participants.

Introduction

> Tomorrow night's game is a celebration of Indigenous footballers, so we can expect some magic from the talented Aborigines in both line-ups. This so-called blockbuster is in need of some magic from (Essendon) Bomber Dean Rioli and Sydney's Michael O'Loughlin. (Sydney) Swan Goodes summed up his frustrating talent by kicking four goals from full back last week against the Bulldogs, but while all three provide flashes of brilliance, consistency is lacking.[1]

Our introductory quote is indicative of the type of media reporting associated with the participation of Indigenous footballers. Such reporting is characterized by an implied performance uniqueness which draws upon racialized thinking. However, it is far removed from conventional understandings of racism which involve exclusion, derogation and unambiguous prejudice. By contrast, the commentaries are clearly supportive of inclusion and regularly concur with the confident self-positioning on race relations proclaimed by the Australian Football League (AFL). Drawing upon the newly elected President of the USA's 'new foundation', the CEO of the Australian Football League addressed the commencement of the 2009 season by intoning a mission statement that placed the League in a position rivalling the Australian government. In a speech entitled 'Above and Beyond: League's Duty in Hard Times', the CEO extolled the virtues of the AFL as an agency of considerable progress. He averred:

> Australian Football is in a fortunate position to be part of our community's revival. Over the past several years, we have achieved President Obama's 'new foundation' and we have used that to provide our game, our clubs, our players and our supporters with a 'lasting prosperity'.

A prosperous game is one that can engage with our supporters in all areas, and we make this vow – in these difficult times we will extend our engagement in as many areas as we are able.[2]

Well known journalist Patrick Smith concurred and followed with his own view regarding the impact of the AFL beyond the confines of the various stadia and club rooms:

> The AFL sees itself as more than a football code. It is an agent of social change. It introduced a formal racial vilification code before other sports; it tested for illicit drugs before other sports. It has this month introduced a personal code of conduct that will apply to all players and officials. Demetriou has told his executive they have the opportunity to make great change to football and, through it, the community. His team are good listeners.[3]

Much of the enlightened stance the League has embraced over the past 15 years occurred against a backdrop of national hard-line political conservatism and social xenophobia. The prime minister of that period drew heavily from populist and assimilationist notions of nationhood.[4] During this time sport provided a recurring opportunity for organizations and governments (mostly controlled by white middle-class men) to celebrate unprecedented progress in race relations as evidenced by the achievements of individuals such as Cathy Freeman and Michael Long. Freeman was an international celebrity. Long's celebrity was contained within Australia. Within Australia, the AFL draws the highest attendances, attracts the largest media coverage and maintains a playing presence in every state and territory. It is widely promoted as 'the national game' and a sport which is a pioneer and frontrunner in race relations.

We examine and contest the assumptions surrounding these proclamations. We begin by providing a social context in which the AFL competition takes place and also profile Indigenous Australians and indicate their participation and contribution in Australian football. We draw upon narratives from key participants in the sport and situate their narratives and ideas within the theoretical notions of Hall regarding inferential racism, as well as Jhally and Lewis' work on enlightened racism.[5] We discuss how the containment of Indigenous participation is framed along common assumptions centred around biological determinism, stereotyped ideas about ambition many of which have enjoyed currency in Australian society since the early nineteenth century. Given this continued structural shortcoming, we conclude by arguing that the race relations that occur in the AFL reconfirm colonialism rather than forge a situation of reconciliation which remains far from complete. Reconciliation requires nothing less than the establishment of a fully operationalized Indigenous Australian team in the expanded Australian Football League. We also suggest how this can be achieved while addressing the objections and concerns of the alliance.

The Australian football landscape

Despite its relatively modest national population, four different football codes contest the Australian winter sports landscape. Australian Football and Rugby League are clearly the most popular and mediated team sports during the Australian winter. Football has its bases in the southern and western cities of Adelaide, Melbourne and Perth. Rugby League is the most popular sport in Brisbane and Sydney. The AFL teams (re)established in Sydney and Brisbane were originally suburban-based Melbourne teams who were on the brink of financial extinction at the time. The South Melbourne Swans became the Sydney Swans and the Fitzroy Lions became the Brisbane Lions. The NRL has also attempted to establish teams in the rival AFL market. This venture failed in Adelaide and Perth. The Melbourne Storm remain and have won two league titles. Despite their on-field success, the Melbourne Storm rely on 'outside' assistance and are 100% owned by News Limited. Nevertheless, the NRL is the sport of choice in New South Wales and Queensland. Such is the popularity, that it maintains NRL teams in several regional cities. Irrespective of relative popularity, both sports have recently been sites of Indigenous overrepresentation. This is in stark contrast to other 'national' sports such as cricket, rugby union and soccer.

The pervasiveness of sport in Australia has been well documented and the level of participation has been consistent for several decades. There have been higher levels of participation with younger age groups and males participate at a higher rate than females. However, approximately 32% of all Australians were involved in playing or organizing sport during 2002.[6] While these figures represent a very high rate when compared with other nations, they are far below the levels of participation in sport for Indigenous Australians. According to the ABS (2005) almost 40% of Indigenous females, and over 50% of Indigenous males participated in sport during 2002. The popularity of sport among Aborigines and Torres Strait Islanders has been noted and has drawn the attention of researchers seeking to investigate, and inevitably challenge, the widespread assumptions connected to Indigenous participation and performance.[7] The sociocultural research literature centred upon Indigenous Australian sport participation has concerned itself with stereotyping, racialized mediation, experiential reality of Aboriginal basketball, and purging of white guilt in Australian football and Rugby League.[8]

Historical context: race relations in Australia

The Indigenous peoples of Australia are the inheritors of the oldest continuous cultures in the world. According to archaeological research, they have occupied the Australian continent for at least 40 millennia.[9] Indigenous peoples across Australia developed highly successful and stable societies that sustained a diversity of cultures and languages. The societies that emerged in Australia adopted decision-making processes in which the virtues of equality, respect and consensus politics were highly valued. These political systems have been described as constituting 'pure democracy' because every individual in society had direct input into decision-making processes. In Indigenous Australia, every person functioned as a self-determining entity with responsibilities to govern their own actions and the collective actions of their society.

The arrival of the British in Australia during the last quarter of the eighteenth century witnessed the destruction of these hitherto self-governing societies. The impact of British colonization for Indigenous peoples in Australia was catastrophic, mirroring the destructive colonial projects in the Americas and the Pacific. Dispossession of land, the smashing of culture and language, and the denial of common law rights that Indigenous peoples possessed as British subjects succeeded in transforming once proud and independent peoples into passive welfare recipients dependant on the charity of colonial governments. A significant factor in this transformation was the colonial policy of 'Aboriginal Protection'. Shaping the relationship between Indigenous and non-Indigenous Australians during the period 1836–1972, the policies of Aboriginal Protection placed Indigenous people on missions and reserves where they became segregated from non-Indigenous Australia. Denied rights by a legislative and regulatory framework that severely curtailed the ability to control their own destiny, Indigenous people could not work, marry or parent their children without the approval of colonial authorities. The federation of the six British colonies in 1901 added a further layer of discrimination with two racist constitutional sections effectively excluding Indigenous people from Australian citizenship. The deliberate transformation of Indigenous Australia from independent and self-determining peoples into passive recipients of government handouts has had several negative consequences that continue to impact on race relations in contemporary Australia.[10]

Profile of Indigenous disadvantage

The consequences of colonialism are no more clearly illustrated than in national measures of social and economic wellbeing which indicate that the first Australians are among the last Australians in terms of income, wealth, employment, education and health status. Indigenous people continue to experience an average life expectancy 17 years below that achieved, expected and demanded by non-Indigenous Australians. The gap in life expectancy is given substance by the catalogue of disease that continues to place Aboriginal people at a distinct disadvantage from the moment of birth. Infant mortality rates remain double those experienced by other Australians. Indigenous people are 3 times more likely to have cardiovascular diseases, 1.3 times more likely to develop cancers, 3.9 times more likely to develop respiratory diseases and 7.5 times more likely to be impacted by diabetes. To these 'lifestyle' diseases of the First World can be added the infectious diseases normally associated with the Third World which finds Indigenous people 7 times more likely to contract TB, 8 times more likely to contract Hepatitis A and 3 times more likely to contract Hepatitis B. Finally according to measures of mental health, Aboriginal people remain 2.5 times more likely to self-harm than non-Aboriginal Australians.[11]

The poor heath profile of Indigenous Australia is closely linked to a social and economic status that sees Indigenous people remain at the bottom of the national education and employment ladder. During a time of unprecedented economic boom the unemployment rate for Indigenous people remained three to four times higher than the national rate at 30%. Median income for Indigenous Australian is significantly lower than that enjoyed by others Australians. Although primarily due to a persistent reliance on welfare, median income also remains lower because Indigenous people earn less money within the same occupational categories than others Australians. For example, in 2001, the median income of Aboriginal managers was 81% of the non-Aboriginal median, for professionals it was 73% and for labourers just 56%.[12]

Indigenous peoples continue to experience unacceptably poor outcomes in education. The highest level of formal education achieved for 33% of all Indigenous Australians is Year 9 or below compared to 16% for all other Australians. The comparative disadvantage of Indigenous people in education becomes even more apparent when grade progression rates are considered: 89% of Aboriginal students progress from Year 9 to Year 10, compared to 99% of all other Australian students. This state of perennial underperformance at the secondary level continues in higher education where Indigenous people are under-represented in all levels of study from Bachelor level degrees to PhDs. In order to achieve parity with non-Indigenous Australia, Indigenous enrolments in Bachelor degrees would need to increase by 115%, at Masters level by 414% and at PhD level by 282%.[13]

Racism and the national psyche

The profile that emerges from these statistical data indicates the influence that nineteenth-century politics continues to exert over Indigenous Australia today. However, we argue that the fundamental significance of this empirical evidence rests not in the statistics themselves but in the national psychological and discursive exclusions of Indigenous people that underpin their continued marginality in almost every aspect of contemporary Australian life. Perhaps a more important consequence of past colonial practice has been the popular acceptance of racist ideas, both scientific and Christian, which provided the rationale and the justification for Australian government to formally discriminate against Indigenous people. What once informed the policy agendas of colonial governments and the research agendas of the colonial academy continues to inform popular representations of Indigenous people that are found littered throughout Australian literature, film and media. As Marcia Langton, a leading Indigenous academic, once famously observed, the vast majority of Australians 'know' Indigenous people through the stories of former colonists.[14]

Reinterpreted in contemporary popular culture the vast majority of Australians come to 'know' and 'understand' Indigenous people through the various representations constructed for their consumption by non-Indigenous people from James Cook to John Howard and Howard Sattler. Functioning as ideology and forming a hegemonic consensus on the racial and cultural characteristics of Indigenous Australia, the stories of former colonists have been primarily concerned to define Indigenous peoples as inferior opposites of a contemporary Australian national identity from which they are excluded. Defined racially by whiteness, culturally by an adherence to British values and a masculinity that sought to place the white Australian male as a superior type of Briton, the Indigenous people came to represent the racial and cultural opposite of the idealized image of Australian national character and national values. The imperatives of Australian racism conceived that Indigenous people were racially inferior and culturally defective according to the iron laws of biology and natural selection. The Indigenous people of Australia accordingly became associated with the most negative and debasing stereotype which characterized them as primitive, stone-age, savage, the missing-link, monkey-like, child-like, over-sexed, physical, unintelligent, incapable, irresponsible, lazy, parasitic, dishonest, violent, drunkard etc. etc.[15]

The notion that the present day disadvantage of Indigenous people is their own fault and not the legacy of the inhumanity inherent in the colonial project stems from understandings of racial and cultural hierarchies that are deliberately designed to remove the legacy of Australian colonialism from public consciousness. Hence, to this day, it is considered socially acceptable and indeed 'common sense' for non-Indigenous Australians to conclude that the lower income, employment, education and health status endured by Indigenous people today is the result of racial/cultural attributes which render them too 'lazy' to find and keep a job and too 'stupid' to get an education or take proper care of their own health. Indigenous leaders who speak up about the social and economic problems that affect the wellbeing of their people are often responded to by the 'mainstream' media with calls to 'let go of the past' and be thankful for the many benefits brought to them by a 'benign' and 'good' colonialism that delivered the natives tea, law, cricket and the other trappings of British civilization.

The entrenched and persistent nature of non-Indigenous (mis)representation of Indigenous people has been sustained because the formal policy agendas of Aboriginal Protection and segregation were replaced with the contrary policies of Assimilation in the 1960s and Self-determined Integration in the 1970s. Hegemonic racism and the negative attributes associated with Indigenous people continued to influence, direct and frame the terms of the relationship between Indigenous and non-Indigenous Australia. The new demands for Indigenous people to assimilate/integrate to the 'mainstream' norms of

Anglo-Australia occurred within the context of lingering doubts about Indigenous capability to meet the challenges and responsibilities associated with political citizenship and participatory engagement in the economics of the free market. Old colonial stories through which non-Indigenous Australia 'understood' and 'knew' about 'the Aborigines' continued to shape national attitudes towards Indigenous people. In the age of assimilation, integration and self-determination Indigenous people became marginalized through a particular discourse that positioned Aboriginal racial and cultural deficit in representations of the Indigenous person as corrupt politician and incompetent administrator. As a result the self-determination in substance became a policy that encouraged limited self-management in which Indigenous people were co-opted by Australian governments to fill low skilled jobs within the public service and 'Aboriginal organizations' established by the Federal government. Although seemingly progressive, the policy agendas of assimilation and self-determined integration remained captive to the longstanding ideas that positioned Indigenous people at the bottom of racial and cultural hierarchies, an oppositional counterpoint to the top of the hierarchical tree, a position that Anglo-Australia strenuously proclaimed itself to occupy.

In the 1990s the Australian government (re)shaped the relationship between Indigenous and non-Indigenous Australia according to the new agenda it called Aboriginal reconciliation. To many this change signalled a new and positive beginning in the fraught history of Australian race relations. However, the most recent shift in the terminology of Australian government policy did nothing to displace the fundamental ideas which frame the Indigenous and non-Indigenous relationship. Consistent with earlier policy regimes, reconciliation positioned non-Indigenous Australia as leaders in a process that perversely placed responsibility for the successful resolution of the (post) colonial condition on Indigenous people. This facet of reconciliation became obvious during the period of the Howard Liberal Government that retained the policy but shifted responsibility for its success from its own administration to the underfunded and resourced National Council for Reconciliation.

Indigenous presence in the AFL

One of the often-noted aspects of Australian men's team sports in the 1990s was the emergence of a growing presence of Indigenous (Aborigines, Torres Strait Islanders) recruits into the Australian Football League (AFL). The AFL comprises 16 teams/clubs – 10 in the greater Melbourne metropolitan area, 2 from Perth, 2 from Adelaide, and 1 team in each of Brisbane and Sydney. At the beginning of the 2009 season, 71 Indigenous players are officially listed. Indigenous players are not found in equal numbers across the League. In fact, approximately two thirds are found in the clubs outside the Melbourne metropolitan area. Several Melbourne clubs have not had a strong record of recruiting Indigenous players. In addition, much of the period coincided with the considerable increase in mass media stories, narratives of the reasons and the impact surrounding the six-fold increase in Indigenous player representation in the AFL, court cases dealing with Indigenous Land Rights (Yorta Yorta in northern Victoria), the Stolen Generations Report (and former Prime Minister John Howard's refusal to say Sorry), and a number of racial vilification cases in the AFL. Despite the increase in Indigenous players, however, a recent study[16] found Indigenous AFL players were assigned into non-central field positions that place an emphasis on speed and quickness and away from positions widely believed to require leadership and intellectual skills. Furthermore, despite comprising approximately 10% of AFL players (as compared to 2% of the national population), Aborigines and Torres Strait Islanders are still absent from team or club management positions.

There have been numerous accounts regaling the AFL as the leader in Australian sports organizations with respect to opportunity access and positive race relations. It is a common practice for key stakeholders such as journalists to extol the virtues of the AFL as pioneer and leader amongst sports organizations and also suggestive of such amongst *any* organization. The common-sense reality is the production of shared language about Indigenous footballers – stereotypes, beliefs and ideologies reinforced in the routine narratives of everyday thought. The identity of Indigenous AFL players is mostly constructed and maintained by an alliance including managers, coaches, players, media commentators and sports scientists. In this essay, we draw upon the narrative data provided by two key groups: journalists and recruiting managers.

Data sources: journalists and recruiting managers

Our key data sources play vital and key roles in the dissemination of Indigenous participation and performance. They are immersed in the AFL and, as with all of the recruiting managers, many journalists are assigned entirely to football. They operate in markedly contrasted domains. The narratives of journalists are public and thus readily accessible. The narratives of recruiting managers are intended solely for reading within the club.

Journalists serve a key role in deploying and disseminating dominant meanings of public performance. As Turner argues, 'media texts offer especially rich opportunities to observe the cultural construction of meaning, locations where we can see the social production of ideas and values happening before our very eyes'.[17] Despite their claims to objectivity, journalists in particular, and the mass media in general, selectively construct particular narratives which serve certain interests and not others. Journalists writing about Indigenous sports participation and performance frequently emphasize the race relations 'achievements' of the AFL. They effectively reinforce that status quo of established power and race relations. For the specific purpose of this project, we combed the major newspaper outlets for any reports. Our raw data sources were from *The Age, Herald Sun, Daily Telegraph, Sydney Morning Herald* and *The Australian.*

The aggregation of media ownership in Australia means that the majority of newspapers are owned and produced by News Limited or the Fairfax Group. News Limited (owned by Rupert Murdoch) is responsible for the *Herald Sun* (Melbourne), *Daily Telegraph* (Sydney) and *The Australian*. Fairfax publishes *The Age* (Melbourne) and *The Sydney Morning Herald*. Between them, these newspapers account for the highest circulation figures and the majority national readership. Our analysis was not intended as a standard content analysis. Rather, we searched for reports which contained specific Indigenous ambition and performance reference, and were representative of broad themes.

Journalists have to negotiate the inherent tension between insider and outsider. Such is their sometimes vague and unclear role that two club presidents also serve as TV commentators during the season. This practice has rarely been criticized along conflict-of-interest lines. Rather, it has occasionally been questioned because of the perception that it may contribute to work overload – failing to pay full attention to the management of the club.

Recruiting managers are employed by all clubs. They are ideal sources for data regarding the logic and rationale for recruiting Indigenous players, they are uniquely positioned as AFL 'insiders', and they function as gatekeepers with their decisions determining who gains admittance. Although each provided consent for disclosure, the identities of individual managers have been rendered anonymous in this study.

We arranged and compiled narrative data according to the key themes of understanding – enlightened racism and inferential racism.

Enlightened brilliance

There would be little or no debate that professional sport in Australia has left behind the practice of overt racism. There were many reported incidents over several decades. However, even leading Indigenous figures such as Michael Long have joined the chorus. Long now serves as the AFL manager of Indigenous development. The classic overt racism has been replaced by a bevy of sports figures strongly and enthusiastically serving as advocates for increased opportunity and access. For example, Australian cricket legend Dennis Lillee, now serving as Fast Bowling Consultant, exemplified this sentiment in speaking about the potential for Indigenous talent to add to the fortunes of Australian cricket when he said:

> Fast bowling requires what we call fast twitch muscles and you only have to look at them playing football and see how quick they are and how dynamic they are. Then you can relate certainly that that muscle movement would go very well for fast bowling.[18]

Lillee's comments signify racialisation of human performance but were not challenged as such. While specifically intended as declarations for support of Indigenous opportunity, similar notions of racialisation were made by AFL coaches.

> It's exciting, most of our Indigenous boys have got a natural talent in the way they play, a lot of speed and run and carry. They play with freedom. I mean that's one of the things I love. They don't have any fear and they play the game very naturally and that's the way Jarrad plays his footy.

Former AFL coach Kevin Sheedy has been routinely credited by the AFL, journalists and supporters as being the vanguard of Indigenous participation in the AFL. He was quoted as saying:

> [T]he skills of the Aboriginal and Islander players had been a godsend for the competition. We've struck gold with the Indigenous players. You think you're a coach and then you get some really wonderfully talented people and they actually teach you how to coach. Indigenous players, they don't need a compass and a protractor. They know the angle coming into the goals.[19]

Journalists also regularly extol the 'special' qualities of Indigenous footballers:

> I don't think it is just my imagination, but I believe that many of the AFL's Indigenous players bring that joy to the game at the highest level. It seems that Indigenous players are some of the most creative and intuitive in the league.[20]

These quotes provide evidence of what Jhally and Lewis refer to as enlightened racism. They drew upon the examples of popular American television programmes which provided an idealization of race relations favoured by white Americans. Far removed from the crude behaviour associated with racial vilification, Jhally and Lewis refer to enlightened racism as a form of racism that constructs positive images of Black America while hiding cultural and economic inequalities. The popular black television characters favoured by white America are confined to a limited and finite range of attributes.

Likewise, the controlling alliance in the AFL is able to construct positive images of Indigenous footballers without confronting the structural inequalities of the sport. That is, Indigenous participation is now celebrated by the alliance but is contained and limited to playing roles. The evidence presented elsewhere strongly suggests that this participation, with minor exceptions,[21] excludes access to leadership and decision-making positions.

Inferential racism: explaining Indigenous ambition

Inferential racism is an idea established by Stuart Hall's work on media studies in Britain when writing about the involvement of Black Britons in everyday life.[22] Racial predicates, according to Hall, are pervasive and ingrained into everyday discourse. Likewise, the production of shared ideas about Indigenous footballers – to 'kick the freak goal' or 'do the magical stuff' – is reinforced in the routine narratives of everyday thought of many managers and journalists in particular. Clearly, everyday, taken-for-granted understandings of race and racial difference permeate the working environment of Australian football. When discussing the reasons for the obvious lack of opportunity for Indigenous players after their career, several managers drew upon such discourse when providing explanations of Indigenous ambition. This was in response to one of the standard questions which was presented in each interview, 'Are we on the brink where Aboriginal players once their playing careers end will start to enter the management area?' As one of the recruiting managers told us:

> I can't think of any Aboriginal player that ever had anything to do with, that have had any interest in money at all, but these guys are making a fortune. In first six months or twelve months, as I said, he didn't say much, but he had three cars he should never have had, he went bought cars, what have you bought that thing for, you know, he say 'is it any good' you'd say, 'no it's not', he go and trade it in and lose $5000 in two weeks on it, had no respect, no interest in money, most of his money went home to Darwin to look after the family and all that sort of stuff.[23]

Others replied in a similar sceptical tone:

> We are sitting there saying 'are they bullshitting us?' They just lead a simple life, you come round to our place, we go home, you come round next year, I'll give you the best kangaroo steaks, everybody comes to eat, the neighbours smell what I'm cooking and they're there, and you're thinking: Can they become coaches? They live more day to day.

> I'm not sure about that. Look Mick McLean has been very much a natural leader and rated as such but I don't know with a lot of the Aboriginal boys that they like to lead. There happy to go do their thing, play the game and with the skills thing, but I don't know if they want to get embroiled in all the rigmarole that goes with being an assistant coach and attending team meetings and standing up and being the backline coach saying 'well, look. This is what I think we should do'. I think, by and large, perhaps it doesn't suit the average Aboriginal temperament to do that.[24]

Some managers were more optimistic and open to the idea and suggested that eventually coaching roles would be offered to, and accepted by, Indigenous players. For example, one manager said:

> Michael Long appears to be a person who just might coach one day, he just seems to have a good feel, when you hear him and listen to him and whatever. He's a special quality person. Maybe we're just seeing that in the next couple of years. I was just watching the basketball the other night, I'm a gridiron fan, there is Negroes [*sic*] coaching in the NFL and the NBA, so maybe the progression is maybe it's taking a bit longer, and maybe the numbers haven't been there in the first place. Like, we're talking about a fairly small number of aboriginals playing league football. So I suppose it will come from the players who have played AFL football.

> They really love playing the game, the playing part of it, is the part they love and perhaps because everything comes so naturally to them, that perhaps they didn't take in the fact of the teaching part of the game, normally you don't have to go to an Aboriginal boy and teach him how to kick, because he's already got that skill, it's become a natural thing, you don't have to teach him how to mark the ball, so perhaps they would find it very hard then to go and teach that technique, because it's so natural to them, and as I said, they love the game,

so it's just the playing part of it, that once the playing part was finished, they couldn't see any enjoyment in the rest of it, the coaching side of things, perhaps that has something to do with it.[25]

In a story regarding the provision of a sports programme by police, the reporter simultaneously extolled the virtues of access and opportunity but clearly drew upon the familiar 'natural athlete' belief when writing 'but as we've seen in agility sports such as football, Aboriginal people have a natural sense of balance and are very athletic'.[26]

These reflections from managers and journalists not only provide further evidence of inferential racism but also provide evidence of the persistence of racialized thinking. The universally condemned blatant racist talk is usurped by a far more subtle, but equally insidious, racialized logic[27] and more socially acceptable discourse associated with racial science.[28] Consequently, the abiding racialized stereotypes typify Indigenous participants as limited to 'natural', 'brilliant', 'magical' playing roles but rule out potential for leadership and/or management roles.

Reconciliation meets Australian football

While the emergence of Aboriginal reconciliation constitutes an important development in the history of Australian government management of Indigenous affairs, this development has also been important in the evolution of the Australian Football League (AFL). Formed in 1990 at the same historical moment as Aboriginal reconciliation, the AFL quickly became an enthusiastic and high profiled advocate of the reconciliation cause. In 1993 the AFL celebrated the International Year of the World's Indigenous Peoples. During the pre-match entertainment of the 1993 Grand Final, the culture of Australia's Indigenous peoples was highlighted. In a game won by Essendon, Aboriginal footballer Michael Long and his mentor Kevin Sheedy, the non-Indigenous coach credited with bringing Indigenous players to the AFL, established themselves as symbols of reconciliation in Australian Football and of AFL commitment to Indigenous Australia. In the time since the 'watershed' 1993 season the AFL has deliberately established itself as the national sporting body that 'knows' and 'understands' Indigenous people. Aware of the need to position Australian football as a sport welcoming and inclusive of Indigenous people, the AFL introduced a number of initiatives designed to draw attention to its reconciliation credentials. 'Dreamtime at the G', the bi-annual Indigenous All-Stars games, recognition of an Indigenous 'Team of the Century' and institution of the 'Marn-Grook Cup' have all functioned to position the AFL as the leading Australian institution to pursue and achieve positive outcomes in the cause of reconciliation. To this end the AFL regularly supports these claims by citing the over-representation of playing personnel drawn from Indigenous backgrounds.

With the abiding assistance of a bevy of registered writers, the AFL elevates itself as the purveyor of social justice well beyond the parameters normally associated with a sports administrator. The normal strictures of team sport all but eliminate any prospect of self-determination. Such are the embedded traditions (invented or otherwise) and practices, that all new recruits are expected to be a 'good fit' for the team and the club. In short, recruits must readily acquiesce to established practice, values and belief systems. The recruitment of players is a complex endeavour that inevitably results in a team base that necessitates player migration from the home town or locality. As a professional sport it carries on the outmoded and nationally discredited practice of integration and assimilation.

The prospects for Indigenous players also have to be considered against the backdrop of the accelerated and dramatic downsizing and withdrawal of facilities in rural and regional Australia given that the majority of Indigenous players come from these areas. Additionally, while there is pressure to reduce the size of team lists, the number of teams in the competition is being increased. Stylistically and organizationally there is a wholesale current practice of clubs and teams being managed, coached and selected by non-Aborigines. Despite the unprecedented recruitment of Indigenous players, there has not been any change in off field opportunity. The boosters of the AFL policy disregard the continued concentration of Indigenous players in Indigenous positions. That is, the increased numbers are celebrated as a sign of progress in race relations and opportunity buti in effect, it is more of the same. The next necessary step for the AFL is to follow the pathway established at the national and move on from integration and assimilation to reconciliation. The barriers that are entrenched at the national level are mirrored at the AFL. That is,

> The great lesson that stands out is that non-Aboriginals, who currently hold all the power dealing with Aboriginals, have to give up the usually well intentioned efforts to do things for or to Aboriginals, to give up the assumption that they know what is best for Aboriginals ... who have to be led, educated, manipulated, and re-shaped into the image of the dominant community. Instead, Aboriginals must be recognised for what they are, a peoples in their own right with their own culture, history and values.[29]

National Indigenous Television (NITV) was established in 2007. It is free to air in Northern Territory and part of the cable television package elsewhere in Australia. Sport features regularly on NITV with broadcasts of cricket, basketball, football and netball. Two weekly programmes – The Marngrook AFL Footy Show and The Barefoot Rugby League Show – are 2-hour programmes produced, managed and hosted entirely by Indigenous staff. The shows include segments and guests and follow the standard format as other AFL and NRL shows. They are clearly distinguished from the structure of the AFL which is produced, managed and hosted by non-Indigenous staff. The current sizeable Aboriginal talent pool has been primarily sought for 'magical', 'uncanny', 'breathtaking flair' on field abilities. Despite the boast of increased numbers, some aspects remain wholly unchanged. Recently in Melbourne, the headquarters of the AFL and base of 12 of the 16 clubs, the NRL conducted a promotion for the forthcoming State of Origin Rugby League challenge match between NSW and Queensland. The launch focused upon three individuals – the respective coaches and the MC. Notably, the coach of NSW (Craig Bellamy) was the exception. That is, both the MC (Gordon Tallis) and the Queensland coach (Mal Meninga) are Indigenous. Nothing was made of this because all individuals have long held leadership roles in the NRL. Meninga has been a coach and selector for many years. Tallis is a media commentator with Fox Sports TV. Unlike the National Rugby League, there are no head coaches, no selectors, no commissioners, and no recruiting managers in the AFL.

The next stage needed for the AFL to move towards reconciliation is the requirement for Indigenous leadership opportunities off the playing field. This can readily be achieved via the establishment of an Indigenous-led AFL team. However, the AFL and the controlling alliance of newspaper journalists and coaches have strongly rejected any possibility of the establishment of an Indigenous-led AFL team. During the launch of an event entitled Cross Cultural Week in 2000, Aboriginal leader Charles Perkins referred to the AFL as engaging 'racism at the highest level' because the AFL had rejected the idea of establishing an Aboriginal Australian Football tournament. Perkins said: 'They didn't agree with Aborigines playing football together ... That's racist talk ... that came from the AFL. That's disgraceful. The AFL has got a lot to learn.'[30] The AFL responded by declaring that, 'The AFL could not support any football competition for one group only that precluded other players from competing on the basis of religion, colour or race.' Perkins' comments drew disdain and hostility such as the opinion expressed by the high circulation *Herald Sun* newspaper:

> Charles Perkins' comments yesterday are an insult to those in football who have committed themselves so heavily in time and spirit to give due respect and recognition to black Australians. Ever since Kevin Sheedy alerted us to the riches in the Aboriginal Community, the situation has improved every year.[31]

Indeed former coach Kevin Sheedy has come to personify the social impact claim that the AFL has assumed in respect to Indigenous participation in the game. As a pioneer of Indigenous player participation in the 1990s Kevin Sheedy has been portrayed as the key figure of reconciliation in sport, a portrayal enhanced by his role as father figure and mentor to Michael Long. Yet, the extent of Sheedy's support for Aboriginal participation in Australian Football and that of the AFL itself was recently revealed when he spoke out against the formation of an Indigenous team franchise joining an expanded national competition. Sheedy, one of the prime movers in fostering Aboriginal and Islander talent in the sport, said any move towards an exclusively Indigenous club could undo much of the bridge-building that the AFL has achieved with the Indigenous community. The former Essendon coach said he would rather see Aboriginal talent spread throughout all AFL clubs, including the two new franchises at the Gold Coast and western Sydney. 'Why would you want to do that?', Sheedy said of creating an all-Indigenous AFL club:

> The one thing that really makes our game is spreading the talent right throughout the whole nation. Otherwise it ends up becoming exactly what you don't want. I would rather have the spread of (Indigenous) players so we build a nation together. That's not probably nowhere near where the AFL would want to go. They want a spread of talent, so let's enjoy it in everybody's camp.[32]

The forthright comment by Sheedy unwittingly exposes the true nature of the relationship between the AFL and Indigenous Australia. Instead of the highly progressive institution that the AFL brand proclaims itself to be in the public arena, the participation and inclusion the league so proudly and loudly proclaims is in fact severely restricted to on-field playing roles. In this way reconciliation is limited to what is possible within the current institutional power structures of the AFL. As an institution formed in the same decade as the Australian government, the AFL continues to reflect the colonial heritage of its origins. The AFL, like the Australian Government, remains a place of whiteness dominated by middle-aged, white 'Anglo-Saxon' men. In other words the AFL is an organization whose current power structures reinforces rather than breaks down the colonial domination and dependence of Indigenous Australia. Indigenous Australians are acutely aware of this, as the response to Sheedy in the *National Indigenous Times* indicates. Alerting us to the strong parallels that exist between the limited approach the AFL and Australian government have adopted in respect to reconciliation and Indigenous self-determination, Chris Munro writing on behalf of Indigenous Australian interests asks:

> Am I hearing this right? Is this Kevin 'the much-lauded champion of Indigenous football talent' Sheedy talking? I can understand the AFL wanting to pour cold water on the whole concept. That's a given. An all-Aboriginal team would be viewed as 'race exclusive' and 'insular' in the wider public eye. For a football code in the delicate stages of expansion into the western suburbs of Sydney, not to mention the bright lights of the Gold Coast, lending

weight to such an idea in modern day Australia would be public relations suicide. Just ask successive federal governments what happens when you propose to formally embolden and individualise a group of Aboriginal people – you rapidly lose the hearts and minds of mainstream Australia. ATSIC springs to mind. Ask Joe Regular his thoughts on the elected advisory commission, and you'd get a response along these lines: 'Corrupt mate. They were all dishonest, and half of them were skimming off the top.' I'm hoping most blackfellas know this is utter rubbish, and the nine successive independent audits prove it, but like it or not, that's the streak of mud that's stuck to ATSIC since its demise in 2005. So unfortunately, whether you're talking sport or politics, mainstream Australia's your bread and butter.[33]

Munro succeeds in exposing the AFL's claims to be a leader in race relations as being seriously flawed and the league's approach to Indigenous Australia as unremarkably consistent with the past and present practices of Australian government that can rightly be described as neo-colonial. The opposition Sheedy (and the AFL) has to the advent of an Indigenous team franchise joining the national competition might be read in purely sporting terms, that an All-Indigenous team would come to dominate the competition and dampen public interest in the code. Adopting a more critical reading we believe that such opposition says much about the racism that continues to inform the AFL and its relationship with Indigenous Australia. The formation of an Indigenous team requires not only playing personnel but a group of non-playing personnel to successfully manage and operate the franchise. Opposition to an Indigenous team in the AFL reiterates the racist imperatives of colonial Australia which tells non-Indigenous Australia that Indigenous people are incapable of management, self-determination and facilitating their own success. While accepting sporting arguments against an All-Indigenous team, we believe that a franchise controlled by the Indigenous Australian football community should one day soon be admitted to the AFL. What better way to achieve reconciliation and anti-colonial, anti-racism in sport than to dream of a situation in which Indigenous CEOs and coaches control the playing destinies of kids from the white ghettos of Adelaide, Melbourne and Perth.

Concluding remarks

The coalition of AFL-accredited journalists, the front office and respective clubs comprises a controlling alliance which effectively obtains persistent domination of subordinate groups such as players, supporters, television viewers and newspaper sports section readers. This is not an overtly coercive act or process but a result of the partly unconscious act of acquiring rules, dispositions and values. This occurs through the elaboration and penetration of ideas and assumptions – such as those pertaining to Indigenous biological determinism, Indigenous ambition, and the AFL as a pioneering leader in race relations – into common sense and everyday practice.

While acknowledging the relative success of the AFL in raising public awareness of Indigenous Australia, our research draws attention to the work yet to be done. Adopting a critical approach we have sought to show how the stories of former colonists that Langton speaks about continue to shape contemporary knowledge about, and relationships with, Indigenous people within the professional Australian Football industry coordinated and controlled by the AFL. We argue that the current situation in which the increase of Indigenous playing personnel has not been met with similar increases in the promotion of Indigenous Australians taking up positions of power and authority in the AFL in non-playing positions – from coaching staff, recruiters, administrators, player managers to club and league board members – is indicative of old racial and cultural prejudices persisting in new and less obvious forms. Relating these ideas to the theoretical insights of Hall, and Jhally and Lewis we believe that genuine reconciliation and self-determination within the context of the AFL will require nothing less than the formation of an Indigenous AFL franchise that is controlled by Indigenous people and which enables them to participate in Australian Football on their own terms. The Indigenous franchise is not intended as an Indigenous-only organization. Indeed, the Indigenous leaders would and should be able to recruit the best and most suitable players. The Indigenous franchise may indeed have more non-Indigenous than Indigenous players. The establishment of an Indigenous AFL franchise will allow the AFL and its alliance of boosters to genuinely lay claim that it is 'an agent of social change' by providing and supporting genuine leadership and management opportunities for Indigenous Australians. At the moment, race relations are simply more of the same.

Notes

[1] *Herald Sun*, May 24, 2002, 108.
[2] Demetriou, 'Above and Beyond'.
[3] P. Smith, 'Sodden League dries out as AFL expands'. *The Australian*, March 21, 2009. http://www.theaustralian.news.com.au/story/0,25197,25217464-12270,00.html.
[4] Hallinan and Hughson, 'The Beautiful Game', 4.
[5] Hall, 'The Whites of Their Eyes'; Jhally and Lewis, *Enlightened Racism.*
[6] Australian Bureau of Statistics. It should be noted that here is considerable discussion concerning the meanings of these figures. For example, Spaaij and Westerbeek have noted that a person only needs to play sport once during the 12 months prior to interview to be included in the participants category. Spaaij and Westerbeek, 'A Healthy Active Australia?'
[7] Godwell, 'Playing the Game'.
[8] For extensive discussion and analysis see Hallinan, Bruce and Coram, 'Up Front and Beyond the Centre Line'; Hallinan, 'Aborigines and Positional Segregation'; Tatz, *Obstacle Race*; Coram, 'Race Formations'; Hallinan and Judd, '"Blackfellas" Basketball'; Judd and Hallinan, 'Hoop Dreams'; Bruce and Hallinan, 'Cathy Freeman'.
[9] Mulvaney, *Australian Aboriginal Prehistory.*
[10] Chesterman and Galligan, *Citizens Without Right*; Broome, *Aboriginal Australians*; Broome, *Aboriginal Victorians.*
[11] Australian Bureau of Statistics, *Online Resources.*
[12] Ibid.
[13] Indigenous Higher Education Advisory Council, *Online Resources.*
[14] Langton, 'Well, I Heard it on the Radio'.
[15] Attwood and Arnold, *Power, Knowledge and Aborigines.*
[16] Hallinan, Bruce and Coram, 'Up Front and Beyond the Centre Line'.
[17] Turner, 'Media Texts and Messages', 203.
[18] Phil Mercer, BBC Sport Online, 19 August 2001.
[19] Hand, 'Sheedy Shoots Down Idea of Indigenous AFL Club'.
[20] Interview data.
[21] Michael Long's position as the AFL's manager for Indigenous development is a notable exception. However, in this role there is relatively little power in decision making of the AFL. Chris Johnson is an assistant coach for Brisbane. There are approximately 150 assistant coaches in the AFL.
[22] Hall, 'The Whites of Their Gyes'.
[23] Interview data.
[24] Ibid.
[25] Ibid.
[26] H. Heard, 'Police Reach Out To Youth on Melbourne River'. *Melbourne Leader*, February 10, 2009, 12.
[27] Bonilla-Silva, *Racism Without Racists.*
[28] St Louis, 'Sport, Genetics'.
[29] Johnston, *Royal Commission into Aboriginal Deaths in Custody.*

[30] M. Sheahen, 'Perkins Looks a Right Charlie Now'. *Herald Sun*, May 25, 2000, 65.
[31] Ibid.
[32] Hand, 'Sheedy Shoots Down'.
[33] C. Munro, 'No Chance for 'our' own Team Without Sheedy'. *National Indigenous Times*, July 23, 2008, 20.

References

Attwood, B., and J. Arnold. *Power, Knowledge and Aborigines*. Bundoora: La Trobe University Press/National Centre for Australian Studies, Monash University, 1992.
Australian Bureau of Statistics. *Online Resources*. April 2009. http://www.abs.gov.au/websitedbs/c311215.nsf/20564c23f3183fdaca25672100813ef1/173914dcaa00b9e4ca2571ff001aca91!OpenDocument.
Bonilla-Silva, E. *Racism Without Racists: Color-Blind Racism and the Persistence of Racial Inequality in the United States*. Lanham, MD: Rowfield and Littleman, 2003.
Broome, R. *Aboriginal Australians: Black Response to White Dominance, 1788–1980*. Sydney: Allen & Unwin, 1982.
Broome, R. *Aboriginal Victorians: A History since 1800*. Sydney: Allen & Unwin, 2005.
Bruce, T., and C. Hallinan. 'Cathy Freeman: The Quest For Australian Identity'. In *Sports Stars: The Cultural Politics of Sporting Celebrity*, edited by D.L. Andrews and S.J. Jackson, 257–70. London: Routledge, 2001.
Chesterman, J., and B. Galligan. *Citizens Without Right: Aborigines and Australian Citizenship*. Melbourne: Cambridge University Press, 1997.
Coram, S. 'Race Formations (Evolutionary Hegemony) and the "Aping" of the Australian Indigenous Athlete'. *International Review for the Sociology of Sport* 42 (2007): 391–409.
Demetriou, A. 'Above and Beyond: League's Duty in Hard Times.' March 20, 2009. http://www.afl.com.au/tabid/208/default.aspx?newsid=73442.
Godwell, D. 'Playing the Game: Is Sport as Good for Race Relations as We'd Like to Think?'. *Australian Aboriginal Studies* 1 (2000): 12–19.
Hall, S. 'The Whites of Their Eyes: Racist Ideologies and the Media'. In *Gender, Race and Class in Media: A Text–Reader*, edited by G. Dines and J.M. Humer, 18–22. Thousand Oaks, CA: Sage, 1995.
Hallinan, C.J. 'Aborigines and Position Segregation in Australian Rugby League'. *International Review for the Sociology of Sport* 26 (1991): 69–81.
Hallinan, C.J., and J. Hughson. 'The Beautiful Game in Howard's "Brutopia": Football, Ethnicity, and Citizenship in Australia'. *Soccer & Society* 10 (2009): 1–8.
Hallinan, C., and B. Judd. '"Blackfellas" Basketball: Aboriginal Identity and Anglo-Australian Race Relations in Provincial Basketball'. *Sociology of Sport Journal* 24 (2007): 421–36.
Hallinan, C.J., T. Bruce, and S. Coram. 'Up Front and Beyond the Centre Line: Australian Aborigines in Elite Australian Rules Football'. *International Review for the Sociology of Sport* 34 (1999): 369–83.
Hand, G. 'Sheedy Shoots Down Idea of Indigenous AFL Club.' July 17, 2008. http://www.theroar.com.au/2008/07/17/sheedy-shoots.
Indigenous Higher Education Advisory Council. *Online Resources*. April 2009. http://www.dest.gov.au/sectors/Indigenous_education/programmes_funding/programme_categories/support_for_education_providers_staff/Indigenous_higher_education_advisory_council.htm.
Jhally, S., and J. Lewis. *Enlightened Racism: The Cosby Show, Audiences and the Myth of the American Dream*. Boulder, CO: Westview Press, 1992.
Johnston, E. *Royal Commission Into Aboriginal Deaths in Custody*, National Report, 5 vols. Canberra: AGPS, 1991.
Judd, B., and C. Hallinan. 'Hoop Dreams: Constructing Aboriginal Sport Identities in Regional Victoria'. *Journal of Australian Indigenous Issues* 11, no. 4 (2007): 17–24.
Langton, M. 'Well, I Heard it on the Radio and I Saw it on the Television. An Essay for the Australian Film Commission on the Politics and Aesthetics of Filmmaking by and about Aboriginal People and Things'. Sydney: Australian Film Commission, 1993.
Mulvaney, D.J. *Australian Aboriginal Prehistory*. Nelson: Melbourne, 1970.
Royal Commission into Aboriginal Deaths in Custody. 1991. http://www.austlii.edu.au/au/other/IndigLRes/rciadic/.

Spaaij, R., and H. Westerbeek. 'A Healthy Active Australia? Sport and Health Policy in Australia'. In *Using Sport to Advance Community Health: An International Perspective*, edited by H. Westerbeek, 59–89. Nieuwegein: Arko Sports Media, 2009.

St. Louis, B. 'Sport, Genetics and the 'Natural Athlete: The Resurgence of Racial Science'. *Body & Society* 9 (2003): 75–85.

Tatz, C. *Obstacle Race*. Sydney: UNSW Press, 1995.

Turner, G. 'Media Texts and Messages'. In *The Media in Australia: Industries, Texts, Audiences*, edited by S. Cunningham and G. Turner, 293–347, 2nd edn Sydney: Allen & Unwin, 1997.

Social functions of high school athletics in the United States: a historical and comparative analysis

Ruud Stokvis

Amsterdam School of Social Science Research, University of Amsterdam, Amsterdam; W.J.H. Mulier Institute, Centre for Research on Sports in Society, The Netherlands

In the United States competitive sport is part of the extra-curricular program of high schools. In the Netherlands, on the other hand, competitive sport is practiced in private clubs which are completely independent of the high schools. The consolidation and continuity of this difference can be explained by the importance of the integrative function athletics acquired in the US high schools. These schools have a much more heterogenic body of pupils in terms of talents and social class than most Dutch schools. The prevalence of ceremonies, rituals and symbols surrounding high school games in the US enhances this integrative function. In Europe these ceremonies are nearly absent in games and matches between private clubs for boys and girls of high school age. The integrative function of athletics in American high schools contributes to the motivation of students to participate in the school system and to the prevention of students dropping out.

Introduction[1]

To understand the influence of extra-curricular sport on the American high school it is instructive to compare the different ways in which sports for boys and girls of high school age are organized in the United States and the Netherlands. In the US competitive sport is organized as an extra-curricular activity within the schools, and a number of regular teachers also act as coaches. In the Netherlands competitive sport for boys and girls is practiced outside the school system in voluntary associations, which are completely independent from the high schools.[2] Comparison of these different institutional arrangements generates questions which one would not ask if one just looked at the arrangements in one country. For Americans the question might be why in the Netherlands competitive sport for boys and girls is organized completely outside the school system in separate voluntary associations.[3] From a European perspective one is inclined to ask why competitive sports are so important in high schools. This essay deals with this latter question.

The first task is to look to the origins of these institutional arrangements. Both date from the end of the nineteenth and the first decades of the twentieth century. However, the striking point is that these arrangements, once they were established, show a remarkable continuity. One explanation for the continuity of the American system might be found in the work of James Coleman. In his study *Athletics in High Schools*, Coleman argued that the importance of athletics in high schools can be explained by considering the important functions it has for the survival of the schools.[4] Firstly, it stimulates students who are not interested in learning to participate in the school system because of their involvement with its athletic teams, as participants or as supporters. Students who do not excel in learning more theoretical subjects may acquire prestige in the school because of their athletic abilities. In this sense, athletics is a powerful weapon in the motivation of students to participate in the school system.[5] Secondly, the high school team can function as a focus of interest for the local community of the school. High school sports may be one of the few areas in which a local community can acquire prestige in a larger region.[6] In this way the school team can stimulate the support of local businesspeople for the school. This typical functional analysis dates from the beginning of the 1960s, the highpoint of structural functionalism in sociology. Before, as well as after the 1960s the American high schools have functioned in a changing social context. We can obtain a better view on the nature of the functions of athletics for high schools if we study them from a historical and comparative perspective.[7] Our argument on the functions of extra-curricular sports for the American high schools is strengthened if we can show simultaneously that these functions are less important for the survival of the continental schools.

The data

Data about the present place of sport in American high schools were obtained during a study trip through South and Western Texas in October and November 2007. During these months I talked with many coaches, teachers, school officials and journalists about high school sports and I watched many matches of high school teams. One week I was the guest of the Athletic Department of the Houston Independent School District (HISD). This district has 97 high schools with approximately 90,000 students. The department organizes the athletics competitions and controls all accommodation and facilities for the competitions. During the day I followed the activities of the coordinators for the different sports and in the evenings they took me to the games and introduced me to a great many people involved in the competitions. I also followed during one week the athletic activities at a high school in San Antonio, interviewed most of the coaches and some officials there, followed the games of its volleyball and football teams and watched some PE lessons. For some time I was a guest at high schools in Pecos and Odessa and had the opportunity to talk with coaches, teachers and officials and watch a number of games and races (swimming). In Austin (Texas) I met three journalists with whom I had long conversations about the place of sports in American high schools and colleges.

My choice for West Texas and especially Odessa was inspired by Bissinger's book *Friday Night Lights* on the place of a high school football team in the social life of the population of Odessa.[8] To the data from the interviews, discussions and observations I added information from several local newspapers. I also made use of the documentation which was available at the HISD and the schools I visited and which I could find on the schools' websites. The history of the relationship between athletics and high schools in the US is based on the available literature. Hardly any research has been done on the development of the relationship between high schools and sport clubs in the Netherlands. The description of the situation in the Netherlands is based on archival and documentary research in connection with earlier research projects conducted by the author.[9]

Sport as an extra-curricular activity

Extra-curricular activities in American high schools are activities which do not belong to the teaching programme of the schools, yet they are organized and administered by the school and its teachers and other officials. Among these activities are debating, drama (one-acts), writing, mathematics, music, exercise and athletics. One can find some of these activities also within Dutch high schools. The main difference is the greater importance which is attached to these activities in the American high schools. More facilities and equipment are available within the American schools. Next to their teaching job many teachers in American schools are paid for directing or coaching in the extra-curricular programme. The American schools allocate more money for these activities. More students are involved in them compared with the Dutch schools and these activities are much more important in the daily life of the school.

The importance of these activities in school life is generated by the highly competitive way in which they are organized.[10] Competition with representatives of other schools is the main motivational force behind these activities. Within the Dutch school system just a few of these activities are organized in competition with representatives of other schools; most of them are non-competitive. The purpose of the drama and music activities is to prepare the participants for a performance for other students and eventually their parents. Most athletic activities within the school are organized as forms of physical education.

To realize the inter-school competition in the US the schools are organized in a system of districts, regions and the state levels. The best schools of a district participate in a regional competition and the winners of the regional competitions compete in the state championship. On the district and state levels there are organizations with paid professionals to organize, coordinate and supervise these competitions and to maintain the rules.

Some of the most important rules are meant to protect students against over-involvement in extra-curricular activities at the expense of their schoolwork.[11] As part of the competitive setting every school tries to be represented by its most talented and best-prepared students in each field of activity. Recruitment is also based on fierce competition among those who strive to represent their school in a certain field. To avoid these competitive pressures forcing students to neglect their schoolwork, there are rules concerning the amount of time they are allowed to practice and the level of grades they must attain to be allowed to participate in extra-curricular activities.

Since 1913 the inter-school competitions in Texas are administered and supervised by the University Interscholastic League (UIL). In other states similar coordinating and supervising organizations have been established.[12] The UIL is a department within the *extension division* of the University of Texas. In this division the University has organized all its services to the wider society. The UIL publishes a yearbook containing the rules for the extra-curricular activities of the high schools. In 2007 this book contained 265 pages of small print. Each school tries to obtain a competitive advantage by adopting new ways of practicing and recruitment. To control the ways in which the schools try to compete and to protect the educational interests of the students, the finest detail for each activity has to be regulated.

In the Netherlands, the majority of boys and girls of high school age practice competitive sport as members of clubs providing specific sports, which are completely independent from the school system. Sport clubs in the Netherlands (and many other European countries) obtain their finances through member contributions and through subsidies from the communities to which they belong. Because of these subsidies member contributions are relatively modest and affordable for most people. These subsidies can be compared with the funds the US School Districts obtain from their communities for athletics, to be distributed among the schools. In the US, in addition to these subsidies schools can acquire money from boosters (local sponsors), from the sale of tickets for the inter-school matches and from the income of concessions in the stadiums.

It is difficult to compare the income of Dutch sport clubs with the income of the athletic departments of the US schools. Probably the high schools in the US are able to direct more money to competitive sports. Sport clubs in the Netherlands may have similar amounts of money available, but they distribute these funds among members who are active in competition and members who practice their sport in a less competitive, more recreational way. Judged on the basis of the available equipment and facilities at the local level, the total amount of tax money which is being spent on sport for boys and girls in the US and in the Netherlands (and other European countries) will not differ substantially. It is likely that in the US a larger share of the total amount is directed towards competitive sport for boys and girls.

Origins of the relationship between schools and athletics

The United States

In the US as well as in Europe the development of organized education for boys and later girls after their 12th or 14th year of age brought these youths together in the collective settings of the school and its classes. During the second half of the nineteenth century on both sides of the Atlantic the boys especially used these newly formed collectivities to organize clubs for activities outside their official courses. Their teachers remained outside these clubs most of the time. In the US the formation of clubs resulted in disciplinary problems for school officials, which can be compared with what is known about the disciplinary problems in English public schools half a century earlier. Dunning and Sheard described how English school boys organized themselves in groups in which older pupils acted as leaders.[13] Groups of pupils created disciplinary problems inside and outside of the schools. People from the neighbourhood complained about the inconvenience of the games and pastimes of these boys. In the English public schools around the 1850s this disciplinary problem resulted in reforms that gave the teachers and other school officials more authority over the students and the way they spent their leisure.

Half a century later, we observe a similar process in the US. Anticipating the behaviour of older students in colleges and universities, high school students in the US organized themselves in fraternities and sororities. Membership could be acquired through election by sitting members and after a period of hazing. The existence of these clubs and its membership was kept secret within the school, yet these clubs played an important role in the daily live of the schools. Leading members of these fraternities also dominated the students' collective leisure activities, including sports such as football, baseball and basketball. Teams representing different schools played each other and sometimes high school students also played against freshman teams from colleges or universities and against teams made up of young workers or employees. Competition between these types of teams was already so fierce that some teams hired players from outside the school, so called 'ringers', to reinforce the school team. This practice could result in school teams without any player who was an actual student of the school. Sometimes these teams became involved in conflicts which came to the attention of the wider public, while no student of the school was actually a member of the team. School officials were confronted with actions of student clubs that discredited the school's reputation, even though the officials were unable to influence these activities. Few officials immediately recognized the pedagogic potential of athletics. Initially, during the last decades of the nineteenth century, school officials considered athletics itself as an unworthy activity related to the atmosphere of bars and dominated by idlers.[14]

Until the 1920s, officials in many schools struggled with students, organized in fraternities, for control over the students' extra-curricular activities. In a number of cases conflicts about the authority over school teams became so heated that students' parents went to court, appealing to the Constitution to defend the rights of their children to form their own associations.[15] During this period school officials became more aware of the pedagogic potential of sports. This was stimulated by a more general movement on the national level to use sports as a means to strengthen and enable the population.[16] School officials dropped their objections towards sports, but agreed that they should be brought under the supervision of the school authorities. They obtained more control by nominating and paying for the coaches and by providing facilities and equipment for athletics. Most of the coaches and trainers were school teachers with a special interest in a branch of sport.

The Netherlands

Fraternities seem to have been absent within Dutch schools for children and young people between 12 and 18 years old. Within many schools students founded school unions which organized some extra-curricular activities, but seldom on a competitive basis against other schools. In some schools they also organized also intra-school sport tournaments. These unions generally cooperated with school officials. Compared to the US, in the Netherlands the balance of power[17] between school authorities and students was more in favour of the authorities. Within the schools, students were less organized and their parents acted more in line with the school authorities and not against them. There is no evidence for the existence of exclusive, secret societies in Dutch schools.[18] No cases are known in the history of Dutch education similar to the US parents who took their children's high school to court because the school authorities did not approve of their children's clubs.

The power balance in favour of school officials may offer one explanation for the absence of exclusive student clubs within Dutch schools. Another fundamental difference between US and Dutch schools might also be relevant in this regard. In the US the high school was, with the exception of certain private schools, the only type of advanced education for children in the age category between 12 and 18. In principle the high school was intended for all American children independent of their social class. During the nineteenth century in the Netherlands, the limited group of students who attended school after they were 12 or 14 years old was always divided between different types of schools, corresponding to the social position of their parents. The gymnasium was meant for the children of the elite, 'higher bourgeois schools' (HBS, literal translation of the official name) for children of upper-middle-class families, and there were also separate schools (the ULO and MULO) for some of the children of lower-middle-class families. The students at each school formed, in terms of social status, a relatively homogeneous category in which no need for further exclusive association arose. In practice, during the greater part of the nineteenth century, the American high school was also an institution for the children of the local elites who aspired to attend a college or university later. Most of the other children did not choose to attend school after the age of 12 or 14. Yet, the students who attended the high schools in terms of social class probably formed a somewhat more mixed category when compared with the students attending Dutch schools.

In spite of the rather low degree of student organization within Dutch high schools, students did organize sports clubs outside the schools, completely independent of the school officials. The founders of Utile Dulce (UD, 1875) in Deventer, the oldest existing cricket club in the Netherlands, were fourth and fifth year students of the local gymnasium and some students of the local HBS. The founders of the Dordrechtsche Football-Club (DFC, 1885) were high school children aged 13 and 14. A few months after the establishment of this club some older high school boys established a competing club in Dordrecht. Two years later even some elementary school pupils, aged 9 and 11 years, established a club in this town.[19] Pim Mulier, who would become one of the most important founding fathers of Dutch organized sport, was 14 when he took the initiative to found the first Dutch soccer club, the Haarlemsche Football-Club (HFC). Later, in a book on the origins of organized soccer in the Netherlands, he accentuated the important role of school boys in the early development of the sport.[20]

Dutch high school (and sometimes even elementary school) students were as active as their American counterparts in the formation of sport clubs. However, even from the nature of the club names one can learn that these clubs had no relationship with their schools. The clubs founded by the Dutch boys were meant for their local social equals. Young boys of the local, rather limited, social elites formed clubs on a socially exclusive basis. Therefore, if they did not use a Latin or patriotic name for their clubs they gave them the name of their locality. They felt that they represented the local elite in the field of soccer and other sports. Already before 1900 in sports such as cricket, soccer and hockey, club members managed to found national associations which standardized the rules of their sports and administered the competitions on a national level. Because the clubs which founded the national associations were completely independent from the schools, these associations came to function entirely outside the school system. This pattern for the organization of sport, once established in the older sports, became the organizational model for all sports.

Even in a sport like netball, a sport which was introduced in the Netherlands in 1903 completely from within the school system by school officials,[21] the clubs formed a national association independent from the school, similar to the older sports. This is remarkable because these clubs had a very close relationship with the schools where they were founded. The students who established the first netball club in 1903 came from a new progressive school. The name of this club does not show its relationship to the school; just like the older clubs in other sports the founders chose their locality as the point of identification: De Eerste Amsterdamsche Korfbalclub (DEAK = The First Amsterdam Netball Club). However, the clubs which followed did use the name of their school to identify themselves. In Amsterdam, these clubs include: De Eerste Vijfjarige (DEV = The First Five-year High School), De Derde Vijfjarige (DDV = The Third Five-year High School), De Vierde Vijf (DVV = The Fourth Five-year High School), De Eerste Driejarige (DED = The First Three-year High School), De Vierde Driejarige (DVD = The Fourth Three-year High School), Korfbalclub Vijfde Driejarige (KVD = Netball club Fifth Three-year High School), Openbare Handelsschool (OHS = Public Trade School) and Kweekschool voor Onderwijzers (KVO = School for Teachers). In spite of the close identification of the clubs with the schools, netball players organized themselves in a national netball union which functioned completely outside the school system.

In the US and in the Netherlands we see two different reactions from school officials to the establishment of sport clubs by students. In the US school officials decided to control the sporting activities of their students by bringing them under school administration, whereas in the Netherlands school officials dissociated themselves from the pastimes of their students as much as possible. Yet, in both countries initially there was not much sympathy among the school officials for sports. In the US football in particular was condemned by some officials as brutal and unfit for high school and college students.[22] One of the first Dutch sport journalists, Jan Feith, called the first soccer and rugby players 'martyrs' who had to bear the torments and tortures of stiff schoolmasters and fearful conservative parents to be able to practice their sports.[23] We now have to explain these different organizational arrangements.

The split between school and sports in the Netherlands

A very obvious difference between US and Dutch schools during the second half of the nineteenth century was the fierce resistance of physical education teachers against sport in the Netherlands. Since 1862 Dutch physical education teachers were organized in a professional association. Their profession came into existence after the introduction of physical education as a compulsory course in the Dutch high schools. This resistance was based on a mixture of ideology and professional interests.

The Dutch physical education teachers modelled themselves on the German pedagogues who became popular with the growing nationalism in Germany and other European countries during the nineteenth century. According to these pedagogues the purpose of physical education was to strengthen and revitalize the national population. For that reason they tried to pursuade the government to offer physical education to all children of school age and to finance the facilities to realize this. According to Mandell they propagated 'induced sports'.[24] These are sports which are organized by state-officials with the purpose of strengthening the population. However, in contrast with the ideals of most physical education teachers, their students preferred to participate in the new modern 'hip' sports which were introduced from England. The students met each other at the schools, but organized their sporting activities during after-school hours on their own initiative, outside the jurisdiction of school officials. The pro-German physical educationalists did not like these sports from England. In their professional journals they defined the interest in sport as an 'English illness'[25] and as a 'cancer for a responsible formation of the young'; sports without professional supervision would result in over-involvement and neglect of school work.[26] Their dislike was reinforced by the aversion of many parents and other authorities for the rather 'rough' new games of the students. The resistance of physical education teachers was also based on their professional interests. In a certain sense students, through their sporting activities, obtained the physical training they needed to compensate for the hours they spent sitting in their classes. Sport threatened to make the jobs of physical education teachers redundant. This resistance of a well-organized professional association of physical educational teachers seems to have been almost entirely absent in the United States.[27]

The fusion of schools and athletics in the US in the twentieth century

Having analysed the origins of the different ways in which the relationships between school and athletics have been structured in the US and the Netherlands, we still have to explain the tenacity of this difference. Why did this difference endure for the rest of the twentieth century and after? It probably was not just a case of path dependency, in the sense that a certain constellation of relations, once established, endures because it becomes involved in a wider system of relations which stabilize the initial constellation.[28]

The school is a natural field for the recruitment of teammates to play sports. In the Netherlands, the actions of physical education teachers probably would not have led to a permanent separation of school and sport if no other factors had been involved. I would argue that athletics meant much more for the stability of American high schools because these schools had already acquired during the first part of the twentieth century a far more heterogeneous student population compared to the Dutch schools. In American schools sport developed an important cohesive function,[29] for which there was no need in the more homogeneous Dutch schools. The relatively homogeneous social composition of the Dutch schools created few problems with the cohesion of these schools. In the Netherlands there was no need for arrangements, like athletics, which could strengthen the cohesion of the schools.

During the latter part of the nineteenth century in the US as well as in the Netherlands students who attended high school belonged to the upper classes and expected an education which would prepare them for college or university. In this period children of the middle and lower classes started working at the age of 14 after eight years of elementary school. Later, from the start of the twentieth century, the American high school lost its elite character. Between 1890 and 1918 the number of students multiplied sevenfold.[30] The social composition of the high school became more heterogeneous, first through the entrance of students from the middle and lower classes and later through the entrance of students from immigrant groups. After the 1960 desegregated schools also absorbed students of the black population and students from Asia, South and Middle America. Most of these new students did not aspire to an education which prepared them for college or university. They were more interested in vocational courses through which they could prepare themselves for manual trades. Alongside the academic courses the schools began to offer all kinds of vocational courses oriented to the local and regional industries and trades.

During the economic crisis in the 1930s the schools became involved in the fight to reduce unemployment. By keeping boys and girls at school as long as possible, the schools assisted in the prevention of unemployed young people aimlessly wandering through the streets, who were considered a risk for disorder and crime. In Angus and Mirel's words,[31] the schools added a 'custodial function' to their existing functions. The high schools evolved in the direction of custodial schools for young people. Educational programmes were adapted to this function. The schools introduced courses which were meant to attract the attention of youngsters who were thought not to be interested in academic or even vocational subjects. A new type of courses, so called life-education subjects, was introduced. These were courses such as: 'maintaining health and fitness', 'exploring vocations and vocational efficiency', 'developing successful social relations', 'learning the right use of leisure' and 'the American teenager and interior decorating'. Only after 1970 school officials started to reverse this tendency to lower the general intellectual level of the educational programmes. However, they succeeded only partially.[32]

Angus and Mirel give little attention to the evolution of the place of extra-curricular programmes within schools during the twentieth century. The growing interest in these programmes, the time and money spent on them and the elaboration of the ceremonies and rituals connected to them nevertheless fit well with an increase in the custodial function of these schools. It makes it understandable that every teacher, coach and official I spoke with during my journey through Texas emphasized that without an athletics programme and other extra-curricular activities the number of drop-out students would strongly increase. According to these respondents many students lived without much parental care and control, and without the school providing care for them they risked becoming members of street gangs.[33] Based on available statistics they might be right (Table 1). In Amsterdam (the Netherlands) the drop out ratio in 2005 and 2006 was on average 16%; in Houston (US) this percentage was 12.5%. In both cities this ratio was very unevenly distributed between ethnic groups.

Coleman touched on this integrative function when he stated that athletics motivates students who are not very interested in an intellectual education to participate in the school

Table 1.   High school drop-out rates in Houston and Amsterdam, 2005/06[34].

Houston		Amsterdam	
Average drop out rate	12.5	Average drop out rate	16
African American	11.9	Surinam	25
Asians	4.2	Antillean	23
Hispanic	15.3	Turkish	26
White	5.2	Moroccan	23
		Other non-western aliens	19
		Western aliens	13
		Dutch	10
Number of students	89.396	Number of students	65.731

system. However, he misses the point that during the twentieth century the American high school had become a very heterogeneous organization in terms of the backgrounds of its students and the nature of its educational programmes.[35] These schools risked disintegration if all kinds of integrative mechanisms had not evolved. The extra-curricular programmes function to influence the motivation of students to participate in an orderly way in school. However, all schools which I visited also have a number of uniformed policemen in the schools to ensure the students behave in an orderly way. Until now in most schools in the Netherlands the need for an internal police force has not arisen, at least not on a large scale.[36]

Ceremonies, rituals and symbols

In Texas, identification of students and teachers with their schools was enhanced by the introduction of ceremonial rituals and symbols in connection with athletic events. Compared with high school sport in the US, in the Netherlands and other European countries most games for boys and girls of high school age are played almost entirely without ceremonies and rituals. In the US, participation in ceremony and ritual can reinforce the emotional energy of students and staff, even for those members of schools who have no special interest in athletics. This reinforces their solidarity with the schools and their identity as part of a collective.[37] In connection with high school football, these ceremonies have integrative functions on four interconnected levels: schools, games, localities and country.

Each school I visited organized a pep rally one day before its football team's match against another school. During a 30- or 45-minute meeting many students and teachers would meet in the gym hall or the school square. During the meeting the school band would play, the cheerleaders would dance and some stimulating speeches would be made. Members of the football team (and sometimes also the girls of the volleyball team) had special chairs, because they were the guests of honour. The school bands were surprisingly large, with at least 40 pupils who, just like the cheerleaders, become more integrated in the school through their participation. On trips to matches in another neighbourhood or town the bus carrying the team and its support staff was always accompanied by a number of buses carrying the band, the cheerleaders, the exercise groups, the flag bearers and the mascot-handlers. School principals and often also other school officials see it as an obligation to be present at most of these matches and generally these matches draw a few thousand visitors.

First team matches are held on Friday evenings and start at seven, when twilight begins. The stadium slowly becomes an isle of light in the darkness. This creates an atmosphere which reinforces the over-all ceremonial set up of the event.[38] In spite of all the preparations of each separate school to manifest itself during the game and to motivate its own students, the whole setting of the game makes it a collective ceremonial event. The entrance of the teams onto the field and the way they do their warm up are all organized to augment the general ritual character of the event. Before the match or during the intermission small ceremonies are held for people who have serviced the school or the community. During the intermission the bands of both sides have 12 minutes to demonstrate their abilities to the public.

The importance of this collective ceremony, not just for the schools but for the local population in general, may be guessed from a newspaper article about a father who is proud that his son serves in the US army in Iraq:

> All of us know the soldiers currently serving over in Iraq and Afghanistan would love to be home with their loved ones watching television or going to a high school football game on Friday night, but instead are over there facing danger every minute so that we can continue to live in a free nation.[39]

Watching high school football is a manifestation of 'the good life'.

In Odessa, Texas, a town with nearly 100,000 inhabitants, I just missed the annual match between two local high schools. Bissinger characterized the meaning of the match between these teams as follows:

> The Permian–Odessa High game had become a clash of values – between the nouveau riche east side of town [Permian] and the older, more humble west [Odessa High], between white and Hispanic, between rich and poor, between the sub-urban style mall and the decrepit, decaying downtown.[40]

Already on the Wednesday before the match the local newspaper informed its readers about the mass of supporters that came to the counters of the local stadium (Ratliff Stadium, with a capacity of 20,000) to purchase tickets. On Thursday there was a similar article, as well as short interviews with the coaches of both teams. On Friday nearly the entire newspaper was devoted to the upcoming match. The same happened on Saturday; the front page was dominated by a photo of the ceremony during the intermission with the high school bands of Odessa (junior high schools included) arranged on the playing field, with around 600 musicians in total. They honoured the firemen and policemen who were former pupils of the Odessa schools and who had died in service.[41]

In a certain sense a high school football game is not just an affair between two schools or between representatives of two localities. It is also a celebration of American society at large. On each athletic field the American flag is present in a prominent position. Just before a game begins everybody is asked to rise and to listen to the American national anthem and, eventually, to sing the anthem. While the anthem is being played people keep their right hand on their heart. As already described in the case of Odessa, time is reserved for small ceremonies to honour people who have serviced their school, town or country. Their names are called and sometimes they are invited onto the field. These ceremonies are attended by a delegation of the Junior Reserve Officers Training Corps (JROTC). It is composed of three or four people clothed in old army, navy, air force and marine-corps uniforms, with shining silver helmets and bearing the flags of their army departments. The presence of all these ceremonies in American high school sport and its near-absence in the Netherlands supports the argument that athletics has an important integrative function for the American high school.

The balance between school and athletics

The ceremonial enhancement I have described for high school football is, in a more modest way, also present at games in other sports. Membership of an athletic team in an American high school is an important position. Students tend to spend much of their time and energy playing in a team. Had no rules limiting their efforts been in place, many students would use time necessary for schoolwork for extra practice. To limit this tendency, the 'no grade, no play' rule has been introduced throughout the state of Texas and in many other American states. The central point of the rule is that every six weeks the grades students have scored for their schoolwork are evaluated. If they fail to attain a certain minimum standard necessary to complete their school year, they are not allowed to play. Every official, teacher or coach with whom I spoke about this rule told me about its salutary influence. Athletically gifted students, who have little interest in their schoolwork, are forced to attain sufficient grades if they want to play. These grades are carefully administered by the school and the coaches. In case of an important game, coaches may feel the temptation to place players in the team who, because of their grades, are not allowed to play. However this is very risky: if coaches act in this way and it becomes known, they will lose their jobs. School officials, officials from the school district and officials of the state organization for athletics (the UIL in Texas) are very keen to maintain the rule.

For athletically gifted athletes there is a lot riding on their being able to play. Their ultimate dream is to be recruited by a professional team after they have finished school. This rarely ever happens.[42] However, once every few years it happens somewhere in the US and this is enough to keep students' fantasies alive. A somewhat more realistic possibility is that the most gifted players in the high school teams are offered a college scholarship to study at a college and play in one of its teams. This is a realistic possibility for the best players of the best teams. Yet, most high school athletes fail to attain this prize. However, the hope for a scholarship is a powerful motivator to perform. Because one can only show one's abilities when one is playing and one is only allowed to play when one has sufficient grades, this 'lottery' stimulates athletic students to perform well in school.

Conclusion

A comparative-historical analysis helps us to locate Coleman's functional analysis of athletics in high schools more explicitly within the context of the development of the position of the high school in American society. The high school represented a democratic ideal to offer all boys and girls an equal educational opportunity. As a consequence, in terms of the nature of its students and its educational programme it became a very heterogeneous institution. This becomes clear after a comparison with Dutch schools. These schools have a relative homogeneous composition in terms of the social backgrounds and talents of their students.

The origin of the difference in the role of athletics in the schools of both countries can be explained only partly in terms of the less democratic structure of the schools in The Netherlands. The organization of physical education teachers played an important role in keeping athletics outside the Dutch schools. However, initial differences were reinforced by the growing importance of the function of athletics in the American high schools to keep the schools together and to create a feeling of collective identity among staff and students, in spite of their increasing heterogeneity. The elaboration of the ceremonial side of the athletic events can be explained in relation to this importance of the integrating function of sport for the high schools.

The integrative function of athletics on the American high school works in three ways. Firstly, students with athletic ambitions are being drawn into the school system not only, as Coleman stated, because they can become popular at school. If they show enough athletic talent their reward may be a college scholarship. The 'no grade, no play' rule forces them to concentrate their efforts as much on their schoolwork as on sport. Another category of students with fewer athletic ambitions is drawn into the school system via activities that are connected with the athletic events. These are the members of the surprisingly (from a Dutch perspective) large school bands, cheerleaders, exercise groups and many other students who are involved in the organization of the ceremonies surrounding the athletics events. The third category consists of those students who are drawn into the school system because they identify with their school teams as fans. The elaborate ceremonial set up of matches contributes to the creation of a collective school identity. Through their participation as fans students and staff acquire positive emotional energy.

Considering the average dropout rates for Houston and Amsterdam, but keeping in mind that we do not know exactly to which extent these percentages can be compared, American high schools – at least those in Houston – seem relatively successful in limiting the number of drop-outs. On the basis of my analysis I think it is fair to state that the impact of athletics plays a significant role. This is not to say that athletics is a panacea for all motivational problems of high school students. Judged from the participation in pep rallies and the number of students visiting games, perhaps one half of the school population shares through athletics in the collective identity of the schools. It would be an illusion to expect that athletics alone can solve all social and psychological problems high schools encounter.

Notes

[1] Research for this study was subsidized by the Dutch Ministry of Health, Welfare and Sport. It is a part of a project on Topsport, National Pride and Prestige executed by researchers connected to the W.J.H. Mulier Institute, Centre for Research on Sports in Society.

[2] The difference between the US and the Netherlands is not absolute. What we discuss in this essay are the dominant patterns in both countries. In the Netherlands out of a total population of 16.5 million, 4.9 million are members of voluntary sports associations. 61% of people between the ages of 12 and 19, who practice sport at least once a year, are members of these associations (Sociaal en Cultureel Planbureau, *Rapportage sport 2008*, 90). In the US boys and girls are also able to participate in sport outside their schools in voluntary associations, commercial sport schools and neighbourhood clubs. In the Netherlands there are some inter-school tournaments, however they are little known and the teams generally don't play an important role in the affairs of the schools. The members of these teams learn their sports in most cases in the voluntary associations.

[3] Americans to whom I explained the European arrangement could only imagine the exclusive and expensive private clubs for some sports (like golf) which exist in the US.

[4] Coleman, 'Athletics in High Schools'.

[5] Participation in athletics reduces student's likelihood of dropping out. See McNeal, 'Extracurricular Activities', 62. In this study I offer an explanation for this function of athletics.

[6] Entering several counties I saw along the road, next to a plate with the name of the county, several times also a plate with an overview of the championships of the local high school football team. Some of these championships had been won more than thirty years previously.

[7] I know of just one other study which compares American high schools with Dutch schools for boys and girls of the same age group: Paulle, *Anxiety and Intimidation*. Paulle attaches less importance than I do to the formal difference between the schools (comprehensive vs. one track) in both countries and different places of extra-curricular activities. He does not even discuss the place of these activities in school life.

[8] Bissinger, *Friday Night Lights*.

[9] Stokvis, *Strijd over sport* and 'De school en de sport'.

[10] The adjunct-principal who introduced me at the Thomas Edison High School in San Antonio told me: 'Everything here is competitive'.

[11] As can be expected, this fierce competition between the schools, especially in the field of football, induces some of the school athletes to use doping (anabolic steroids). Assael, *Steroid Nation*, 244.

[12] O'Hanlon, 'School Sports as Social Training', 7.

[13] Dunning and Sheard, *Barbarians*, 77–80.

[14] Jebsen, 'The Public Acceptance', 15–16; Rader, *American Sports*, 161.

[15] Pruter, 'Chicago High School Football Struggles', 60.

[16] Jebsen, 'The Public Acceptance', 15; O'Hanlon, 'School Sports', 19.

[17] Elias, *Was ist Soziologie?*, 77.

[18] Jansing and Dasberg, 'Onderwijs', 370.

[19] Stokvis, *Strijd over sport*, 9.

[20] Mulier, *Athletiek en Voetbal*, 141.

[21] Broekhuysen, *Het ontstaan*, 14.

[22] Mirel, *From Student Control*, 92.

[23] Zuijderhof, 'Voetbal', 73.

[24] Mandell, *Sport*, 158.

[25] Kramer and Lommen, *Geschiedenis*, 48.

[26] Stokvis, *Strijd over sport*, 73.

[27] Baker, *Sports*, 166, Rader, *American Sports*, 92.

[28] David, 'Clio and the Economics of QWERTY', 332.

[29] Waller, *The Sociology of Teaching*, 115.

[30] O'Hanlon, *School Sports*, 3–4.

[31] Angus and Mirel, *The Failed Promise*, 57.

[32] Ibid., 74, 165, 195.

[33] During an introductory interview at the start of my stay at the HISD, there was a moment when the black cameraman from the district TV channel asked permission to stop recording the interview in order to testify that his son would not have become a successful accountant had he not participated in his high school's football team. In order to participate he was forced to succeed in his exams.

[34] Houston Independent School District, *Facts & Figures*; Dienst Onderzoek en Statistiek, *De staat van Amsterdam IV*, 61, 71.

[35] At the end of the article, Coleman (1961) writes that this integrating function of sports for the schools could be replaced in principle by more intellectually prestigious activities like competitions in music, theatre, mathematics or computing. These competitions do exist. However, Coleman misses the relationship between the prestige of football players and the popularity of football within the school and the enormous prestige of college and professional players and the popularity of football outside the schools and its exalted position in the media. Coleman overestimates the possibilities for the introduction of alternatives for athletics.

[36] Cf. Paulle, *Anxiety and Intimidation*, 88.

[37] Collins, *Interaction Ritual Chains*, 49.

[38] Just before a match, one of the team assistants drew my attention to the wonderful twilight sky and said: 'Don't mess with Friday night football'. This was a variant of the slogan 'Don't mess with Texas', which was used in a campaign to keep the landscape clean and which could be seen along many roads in Texas.

[39] *Dalhart Texan*, November 7, 2007, 4.

[40] Bissinger, *Friday Night Lights*, 156.

[41] *Odessa American*, October 31, 2007 and November 1, 2 and 3, 2007.

[42] Coakley, *Sport in Society*, 306. A fairly recent example is LeBron James, a basketball player who in 2003 at the age of 18 was contracted with the Cleveland Cavaliers.

References

Angus, D.L., and J.E. Mirel. *The Failed Promise of the American High School 1890–1995.* New York: Teachers College Press, 1999.

Assael, S. *Steroid Nation*. New York: SEPN Books, 2007.

Baker, W. *Sports in the Western World*. Totowa, NJ: Rowman and Littlefield, 1982.

Bissinger, H.G. *Friday Night Lights. A Town, a Team, and a Dream*. Reading: Addison-Wesley, 1990.

Broekhuysen, N. 'Het ontstaan van korfbal (1902–1903)'. In *Dat is korfbal. Handboek voor de korfbalsport*, ed. Technische Commissie van de Koninklijke Nederlandsche Korfbalbond Rotterdam: Nijgh & Van Ditmar, 1949.

Coakley, J. *Sport in Society. Issues and Controversies*. Boston, MA: McGraw-Hill, 1998.

Coleman, J. 'Athletics in High Schools'. *Annals of the American Academy of Political and Social Sciences* 338 (1961): 33–43.

Collins, R. *Interaction Ritual Chains*. Princeton, NJ: Princeton University Press, 2004.

David, P. 'Clio and the Economics of QWERTY'. *American Economic Review* 75, no. 2 (1985): 332–7.

Dienst Onderzoek en Statistiek. *De staat van Amsterdam IV*. Amsterdam: Gemeente Amsterdam, 2007.

Dunning, E., and K. Sheard. *Barbarians, Gentlemen and Players*. Oxford: Martin Robertson, 1979.

Elias, N. *Was ist Soziologie?* München: Juventa Verlag, 1970.

Houston Independent School District. *Facts & Figures*. Houston: HISD, February 2007.

Jansing, J., and L. Dasberg. 'Onderwijs'. In *Algemene Geschiedenis der Nederlanden Deel 13*, edited by Th. van Tijn, E. Scholliers, J. Boogman and L. Wils, 129–44. Haarlem: Fibula-Van Dishoeck, 1978.

Jebsen, Jr. H. 'The Public Acceptance of Sports in Dallas, 1880–1930'. *Journal of Sport History* 6, no. 3 (1979): 5–19.

Kramer, J., and N. Lommen. *Geschiedenis van de lichamelijke opvoeding in Nederland*. Zeist: Jan Luiting fonds, 1987.

Mandell, R.D. *Sport: A Cultural History*. New York: Columbia University Press, 1984.

McNeal, Jr. R.B. 'Extracurricular Activities and High School Drop Outs'. *Sociology of Education* 68, no. 1 (1995): 62–80.

Mirel, J. 'From Student Control to Institutional Control of High School Athletics. Three Michigan Cities, 1883–1905'. *Journal of Social History* 16, no. 2 (1982): 83–100.

Ministry of Health, Welfare and Sport (The Netherlands). *Tijd voor sport. Bewegen, meedoen, presteren*. The Hague: VWS, 2005.

Mulier, W. *Athletiek en voetbal*. Haarlem: De weduwe Loosjes, 1894.

O'Hanlon, T.P. 'School Sports as Social Training: The Case of Athletics and the Crises of World War I'. *Journal of Sport History* 9, no. 1 (1982): 4–29.

Paulle, B. *Anxiety and Intimidation in the Bronx and the Bijlmer. An Ethnographic Comparison of Two Schools*. Amsterdam: Dutch University Press, 2005.

Pruter, R. 'Chicago High School Football Struggles, the Fight for Faculty Control, and the War against Secret Societies, 1898–1908'. *Journal of Sport History* 30, no. 1 (2003): 47–72.

Rader, B. *American Sports. From the Age of Folk Games to the Age of Spectators*. Englewood Cliffs, NJ: Prentice-Hall, 1983.

Sociaal en Cultureel Planbureau. *Rapportage sport 2008*. The Hague: SCP/WJH Mulier Instituut, 2008.

Stokvis, R. *Strijd over sport. Organisatorische en ideologische ontwikkelingen*. Deventer: Van Loghum Slaterus, 1979.

Stokvis, R. 'De school en de sport- en spelbeweging in Nederland'. In *Het vergeten lichaam: Geschiedenis van de lichamelijke opvoeding in België en Nederland*, edited by M. D'hoker and J. Tolleneer, 59–75. Leuven: Garant, 1995.

University Interscholastic League. *98th Edition of the Constitution and Rules of the University Interscholastic League 2007–2008*. Austin, TX: The University of Texas, 2007.

Waller, W. *The Sociology of Teaching*. New York: John Wiley, 1970 [1932].

Zuijderhoff, B. 'Voetbal'. In *Het boek der sporten*, edited by J. Feith, 73–103. Amsterdam: Van Holkema en Warendorf, 1900.

The social construction and impact of champions

Joseph Maguire

School of Sport and Exercise Sciences, Loughborough University, Loughborough, UK

This essay addresses the belief that the performances of champions are attributable to either the genetic make-up, or to some notion of genius of athletes. Individualistic and/or behavioural explanations tend to dominate. Yet, such explanations provide a very limited grasp of the genesis of performances and reveal nothing about the stage on which the 'act' is performed, the theatre in which the 'play' takes place or the impact that sport has on society. In emphasizing the cultural making of sport, this is not to dismiss the notion of genius, or overlook the creativity, expressiveness and existential experiences that are part of sport. In fact, champions of sport perform powerful functions for the societies they represent. This essay, then, seeks to capture both the construction of genius and what it tells us about the societies which such champions represent.

The social construction and impact of champions

In the study of art as a social product, it is necessary to debunk 'the romantic and mystical notion of art as the creation of "genius", transcending existence, society and time'.[1] The study of sport is no exception. Sport performances emerge and develop in a network of numerous structural determinants and processual conditions. That is, the practical craft and creativity of champions are in a mutual relationship of interdependence with wider structured processes. Thus, this essay confronts the more usual belief that thrilling performances are attributable to either the genetic make-up, or to some notion of genius of athletes. In this line of thinking, emphasis is placed on the biomedical properties or uniquely individual creativity of performances. Individualistic and/or behavioural explanations hold sway. Yet, such explanations provide a very limited grasp of the genesis of performances. And, in addition, they tells us nothing about the stage on which the 'act' is performed, the theatre in which the 'play' takes place or the impact that sport has on society. This essay seeks to outline some of the features of these overlooked dimensions.

In accounting for sport, like art, it is necessary to probe the production, distribution and reception of athletic performances. While the performance of Tiger Woods is very different from that of Wolfgang Amadeus Mozart, each are perceived as uniquely gifted individuals, exceptions who stand outside of general social structures. However, the products of their brilliance, and the recognition and reception of their performances, are deeply connected to social processes. That is, 'Mozart's individual fate, his destiny as a unique human being and thus also a unique artist, was heavily influenced by his social situation, the dependence of a musician of his time on the court aristocracy'.[2] In emphasizing the social construction, or cultural making of sport, this is not to destroy the notion of genius, or downplay the creativity, expressiveness and existential experiences that are part of the sports world. In fact, champions of sport perform powerful functions for the societies they represent. This essay, then, seeks to capture both the construction of genius and what it tells us about the societies which such champions represent.

Identifying the qualities of champions: the logic of the sports industrial complex[3]

Are champions born or made? Popular science and the media often assert that athletes are born, not made. Such a view hinges on a genetic 'magic bullet' model: the possession of a particular set of genetic factor(s) makes a champion, and therein lies the promise of unlocking a genetic blueprint to sporting talent. One aspect of such a blueprint is the will to win, the desire to compete and to be the best – irrespective of the other genetically predisposed qualities associated with success in a particular sport. In contrast, sport science research highlights the various factors that go into making a champion: for example, modes of preparation, psychological attitudes, carefully planned training and coaching, and adherence to a 'sport ethic' are all relevant to the production of champions. On this basis, it is possible to conclude that it is no fluke of nature that some societies continue producing top talent in specific sports. Examples include Australia and cricket, Brazil and association football, Canada and ice hockey, and Sweden and tennis. Are champions born or made – and is it simply a question of one or the other?

In a commonsense understanding, we can appreciate that genes have a large effect on a person's muscle composition, height and length of trunk, legs and arms. But grasping the complex interplay between genetics and sports performance requires differentiating between genotypes and phenotypes. Genotype refers to the entire genetic identity of an individual, including alleles, or gene forms. This, then, is the hereditary constitution of a person. Crucially, genotypes show no outward characteristics. Phenotype refers to the observable physical or biochemical characteristics of a person and depends on which genes are dominant and on the interaction between genes and environment (an issue that will be returned to). In popular understanding these two are often confused. Put simply, however, genotypes *code* phenotypes. The internally coded, inheritable information of the genotype, carries the critical instructions that are used and interpreted by the (cellular) machinery of the cells to produce the outward, physical manifestation expressed in the phenotype. Crucially, all the physical parts, the molecules, macromolecules, cells and other structures, are built and maintained by cells following the instructions given by the genotype. As these physical structures begin to act and interact with one another they can produce larger and more complex phenomena such as metabolism, energy utilization, tissues, organs, reflexes and behaviours. Given this, it is no surprise that scientists have explored the role of genes in sports performance.

What implications does this have for identifying sporting champions? In this connection several questions arise: Which factor(s) are most important? When, during an athlete's sporting career, is genetics or the environment more influential in shaping behaviour? Why do some athletes seemingly benefit more from training and practice than others? And, how can specific champion potential be identified and developed? Some sport scientists assert that genes are responsible for up to half of the variation in physical performance within a given population. Attention in molecular biology has thus focused on single gene variants to explain the propensity for specific diseases or for impacts on an individual's performance. In particular, the performance of champion sprinters, endurance athletes and even mountaineers has been linked to specific genes. In the light of this type of research, consideration has also been given to profiling the capabilities of champions, the susceptibility of athletes to injury forms and the suitability of individuals to specific roles or positions within a team. Research of this type has also been reinforced by work that seeks to explore the role of inheritance in personality and in skill acquisition. Such work probes whether there is an underlying basis to claims that people are born 'talented' and with a will to win.

One of the more controversial issues that such work throws up is that of gene transfer technology and its use not only in restorative medicine but also to enhance performance of potential and existing champions. Indeed, it is possible to go further and suggest that humanity is on the brink of advances that will see tiny 'robots' implanted in people's bodies – machines and humans will eventually merge. How then, would we compare the champions of the past with those of the future? Despite the outlandish claims and dire predictions the hard evidence suggests that things are not as clear cut as the 'magic bullet' model of genetic sporting excellence.

In searching for candidate genes that contribute to performance variability among athletes, the reality is that there is no clear and conclusive evidence to support the notion that champions are simply born winners. Though the identification of a single gene to explain the performance of champions is the 'holy grail' of molecular biology, in fact many genes act in combinations and 'cooperate' or 'compete' with environmental constraints. Specific studies that assumed a specific link could be established between genetics and performance have found no clear evidence to support such claims. Work on Kenyan middle distance and long distance athletes, for example, in comparing them with non-athletes found no differences in genotype frequency between the groups. In addition, the primary limitation of genetic studies of psychological variation between athletes is that the role of psychological traits in sports performance is relatively unknown. In summary, then, an athlete, like any human, has a particular genetic inheritance, but those genes do not work in transparent ways. They work in combined networks and interrelate with the environment to influence biological function. Champions are not simply born. How, then, are they made?

Champions are made: the identification and production of talent

International sport success involves a contest between systems located within a global context. Sport success depends on several elements: the availability and identification of human resources; methods of coaching and training; the efficiency of the sport organization and the depth of knowledge of sports medicine and sport sciences. These national sport system mechanisms are a necessary but insufficient explanation of international sport success. In addition to these elements sport development within a particular society also depends on the status of that nation in the international sports rank order. Less developed nations tend to under-utilize their talent and performers and/or lose them to more powerful nations in the global sports process. If champions are made, what factors or components contribute to their success?

Sports performance involves the integration of many factors. As observed already, genetics (along with aging) are outside of an individual's control. Yet, a person's physiology, biomechanics and psychology are *trainable*, and the tactics and strategies a champion deploys are *teachable*. In physiological terms it is possible to improve the work capacity of the individual by the adoption of training regimes that relate to the specific demands of that sport. In biomechanical terms the repetition of exercises focusing on precise or gross motor skills can lead to improved physical performance. And, in terms of psychological preparedness, a person can enhance the notion of self-confidence and better tolerate the stressful demands stemming from training and competition. Though these components are teachable and trainable, the success of such measures also depends on identifying different types of athlete. Work done by the Australian Coaching Council identifies two broad categories of champions: those who are genetically talented and those with a highly developed training and performance ethic.[4] This work identified four categories of athletes, using the rather unflattering analogy of horses:

1. Wooden Horse – low fitness/low speed: athletes who are just commencing training or returning from illness or injury.
2. Bolter – low fitness/high speed: athletes who have natural speed and may not find it necessary to do the same volume of work as their team mates. This athlete may have short-term success, but long-term progress to elite competition may be limited.
3. Workhorse – high fitness/low speed: these athletes are training specialists who are extremely dedicated and consistent in their workouts. However, they struggle to lift the quality of their efforts when in a competitive situation. This may be due to excessive training loads, insufficient recovery or inadequate speed work.
4. Thoroughbred – high fitness/high speed: the athlete with a combination of developed fitness and natural speed is likely to have the greatest chance of success and improvement in the long term, when in association with skill and tactical awareness.

Such research does not dismiss the role of genetics but seeks to place it in the context of other factors. In identifying potential and actual champions in both individual and team sports, it is clear that different 'horses' can complement each other, bringing out the best in each other. A successful programme does not happen by chance – there are key elements that have to be in place in order to ensure that quality preparation produces champions. What elements have been identified? There is no substitute for perfect practice – for this makes practice perfect and leads to champion performances. From the available evidence it is clear that focused, effortful and deliberate practice is required to produce excellent performances. It takes 10 years and more of such practice to hone the required skills and develop the necessary experience to be a champion. In the process of making champions, generation after generation, several key factors must be focused on. These include:

1. The development of a long-term training strategy;
2. Tailoring training specific to the stage in the athlete's 'career';
3. Consideration of the intensity, duration and volume of training;
4. Attention given to training cycles and strategies – with relevant structures, phasing and tapering for peak performance;
5. Sensitivity to the balance between over-training and optimal performance.

It would appear that those champions who succeed on a regular basis do so on the basis of the factors identified, but also because, in comparison both with their contemporary competitors and champions of the past they are subject to the following:

1. More sophisticated coaching;
2. Advances in knowledge of, and exposure to, better training methods;
3. Better equipment and access to new technology;
4. A 24/7, year-round, professional and scientific approach to identifying and producing champions;
5. An adherence to the unwritten 'sport ethic' that ensures that champions are 'willing to pay the price' and 'go the extra mile' to be the best.

If these are the key factors and features that are necessary in producing champions, then evidence also exists that suggests what we should avoid. Although 'talent' may be evident at an early stage, if specialization occurs too soon in a person's athletic career then negative consequences follow. Equally, too great an emphasis on competitive games, simulating what happens at an adult level, can also have a harmful effect on producing talent. There is also evidence of selection bias, with coaches favouring children who are born earlier in the year cohort and who have greater physical maturation rather then skill.

Future champions need to be nurtured with a diverse range of movement skills. In addition, in order for the intensity and duration of motivation of potential champions to be maintained, early involvement in sport must be permeated by a play-like spirit. Access to resources and facilities as well as the role of parents and the broader culture must also be taken into consideration. Only when a higher level of performance is achieved is it appropriate to introduce the type of highly structured practices that are the most effective form of preparation and training. The debates and factors outlined above apply across sports.

The debate about 'soccer' talent, for example, revolves around the issues already outlined. How do we identify and nurture the 'stars' destined for greatness in the game? In soccer, as in other sports, there is no clear agreement over what counts as talent. Some sets of criteria focus on technique, attitude, balance and speed while with others the emphasis is on speed, understanding, personality and skill. In addition, these criteria can be interpreted differently and acted upon or not. No matter what criteria are used, the pursuit of excellence that finds expression in great players, such as Thierry Henry, is structured into four main stages: detection, identification, development and selection.

Detection relates to the discovery of potential performers who currently do not play the sport. Identification refers to the process of 'spotting' those players who have the potential for greatness. Development occurs when such talent is nurtured in a suitable training environment. The selection stage relates to the process by which talent is deemed coachable and selectable. This selection tends to be based on either achieved criteria (what the player actually does) or ascribed criteria (preconceived ideas of the coach or scout – some of which may be quite subjective or even flawed), or a combination of both. Here, the focus is on the identification stage.

Predictors of identifying talented soccer players are drawn from several areas. These include the physique of the player, physiological factors, psychological dimensions and sociological considerations. In terms of physique the evidence suggests that young soccer players who succeed in the age cohorts have similar somatotypes (the structure or build of a person, especially to the extent to which it exhibits the characteristics of an ectomorph, an endomorph, or a mesomorph) as older, equally successful, players. But, as noted with athletes in general, there appears to be some element of subjective thinking about, or discrimination bias regarding, players who are more physically mature. This may be especially so in British soccer, with its emphasis on strength and aggression and the onset of competitive football at an early age. Younger, more skilful players may well lose out – something which may happen to a lesser extent in other soccer development systems. The consequence of this is evident at elite level where English players are often compared unfavourably in terms of basic technique with their fellow Europeans.

Physiological predictors follow the seemingly commonsense observation that elite young players achieve higher levels of performance in terms of running and jumping in comparison with less elite players. Better measures of oxygen uptake, anaerobic power, grip and trunk strength and heart volume are cited as indicative of elite performers. Yet, such measures may reflect the fact that such elite performers are already subject to a more systematic approach to training. Indeed, these measures relate to younger players: older, more established players show less diversity in such measures. These physiological predictors may thus be a necessary factor involved in elite performance but on their own they are not sufficient to explain why some players stand out in the team and others do not.

When examining the psychological predictors of elite performance in soccer there are also difficulties. In examining the evidence on profiling, personality and performance the overall conclusion appears to be that there is no clear or consistent relationship with sporting excellence. Recent studies of the changeable states, as opposed to the supposedly fixed traits, of people's personalities (looking at measures of anxiety, self-confidence, motivation and attentional style) also come up short in providing a recipe for identifying soccer greats. In fact, the improvement of psychological skills is more the focus of investigation: players are being equipped to better cope with the demands of elite performance through a variety of psychological training techniques. These, combined with consideration of the cognitive skills required to 'read the game' – anticipation, game patterns and decision-making skills – all suggest that champion soccer players are made, not born. The 'feel for the game' is something you learn. Being a competent or accomplished social actor, and having mastery over social practices, such as art or sport, involves having a 'feel' for the task at hand. This feel for the game is developed and maintained by a person's habitus. In other words, sporting performances are abilities so well honed through practice that they become habituated and part of our second nature. We learn to 'use' aspects of them intuitively. In art and in sport, the quality of performances also swings on a hinge between the learned and the unlearned. The saying 'practice makes perfect' refers to the way in which our unlearned abilities are fused with our learned attributes. In more able performers this process is so well integrated that performances appear 'natural'. Yet, these performances are, in reality, the product of both long-term socialization processes and the sport worlds that enable or constrain such learning.

This learning occurs in a social context: hence, the identification and development of soccer talent varies considerably between countries. The attraction of the sport of soccer (and its subsequent development of talent) is contoured and shaped by the fault lines of a society: social class and ethnicity are two of the main factors to consider. These influences are also reinforced by issues concerning facilities, schooling, parental support, local club structures and the duration of exposure to quality coaching. Inherent talent may, to a degree, have a genetic and physiological basis but the extent to which this talent finds expression and flowers to become a champion of the sport is very much dependent on these social factors. In sum, there is no easy answer to the task of identifying and predicting future stars. The overall conclusion appears to be that a multi-causal approach is required but that, on balance, brilliant soccer players such as Thierry Henry are made.

From the range of arguments surveyed it is possible to conclude that sports performance is the result of interactions among a host of genes and environmental constraints. This conclusion tends to undermine folklore, highly simplistic pseudo-scientific accounts and some well planned research which perpetuates the myth of inherent sporting greatness. The uncritical acceptance of the notion that athletes are born not made has distorted general models for talent identification and development programmes across the globe. While there is no single gene as 'magic bullet', there is evidence regarding the particular stages and phases of a child's maturation and psycho-motor skill development that, if better understood, could provide a sound evidence-based footing on which to intervene and detect, select, identify and develop talent. The 'secret' seems to be careful planning, considerable dedication and sophisticated preparation. While champions may make success and excellence look effortless, what goes unseen are the endless hours of careful practice.

Making sport champions: systems of production and consumption

The British gave modern sports to the world. For a long time, continued success in these sports seemed self-evident. Yet, over the course of the second half of the twentieth century, the decline of Great Britain, in political and economic terms, has been matched by their performances on the playing fields. Old rivals got better and new competitors overtook them in the developing sporting international rank order. This was due in part to the adoption by the Soviet Bloc, from the 1950s onwards, of a scientific, highly rationalized and technologized system for the identification and production of champions. This approach was exemplified by the sports system developed by the German Democratic Republic (GDR). Four key elements have been identified. These include:

1. Scientifically organized and rational selection of boys and girls in early childhood;
2. Excellent facilities and a highly planned approach to coaching and training;
3. Extensive networks of support by scientists from different branches of the natural and social sciences;
4. A very specific focus on achieving success in specific sports where success was more likely and where there was some tradition of German involvement.[5]

This system, with local modifications, was adopted by Australia and Canada. As a result, Team GB was becoming less successful during the 1970s and 1980s at the Olympics, and its component nations (England, Northern Ireland, Scotland and Wales) were being overtaken by other countries at the Commonwealth Games. That decline has now been reversed due to the 'modernisation' of the identification and production of champions in the UK – especially with London 2012 on the horizon. However, as more and more nations adopt some or all of the elements outlined, the intensity of competition intensifies: sporting success has become the equivalent of an 'arms race' in which ever greater resources have to be invested in order to maintain or improve the position of the nation in the medal table. What then are the current ingredients for sporting success and the production of champions in the twenty-first century?

Just as there is no *single* magic gene that explains brilliant performances, the evidence suggests that there is no *single* model that helps explain sporting success and the ongoing production of champions. There are, however, increasing similarities between countries and a formal standardized model of elite sport development has emerged, which has been modified to suit local histories, cultural sensitivities and contemporary political circumstances. Several key elements of this standardized model have been identified and have been drawn together in three clear 'clusters'.[6]

The first cluster is contextual and centrally concerns whether there is the availability of funding and resources. The financial support can be derived from the state and/or the private sector but must be of a level that ensures that athletes can be employed 'full-time' (the days of elite amateur athletes are long gone). Resource issues relate to the quality, access and provision of scientific/medical knowledge.

The second cluster is processual and relates to whether a system of rational, bureaucratic planning and administration exists. Such a system is a necessary component as it enables effective administration to exist within and between different agencies and departments involved in the process. Such an approach ensures that effective priorities are set, detection and identification undertaken, monitoring accomplished, and that 'objective' evaluation occurs. Talent can be detected, resources allocated, rewards distributed and support provided. These concerns apply to the athlete, the coach and the sports administrator.

The third cluster is specific – that is whether there exist well-structured competitive programmes and highly tailored facilities that serve the needs of specific sports. Without these, nations who do produce talent tend to find that there is a 'brawn drain', where such talent is attracted to other countries to train, compete in and, in specific instances, compete for other nations. In contrast, athletes can also be recruited from other countries to represent the nation – this has, in the past, been done on an *ad hoc* basis, but with the 2012 London games looming, a more systematic approach regarding the recruit of foreign migrant athletes may be adopted.

In summary, then, five common themes have been identified in successful elite development systems:

1. Efficiency of administration and organization;
2. Elite facility development in targeted sports and support for 'full-time' athletes in those sports where there are insufficient opportunities for financial rewards from the private sector;
3. Methods of coaching and training;
4. The provision of sports science and sports medicine support services
5. Realistic appraisal of international rank order of sports, opportunities for success, and the hierarchy of competitive opportunities geared towards peaking at prioritized international events, e.g. the Olympics.[7]

The emergence of champions does not happen by chance anymore: the resources of the state and the private sector are involved. This process has developed to such a degree that it can now be said that a sports-industrial complex underpins the identification and production of talent in advanced industrial societies. This complex has four key dimensions: structural, ideological, cultural and institutional. In structural terms, several key groups, including state agencies, transnational corporations, non-governmental agencies and sport associations are involved. A mix of state and transnational corporations (TNCs) are involved in global sport.[8] In ideological terms, states use global sports, and national champions, to promote the values and status of the nation, both internally and externally. National traditions still mean much to people and governments use champions both to promote international prestige and to foster 'soft diplomacy'. The logic of the British state, UK Sport and Team GB is strikingly similar to that of the former GDR and its sports system.

In cultural terms, champions adhere to what is best termed the 'sports ethic'. Four key features of the sports ethic have been identified. These include: a willingness to make sacrifices; a striving for distinction; an acceptance of risk and the possibility of participating while enduring pain; and a tacit acceptance that there is no limit to the pursuit of the ultimate performance. The institutional framework of this complex involves at least four main elements: sports medicine, sports science, sports science support programmes and regional/national centres of excellence. It is in the institutional dimension that champions are actually identified, selected and developed. Exercise physiologists examine the most advantageous biological conditions necessary to train and compete effectively. Biomechanists trace the most rational way specific forces and angles can be utilized for the demands of competitive tasks. Sport psychologists – whether motor learning or cognitive based advocates – plot the optimal mental conditions and conditioning required to reach the performer's peak. Geneticists seek to find the 'magic gene' and contribute to the early stages of the gene transfer revolution that is unfolding. And, as sports science has grown in depth and range, we now see match analysts, and nutrition and related sports medicine specialists, plying their trades.

The rationale and funding underpinning such research ensures that attention is directed at identifying factors that: maximize the development of talent; generate efficient training regimes; contribute to rational performance systems; identify effective recuperation programmes; and highlight strategies that enable performers to cope with pain and injury experiences. Highly rationalized and technologized physical and mental training methods, and scientifically evaluated and scheduled fitness regimes, are designed to produce optimum performance and thereby reinforce the overall impact of the sports industrial complex in the quest for sporting success.

The complex initially emerged, as noted above, in the Soviet Bloc and then in Australia, Canada and in those western/developed nations less restricted by the legacy of an amateur attitude to sporting success and the production of champions. The business of sporting success is now deadly serious and thoroughly professional. Having jettisoned the amateur tradition, the British have been keen to catch up. Under both the Conservatives, and more especially New Labour, UK governments have embraced a 'modernization' agenda – adopting a professional approach to talent identification, production and performance – with advocates of coaching science, sports science and sports medicine recruited to help deliver 'success'. The mission statement of the state-funded UK Sport is clear:

> UK Sport is the agency charged by the Government with providing support to high-performance sport at the UK level, with the aim of achieving sporting excellence on the world stage. The work of UK Sport is all about building a framework for success – developing and supporting a system capable of producing a constant flow of world class performers in a fair and ethical way.
>
> UK Sport takes the lead ... in aspects requiring UK-wide strategic planning and administration, co-ordination or representation. Our focus is on performance, and providing a winning environment.[9]

The logic at work is to ensure the most effective use of funding available from the Lottery. As a result, UK Sport prioritizes both between and within sports, and draws on and further funds the knowledge base of sports science and sports medicine. Their concern is with the coordination of the many strands of sports science and research to make sure that sports are receiving the most appropriate services. The system is thus aimed at producing 'effective systems and strategies ... to help sports monitor and evaluate sports science and sports medicine'.[10] UK Sport has also been explicit as to the logic that was at work in the funding of sports science support and sport associations prior to previous and upcoming Olympic Games:

> Prioritisation criteria focused on: medal potential; evidence of a performance system that should continue to produce a high number of talented athletes; track record; and the significance of the sport in the eyes of the public. In terms of decision-making most attention was given to the criteria relating to: medal potential (which hinges on whether the performance gap to the podium is bridgeable); the number of World Class athletes; and the number of medals targeted. Track record merely provided some confidence in the level of risk in the investment.[11]

Following the logic outlined, UK Sport is keen to highlight the 'success' of state investment in elite sport, and has produced what it terms a 'World Sporting Index'. According to UK Sport this 'works by calculating performances by the world's best athletes and teams in over 60 sports, over a four-year cycle' and thus 'can produce a basic guide to the world's best sporting nations'.[12] Of the top ten, all are industrial nations;

all G8 countries are represented; eight are Western and two are former state socialist/communist societies – here, sport and military-industrial complexes interweave. Through further investment in the performance efficiency model of elite sport development, UK officials hope to maintain or increase their sporting lead. Not surprisingly, then, in the UK Sports Annual Review of 2002/2003, its Chief Executive, Richard Callicott, declared that 'Our Lottery-funded World Class Performance Programme continues to be unashamedly about the pursuit of success – targeting sports and individuals most likely to deliver medals at major events'.[13] Its stated overall aim was even starker: 'UK Sport is committed to a goal: putting the UK among the world's top five sporting nations by 2012.'[14] UK Sport also signed 'co-operation agreements with two Olympic superpowers', China and Cuba, sharing sports science knowledge, access to expert coaching, and facilities.

Such strategies between so-called 'Olympic superpowers' reinforce the structure of the global sports–industrial complex. Its mechanisms of production, experience and consumption involve several elements: the identification and development of talent; its production on a global stage, in a single or multi-sport event; and its consumption by direct spectators or, through the media complex, by a global mass audience. Traced over time, there is a tendency towards the emergence of a global achievement sport monoculture in which administrators, coaches, sports scientists and teachers promote achievement sport values and ideologies, and competitions and tournaments are structured along highly commodified and rationalized lines.

In the production of national champions, nothing is left to chance – it is investment and professional and scientific preparation that count. This is evident in how the knowledge and resources of the sports industrial complex are applied by coaches to prospective champions. Indeed, the intent of any approach to coaching is to ensure that a performance-enhancing environment is created. On this basis, champions can potentially be produced. An integrated approach seeks to provide the means of organizing training and preparation so that the component parts of coaching dovetail well together. In this context integration refers to drawing together all the factors that affect performance into a training plan.[15] This integrated approach enables a prospective champion to recognize strengths, while reducing any weaknesses. In addition, on this basis players such as Tiger Woods can set goals that ensure that a performance peak occurs when it really matters – at a Gland Slam tennis tournament or a Major golf championship. Working with their coach and support staff, the athlete can establish specific phases of development and action plans to improve performance, in both the short and the long term. In more sophisticated integrated approaches to coaching, the identification and development of a champion is structured along three broad timescales. Goals are set for the long term (10–20 years); the medium term (3–5 years); and, the short term (the annual training plan).

The production of champions can be viewed in terms of a career that has four stages. The initial socialization into sport in general and a specific sport in particular must develop a sense of love for, and attachment to, the activity. At this stage, nurturing the play and intrinsic reasons for participation outweigh the pressure to introduce competition. The next stage involves training to train: that is, the athlete begins to develop the skills and capacities to participate, but not to compete 'seriously', in a specific sport. In the third stage, the emphasis is on the athlete training to compete. Even at this stage, however, the long term development of the athlete outweighs the attraction of short term competitive success. In the final stage, the champion trains to perform and win – the focus is on competition priorities and the need to achieve carefully timed peak performances.[16] Over these time scales and stages the coach and athlete develop a systematic analysis of the components of performance for their sport. By identifying and integrating these components into a training programme the athlete is more likely to best develop their talent and express it under championship conditions. Several basic principles of integrated planning have been identified.[17]

Preparation and careful planning are thus key to success in the production of champions. In some sports, and with very talented individuals, the stages outlined may be compressed or overlap considerably. In addition, the basic principles of integrated planning apply as much to team as individual sports: within teams the individual's development must be closely linked to the team plan and structures. Within the agreed style of play, strategy and tactics, individuals must be encouraged to innovate, express themselves and make decisions. Successful teams have group cohesion and individual flair. But what meaning does this production and consumption have for society at large?

Champions of sport and society

What is it to be a champion and why do they mean so much to us? In a simple sense, a champion is someone who is the first among all contestants or competitors and, in this regard, the word refers to the ability of an individual or team to win a contest or championship. Clearly, Tiger Woods or Thierry Henry's membership of the French World Cup winning football team would be examples of this. Yet, the origin of the word indicates a different usage and offers a clue as to why champions are so much more important to us then just their ability to win and why we attach such meaning to them. Its first usage emerged in the context of the medieval tournament and referred to the person who would act as a champion of others; who would defend, support or *champion* a cause.[18]

In this sense, athletes are not simply champions of their sport, but also of their local community and nation and sometimes, humanity as a whole. An example of this par excellence is Muhammad Ali.[19] A champion is said to possess special gifts and exude a certain charisma: they perform 'miracles' and achieve the seemingly impossible. They are our modern heroes: symbolic representations of our cultural values and who we would wish to be. Champions are talented individuals but as heroes they are people whose lives tell stories about ourselves, to ourselves, but also to people from other nations.[20]

People appreciate excellence and have a desire to achieve it, and if not, then at least to share in it. The champion allows us to catch a glimpse of what we could be: by representing us they make us vicariously fulfilled human beings. They are our modern heroes because sport has become the forum in which communal self-revelation occurs.[21] That is, modern sport is a form of surrogate religion and popular theatre in which there occurs the communal discovery of who we are. Sports stadia are contemporary venues in which we can observe champions as heroes and experience the 'sacred', moments of exciting significance, while leaving behind the profaneness of ordinary life.[22]

In this sense, society needs its champions as heroes. They perform the manifest function of achieving sporting success for themselves and their local community and nation. But they also perform a more latent role: they are meant to embody the elements that a society values most. As idealized creations, they provide inspiration, motivation, direction and meaning for people's lives. Champions as heroes act to unify a society, bringing people together with a common sense of purpose and values. That is how modern sport developed. Pioneers of the nineteenth century linked sport to muscular Christianity: unselfishness, self-restraint, fairness, gentlemanliness and moral excellence. This was itself supplementing traditional notions of chivalry: honour, decency, courage and loyalty. These qualities are, as will be discussed further, some of the very attributes associated with the footballer Sir Bobby Charlton, as well as more recent champions. Writing of Thierry Henry, Barry Smart observed:

> A very modest person off the field of play, an individual who values his privacy, Henry is truly charismatic on the pitch, a player whose power and explosive acceleration, outstanding technical ability, exceptional vision and all-round contribution during matches has made him a talismanic figure, one whose ability to perform the extraordinary has excited and enthralled fans around the world.[23]

Despite the sense of nobility that both Charlton and Henry embody, there are, however, threats to the manifest and latent functions of champions as heroes. This stems from issues associated with authenticity and integrity. The status of the champion relies upon the authenticity of the contest. If the contest is tarnished by corruption, cheating or betting scandals then the hero is diminished in our eyes. The contest is no longer either a mutual quest for excellence or societies forum in which communal self-revelation occurs. This lack of authenticity also occurs when the sport becomes too make-believe, is rigged or becomes too predictable. Professional wrestling may produce 'champions' but they are not taken seriously, and they are not our heroes.[24]

The champion as hero also, as noted, embodies the elements that a society holds most dear. But, the integrity of the champion may also be undermined in several ways. The champion may be a flawed genius – either due to the fact that they suffer from hubris and feel they need not dedicate themselves to the level and intensity of preparation and performance required, and/or because their private lives intrude on their status as heroes. Here, the examples of George Best and Paul Gascoigne spring to mind. Our idealized image of them as athletes is shattered, though in the case of Best, we still mourn his death in a profound expression of grief. In addition, our champion may be less a hero and more a celebrity – they are famous but not heroic. David Beckham may be seen in this light.[25] If this is the case, such fame is short lived and they fail one of the tests of a true champion as hero – the test of time. Eddie 'the eagle' Edwards was once famous, but he was neither a champion nor a hero, and is now forgotten. In order to understand why champions mean so much to us and what impact they have, we have to consider the role sport plays in society.[26]

The meaning of sport and the role of champions

Sport is both a separate world, and a suspension of everyday life, yet is also highly symbolic of the society in which it exists. In the context of sport we can both experience a form of exciting significance that we rarely, if ever, encounter in our daily lives, and also conduct a symbolic dialogue with fellow participants and spectators that reveals things about ourselves and others. We are laid bear in sport in a ways which we cover up in everyday life. Sport is a modern morality play that reveals fundamental truths about us as individuals, our societies and our relations with others. Sport, then, moves us emotionally and matters to us socially.[27] That sport performs these functions relates to several reasons that dovetail with, and highlights, the role of champions.

One of the principal features of sport is the arousal of pleasurable forms of excitement.[28] People, it seems, have a need to experience various kinds of spontaneous, elementary, unreflective yet pleasurable excitement in increasingly rule governed and risk-averse societies. In sport, whether as participant or spectator, people quest for this controlled decontrolling of emotions. Here, emotions flow freely and in a manner that elicits or imitates the excitement generated in real life situations. Sports, then, are mimetic activities that provide a 'make-believe' separate setting that allows emotions to flow more easily. This excitement is elicited by the creation of tensions that can involve imaginary or controlled 'real' danger, mimetic fear and/or pleasure, sadness and/or joy. This controlled decontrolling of excitement allows for different moods to be evoked in this make-believe setting that are the siblings of those aroused in real-life situations. Our champions are identified with – in terms of their technical accomplishments but also in terms of the emotions they, and thus, we, go through, in terms of the well-played game or thrilling contest.

Tie-breaks in tennis, penalty shoot-outs in football and sudden death play-offs in golf evoke a range of emotions, so much so that by the end of the contest we are emotionally drained. And, unlike a well performed play or well acted film, we know that what we were witnessing in sport is real and that the outcome was not determined beforehand. Sometimes, our champions fulfil their own and our dreams but, on other occasions, the tragedy of defeat must be endured. A champion, such as Roger Federer, on entering Centre Court at Wimbledon can observe a plaque that displays Rudyard Kipling's poem 'If'. The poem notes, that when you meet triumph and disaster you have to meet those impostors just the same. In dealing with both triumph and defeat in Wimbledon finals Federer has arguably embodied such sentiments.

Only when sports are associated with matters of deep cultural and personal significance do they become important to fans.[29] Major sporting events are thus mythic spectacles where fans are provided the opportunity for collective participation and identification that serves as a means of celebrating and reinforcing shared cultural meanings. It is precisely because sports are a separate world that suspends the everyday world, that they are able to celebrate shared cultural meanings that are expressed through, and embodied by, champions. The anthem, the emblem and the flag associated with sporting contests highlights how champions represent the nation.[30] The England World Cup team of 1966 became World Champions but also have had a collective heroism attached to them. Their success has stood the test of time – it still moves England fans. But it is perhaps the iconic images of Bobby Moore that remain etched in people's minds. This gives a clue to the fact that the symbolism of sport, and the role played by the champion, is even deeper then mere nationalism and patriotism. Bobby Moore symbolized something more then winning.[31]

If social life can be conceived of as a game through which identities are established, tested and developed, then sports can be viewed as idealized forms of social life. Its rules and codes of play (such as in golf etiquette) allow for a fair contest and a true test of ability. The 'true' champion, playing an authentic match, with integrity, is the best expression of this. In this context it is thus possible to establish an identity with greater consensual and authentic certainty then in social life itself. We insist on the authenticity and integrity of the contest – on the strict formal rules and their fair enforcement – because we want any differences of worth between us to be based on merit.[32] In real life our class, race, gender or religion interfere and rig the game of social life and its outcomes. As such, its victors and losers, its champions, are profane deceptive illusions. But, on the field of play, sport outcomes are sacred; they are real and authentic. That is also why champions seek to beat fellow champions: that is the true test. Honour and respect are not achieved by knowing in advance that you will beat inferior opponents. The on-field handshake between Bobby Moore and Pele during the 1970 World Cup match between England and Brazil symbolizes such honour and respect. The 'hand-of-god goal' scored by Diego Maradona, wonderful player though he was, does not.

Sport is thus a symbolic dialogue: it symbolizes the strict requirements of how a dialogue should be conducted.[33] Sport, then, involves a dramatic representation of who we are and who we would like to be. The stadia is a theatre in which we experience a range of pleasures of emotional and exciting significance: the excitement of the played-game, uncertain as to its outcome but its significance lying in what we have invested in it emotionally, morally, socially. Our champions as our heroes express both the myths and revered social values of a society, and the sports ethic that underpins involvement in sport.[34] They have to take risks, to exhibit the hallmarks of bravery and courage and show integrity. That is why we remember them but not necessarily the processes outlined here that underpin their construction.

Notes

[1] Wolff, *Social Production of Art*, 1.
[2] Elias, *Mozart*, 14.
[3] Maguire, 'Challenging the Sports-Industrial Complex'.
[4] Pyne, 'Designing an Endurance Training Program'; Australian Coaching Council Inc., cited in Smith, 'A Framework for Understanding the Training Process'.
[5] For further discussion see Green and Oakley, 'Elite Sport Development Systems'.
[6] These clusters have been identified by Houlihan and Green, *Comparative Elite Sport Development*.
[7] Ibid.
[8] See Maguire, *Global Sport* and *Power and Global Sport*.
[9] UK Sport, *Annual Report*, 3.
[10] Ibid., 10.
[11] Ibid., 7.
[12] Ibid., 29.
[13] UK Sport, *Countdown to Athens*, 10.
[14] Ibid., 10.
[15] See Pyke, *Better Coaching*.
[16] For further discussion see ibid.
[17] Ibid.
[18] For further discussion of sporting heroes see Gilchrist, 'Local Heroes or Global Stars?'; Hughson, 'On Sporting Heroes'; Tännsjö, 'Is our Admiration?'.
[19] Hauser, *Muhammad Ali*.
[20] For general discussion of the role of play, games and sport in civilization see Huizinga, *Homo Ludens*; Caillois, *Man, Play and Games*.
[21] Algozin, 'Man and Sport'.
[22] Maguire *et al.*, *Sport Worlds*.
[23] Smart, *The Football Star*, 199.
[24] Stone, 'Wrestling'.
[25] Cashmore, *Beckham*.
[26] Books abound on sporting champions: see McGovern, *Amazing Athletes*.
[27] Maguire *et al.*, *Sport Worlds*.
[28] Elias and Dunning, *Quest for Excitement*.
[29] Nixon and Frey, *A Sociology of Sport*.
[30] Maguire and Tuck, 'Making Sense of Global Patriot Games'.
[31] Powell, *Bobby Moore*.
[32] See Morgan and Meier, *Philosophic Inquiry in Sport*.
[33] Ashworth, 'Sport as Symbolic Dialogue'.
[34] Coakley, *Sports in Society*.

References

Algozin, K. 'Man and Sport'. *Philosophy Today* 20 (1976): 190–5.
Ashworth, C. 'Sport as Symbolic Dialogue'. In *The Sociology of Sport*, edited by E. Dunning, 40–6. London: Frank Cass, 1971.
Caillois, R. *Man, Play and Games*. Glencoe, IL: Free Press, 1961.

Cashmore, E. *Beckham*. Oxford: Polity, 2004.

Coakley, J. *Sports in Society*. 8th ed. New York: McGraw Hill, 2003.

Elias, N. *Mozart: Portrait of a Genius*. Cambridge: Polity Press, 1991/1994.

Elias, N., and E. Dunning. *Quest for Excitement: Sport and Leisure in the Civilising Process*. Oxford: Blackwell, 1986.

Gilchrist, P. 'Local Heroes or Global Stars?' In *The Global Politics of Sport: The Role of Global Institutions in Sport*, edited by L. Allison, 118–39. London: Routledge, 2005.

Green, M., and B. Oakley. 'Elite Sport Development Systems and Playing to Win: Uniformity and Diversity in International Approaches'. *Leisure Studies* 20, no. 4 (2001): 247–67.

Hauser, T. *Muhammad Ali: His Life and Times*. New York: Simon & Schuster, 1992.

Houlihan, B., and M. Green, eds. *Comparative Elite Sport Development*. London: Butterworth, 2008.

Hughson, J. 'On Sporting Heroes'. *Sport in Society* 12, no. 1 (2009): 85–101.

Huizinga, J. *Homo Ludens: A Study of the Play Element in Culture*. London: Routledge, 2000.

Maguire, J. *Global Sport*. Oxford: Polity, 1999.

Maguire, J. 'Challenging the Sports-Industrial Complex: Human Sciences, Advocacy and Service'. *European Physical Education Review* 10, no. 3 (2004): 299–321.

Maguire, J., and J. Tuck. 'Making Sense of Global Patriot Games: Rugby Players' Perceptions of National Identity Politics'. *Football Studies* 2 (1999): 26–54.

Maguire, J., G. Jarvie, L. Mansfield, and J. Bradley. *Sport Worlds: A Sociological Perspective*. Champaign, IL: Human Kinetics, 2002.

McGovern, M. *Amazing Athletes of the 20th Century*. New York: Checkmark Books, 2001.

Morgan, W., and K. Meier, eds. *Philosophic Inquiry in Sport*. Champaign, IL: Human Kinetics, 1988.

Nixon, H., and J. Frey. *A Sociology of Sport*. Boston, MA: Wadsworth, 1996.

Powell, J. *Bobby Moore: The Life and Times of a Sporting Hero*. London: Robson Books, 2002.

Pyke, F. *Better Coaching*. 2nd ed. Champaign, IL: Human Kinetics, 2001.

Pyne, D. 'Designing an Endurance Training Program'. Proceedings of the National Coaching and Officiating Conference; Brisbane, November 30 to December 3, 1996.

Smart, B. *The Football Star*. London: Sage, 2005.

Smith, D.J. 'A Framework for Understanding the Training Process Leading to Elite Performance'. *Sports Medicine* 33, no. 15 (2003): 1103–26.

Stone, G. 'Wrestling: The Great American Passion Play'. In *The Sociology of Sport*, edited by E. Dunning, 301–35. London: Cass, 1971.

Tännsjö, T. 'Is our Admiration for Sports Heroes Fascistoid?'. In *Ethics in Sport*, edited by W.J. Morgan, 429–40. Champaign, IL: Human Kinetics, 2007.

UK Sport. *Annual Report*. London: UK Sport, 2001.

UK Sport. *Countdown to Athens*. London: UK Sport, 2003.

Wolff, J. *The Social Production of Art*. London: Macmillan, 1981.

Personal and social change in and through sport: cross-cutting themes

Ramón Spaaij

School of Management, La Trobe University, Australia; Amsterdam School for Social Science Research, University of Amsterdam, The Netherlands

The ten essays that make up this special edition of *Sport in Society* serve as a starting point for examining the ways in which sport contributes to, or inhibits, particular social outcomes. In this epilogue I will address, in a concise and exploratory way, the main cross-cutting themes that emerge from the individual contributions as a basis for further discussion and research.

An issue that has been frequently commented upon is that social development through sport is focused disproportionately on Northern modern sports to the exclusion of indigenous games. The most used sport in sport-for-development programmes across the globe is association football (soccer), reflecting the game's global appeal.[1] Other often used sports, though to a much lesser extent, are volleyball, athletics and basketball.[2] In considering the contemporary academic and policy discourses on sport-for-development, it is critical to recall the instrumental use of sport during the colonial period. In their contribution to this volume, Meier and Saavedra explain how sport served as a means of 'civilizing' African societies through its disciplining nature, and as a regimen to teach hygiene, cleanliness and self-control. It could be argued that besides representing modes of (neo-) colonial domination and social control, Northern modern sports carry with them certain 'dysfunctional' aspects of the societies in which they originated, such as a fixation on competition and winning and related practices of violence, cheating and corruption.[3]

The contributions to this special edition appear to challenge this view in two ways. Firstly, they point to the much wider range of sports that may act, in certain circumstances, as agents of personal and social change. Burnett, for instance, discusses the uses of indigenous games, gymnastics, aerobics, netball, rugby, cricket, handball and other games in South Africa. The project in Bam, Iran, also included table tennis and karate in its combination of several sports. Kunz found that children's interest in traditional, indigenous games was very low and that some of these games are not well-suited for children (i.e. certain combat sports). The essays by Spaaij and Hallinan and Judd pay particular attention to the role and influence of Australian football, not only for Australians of Anglo-Saxon descent but also for Indigenous Australians. The latter essay nevertheless paints a rather grim picture of race relations progress in Australia, showing how the Australian sport system, especially the Australian Football League, generates a form of organizational practice that contains and stereotypes Indigenous ambition and performance. This and other contributions highlight that the transformative capacity of sport cannot be taken for granted, and that sport often reproduces or reinforces social inequalities rather than fundamentally contests or resists them.

Secondly, as Kunz points out in her analysis of the Bam project, sport development workers and coaches often seek to modify the sporting environment from one that is based on competition and individual performance to one that focuses on respect, tolerance and inclusiveness. She argues that without these modifications sport would not have contributed such positive effects in the aftermath of the Bam earthquake. In other words, while sports carry particular symbolic and cultural meanings in a globalizing context, these meanings can be transformed and contested at the grassroots level and are therefore always contextual. This, in turn, raises important questions about which sports and sports processes produce what outcomes, for which participants and in what circumstances.[4] While the competitive aspect of sport may 'work' for some people and some purposes, as Klein's essay shows regarding Major League Baseball's impact on economic and community development in the Dominican Republic, it may not work for others. For example, certain sports seem better suited than others to address or change gender relations and to empower young women, facilitating a radical rethinking of things we tend to take for granted. The key, then, is to avoid naive and unrealistic generalizations about the transformative capacity of sport. Instead, we should examine the specific processes and mechanisms that produce beneficial outcomes in particular social, cultural and political contexts and establish the extent to which, and the ways in which, these practices (like those identified by Kay, Kunz, Vermeulen and Verweel, and Meier and Saavedra) are transferable to other contexts.

In regard to these processes and mechanisms, the second issue that cuts across several contributions to this special edition is the way in which sport activities, at least in targeted initiatives, are often intimately connected to other services, such as education and health. Burnett demonstrates how in South Africa a health programme (HIV/AIDS education and training) and a gardening project were developed under sport club leadership. Kay's essay describes how GOAL staff deliberately fostered a structure in which giving and receiving information was integrated with the netball activities, creating a more informal and reflexive educational platform. These practices underline the recognition that it is not about sport itself, but rather about the social issues people seek to address by means of sport activities. There is a strong feeling here that while sport participation is important as an end in itself (i.e., in terms of its intrinsic significance), one needs to 'add things to it' to enhance opportunities for sport to act as an agent of personal and social change. This finding verifies Crabbe *et al*'s conclusion that 'it is the adoption of a personal and social development model which is sacred to sport-based social inclusion programs rather than sport'.[5]

Based on the contributions by Klein, Stokvis, Spaaij, and Vermeulen and Verweel, it can be concluded that such wider connections do not necessarily require elaborate design and planning. Vermeulen and Verweel conclude that both bonding and bridging social capital is found in organized sport clubs as well as in more informal sport activities in public playgrounds. From a different perspective, Klein emphasizes the economic and social capital resources that accrue from the growing baseball industry in the Dominican Republic. Stokvis takes this point further by revealing the significance of US high school athletics in limiting drop-out rates and in creating a feeling of collective identity and common purpose among staff and students despite their increasing heterogeneity.

Looking more closely at the sport-related processes that generate positively perceived personal and social change, the role and the influence of role models and peer leaders, and their personal and social closeness to participants, become evident. The contributions by Meier and Saavedra, Burnett, Kunz and Kay all consider the ways in which role models or peer leaders (especially young women) are involved in sport-for-development programmes at various levels. Their investigations carry forward the growing body of literature which stresses the vital contributions peer leaders and embedded role models can make in social development through sport.[6] They identify some of the conditions necessary for peer educators to have a positive social impact as part of on-going processes of socialization and social communication, and raise important epistemological and methodological questions that will stimulate academic and policy debates on sport as an agent of personal and social change. Meier and Saavedra in particular argue that it is important to be very specific about how sport-based development projects can use role models as a tool or a focusing device for staff and participants, as individuals will not necessarily be receptive to a positive role model which requires a path of individual risk. The predisposition or the particular regulatory focus of an individual and community must be considered when evaluating the use of role models.

More generally, this special edition stresses the need for theoretically and methodologically informed considerations of the social impact of sport. The contributions highlight the multitude of theoretical and methodological frameworks that can be employed to study personal and social change in and through sport, each offering a different, yet not necessarily mutually exclusive, perspective on the subject. Echoing wider calls for engaging with Southern and postcolonial modes of knowledge and experience,[7] some of the contributors explicitly challenge the biases of Northern theories and methodologies, arguing for a radical rethinking of sport-for-development research. Others employ more 'orthodox' theories and methodologies but apply them in novel ways, considering the subject matter from a different angle and generating interesting, often counter-intuitive, insights into the social impact of sport in society. These different approaches help us, each in its own distinctive way, to better understand the ways in which sport contributes to, or inhibits, personal and social change, the directions these changes take, and the circumstances and wider social conditions in which they occur.

Notes

[1] Goldblatt, *The Ball is Round*; Giulianotti, *Football*.
[2] Levermore, 'Sport-in-International Development', 42.
[3] E.g. Maguire, *Global Sport*.
[4] Coalter, *A Wider Social Role for Sport*, 2.
[5] Crabbe *et al.*, *Knowing the Score*, 19. Compare Danish, Taylor and Fazio, 'Enhancing Adolescent Development', 102.
[6] E.g. Nicholls, 'On the Backs of Peer Educators'; Crabbe, 'Avoiding the Numbers Game'.
[7] E.g. Connell, *Southern Theory*; Young, *Postcolonialism*.

References

Coalter, F. *A Wider Social Role for Sport: Who's Keeping the Score?* London: Routledge, 2007.
Connell, R.W. *Southern Theory: The Global Dynamics of Knowledge in Social Science*. Cambridge: Polity, 2007.
Crabbe, T. 'Avoiding the Numbers Game: Social Theory, Policy and Sport's Role in the Art of Relationship Building'. In *Sport and Social Capital*, edited by M. Nicholson and R. Hoye, 21–37. Oxford: Elsevier Butterworth-Heinemann, 2008.
Crabbe, T., G. Bailey, T. Blackshaw, A. Brown, C. Choak, B. Gidley, G. Mellor, K. O'Connor, I. Slater, and D. Woodhouse. *Knowing the Score: Positive Futures Case Study Research. Final Report*. London: Home Office, 2006.
Danish, S.J., T.E. Taylor, and R.J. Fazio. 'Enhancing Adolescent Development through Sports and Leisure'. In *Blackwell Handbook of Adolescence*, edited by G.R. Adams and M.D. Berzonsky, 92–108. Oxford: Blackwell, 2003.

Giulianotti, R. *Football: A Sociology of the Global Game*. Cambridge: Polity, 1999.

Goldblatt, D. *The Ball is Round: A Global History of Football*. London: Penguin, 2007.

Levermore, R. 'Sport-in-International Development: Theoretical Frameworks'. In *Sport and International Development*, edited by R. Levermore and A. Beacom, 26–54. Houndmills: Palgrave Macmillan, 2009.

Maguire, J. *Global Sport: Identities, Societies, Civilizations*. Cambridge: Polity, 1999.

Nicholls, S. 'On the Backs of Peer Educators: Using Theory to Interrogate the Role of Young People in the Field of Sport-in-Development'. In *Sport and International Development*, edited by R. Levermore and A. Beacom, 156–75. Houndmills: Palgrave Macmillan, 2009.

Young, R.J.C. *Postcolonialism: An Historical Introduction*. Oxford: Blackwell, 2001.

Index

Page numbers in *Italics* represent tables.
Page numbers in **Bold** represent figures.